AGE OF
CAGE

AGE OF CAGE

**Four Decades of Hollywood
Through One Singular Career**

KEITH PHIPPS

Henry Holt and Company
New York

Henry Holt and Company
Publishers since 1866
120 Broadway
New York, New York 10271
www.henryholt.com

Henry Holt® and **ⓗ**® are registered trademarks of Macmillan
Publishing Group, LLC.

Library of Congress Cataloging-in-Publication Data

Names: Phipps, Keith, author.
Title: Age of Cage : four decades of Hollywood through one
    singular career / Keith Phipps.
Description: First edition. | New York : Henry Holt and Company,
    2021. | Includes bibliographical references.
Identifiers: LCCN 2021021340 (print) | LCCN 2021021341
    (ebook) | ISBN 9781250773043 (hardcover) |
    ISBN 9781250773036 (ebook)
Subjects: LCSH: Cage, Nicolas, 1965– | Motion picture actors and
    actresses—United States—Biography.
Classification: LCC PN2287.C227 P47 2021 (print) |
    LCC PN2287.C227 (ebook) | DDC 791.4302/8092 [B]—dc23
LC record available at https://lccn.loc.gov/2021021340
LC ebook record available at https://lccn.loc.gov/2021021341

Our books may be purchased in bulk for promotional,
educational, or business use. Please contact your local
bookseller or the Macmillan Corporate and Premium Sales
Department at (800) 221-7945, extension 5442, or by e-mail at
MacmillanSpecialMarkets@macmillan.com.

First Edition 2022

Designed by Meryl Sussman Levavi

Printed in the United States of America

1   3   5   7   9   10   8   6   4   2

To Stevie, of course

IDIOT PUNK:
You look like a clown in that stupid jacket.

SAILOR:
This is a snakeskin jacket, and for me it's a symbol of my individuality and my belief in personal freedom.

—*Wild at Heart*,
screenplay by David Lynch and Barry Gifford

Contents

Introduction: The Meaning of Cage

Early in the 2011 film *Season of the Witch*, two knights whose consciences have led them to flee the bloodshed of the Crusades encounter a cardinal dying of the Black Death. His gaunt face buried beneath makeup simulating the ravages of the disease, the actor playing the cardinal looks almost unrecognizable. But there's no mistaking the voice of Christopher Lee, a sound familiar from movies featuring hobbits, Jedi Knights, superspies, vampires, and all sorts of other fantastic characters. Lee was approaching ninety when he made the film, and though the one-scene role could easily have been played by another actor, Lee's presence has meaning in a film designed—sincerely, if not particularly well—to evoke the spirit of the classic horror films in which he first became famous many years before. Lee arrived with a lifetime piled up behind that appearance, and that lifetime informs it, giving it meaning no other actor could have.

Lee was a childhood favorite of the star playing opposite

him. Like Lee, Nicolas Cage arrived to the film trailed by a history; his was shorter than Lee's, but no less colorful. By 2010, he'd been an Oscar winner, an action hero, the star of quirky comedies, a tabloid target, and an internet punch line. And here he was now, making no attempt to disguise his precise diction or his California accent and sporting perfect teeth of the sort unknown to the Middle Ages, but still capturing the essence of a man whose struggle to control a malevolent supernatural force doubles as a battle with his own soul. As usual, he gave the film his all, whether or not the film deserved it.

Not that many saw it. A critical and commercial disappointment, *Season of the Witch* arrived in the middle of a bad-luck streak of mammoth proportions in Cage's career. But Cage usually operated on a mammoth scale. He'd taken big risks on-screen from the start, steered his career in unexpected directions, and engaged in questionable financial choices (and high-profile romances) that kept him in the headlines. His name could summon up highs and lows of the sort few other actors could boast; nor could few other actors prompt so much discussion as to which were the highs and which the lows. His eccentricity made him stand out early in his career, but it also made him an odd fit for the sort of movies made by the top-level star he became—choices that narrowed as the movies got bigger and Hollywood more risk-averse. He has been the object of criticism for the same qualities that earned him acclaim. Even those who admired him could find their opinions challenged, or find themselves wondering if the actor had, in fact, taken a wrong turn. Though Cage was entering a bumpy stretch in 2010, he showed no signs of going away or making it easier to understand who he was or what he'd do next.

It's complicated, the way we think about movie stars, and it just gets more complicated over time. Some appear at just the right time in just the right place; to paraphrase *The Big Lebowski*, they just fit right in there. But when that time has passed and that place changes, they stop fitting in, and they fade away or move to the margins, struggling to stir more than memories of when we first saw them. Some arrive seemingly indestructible, destined to stick around forever and suffer nothing worse than the occasional dip in popularity. Some reinvent themselves from time to time, shifting with ease from comedy to drama to action. Some come and go so quickly that it takes a moment to recall why we remember their names. Some turn their weirdness and lifelong identification with misfits into a virtue.

Stars work in an ever-shifting world. In *Singin' in the Rain*, Jean Hagen plays an actress whose beauty and expressiveness made her a star of the silent film era but whose shrill voice threatens to make her obsolete with the advent of sound. It's an extreme example of how changes—in technology, in public taste, in the ways movies get financed, and in the venues in which they're seen—conspire to keep actors perpetually off balance. Pity the singing cowboy star when Westerns and musicals go out of style. To stay in the picture, a star has to adapt and hope they don't lose too much of themselves with the changes.

All the while, we change, too. A favorite actor of our youth may start to seem callow in adulthood. A star who once evoked annoyance can become a welcome presence. If we know about a star's personal life, it becomes even harder to separate actor from role. An actor can give the performance of a lifetime, and we might still be thinking of their political views or whom they've dated or their favorite brand of shoe. As the years pile up, information and past encounters can shift the way we look at a star. An actor becomes a palimpsest; no matter how indelible a performance, we can still see the characters they've been before and the real person beneath those characters.

Or so we tell ourselves. We can spend hours watching a star at work, but what of them do we see? A memorable film performance involves sustaining an illusion created from scenes filmed out of sequence and shots captured hours, days, even months apart and pasted together in the editing room. Public personae work much the same way. We're given access to a selection of what a star wants us to see of their lives via photo shoots and talk show anecdotes that collectively create the impression they want to give the world. Sometimes that impression gets away from them, skewed by changing tastes or embarrassing information. Yet, for all we know of them, they remain essentially unknowable. Still, we can try to sort out what they mean.

A few facts. In 1983, Nicolas Kim Coppola made his starring debut in *Valley Girl* under his new, assumed name, "Nicolas Cage." In 1996, he won a Best Actor Oscar for playing an alcoholic screenwriter in the film *Leaving Las Vegas*. In the years that immediately followed, he became one of the biggest stars in the world. In 2009, financial problems tied to extravagant (and colorful) spending habits came to light. At the dawn of the 2020s, you can find the movies that made him famous sharing space with the many low-budget, direct-to-VOD efforts he's made in the past decade on the streaming service of your choice. He's been married five times and has fathered two sons, one named after Superman's Kryptonian name, Kal-El.

If you've picked up this book, you probably know all this. Even the casual movie viewer can list a half dozen Nicolas Cage movies without thinking too hard. He has appeared, as of this writing, in nearly one hundred, usually as the star. They're films of seemingly every variety spread out over four decades. In the process, Cage has become iconic, in both the common and the original sense of the word: he's instantly recognizable but also symbolic of unpredictability of a kind no other actor can claim. He has served as an X factor in an industry often dictated by creative conservativism and timid choices. And though that has sometimes made him a misfit, he continually finds ways to keep working, and to surprise, that ensure that he remain in the conversation long after other stars have been forgotten.

This is a book about the films of Nicolas Cage but also about the changes that have taken place in Hollywood over the course of his career, from his unconventional early work to his unlikely ascent to superstardom to the deflation of his career in an era dominated by franchises rather than stars. It's not a biography; nor does it have much interest in Cage's personal life beyond the ways its known details reshaped his public image and exerted an impact on his career. It's a book about sweeping trends and small disruptions as observed through the lens provided by the career of an unusual and divisive actor, one who has appeared in virtually every sort of movie made over the last four decades, from sweet romantic comedies to assaultive action films, while at almost every point staying true to his artistic impulses, strange as they sometimes seemed. It is also about how, when he played it too safe, it often backfired. It's a book about the choices and waves of change that sometimes brought Cage to the top of the industry and sometimes to its depths; how he ended up in each place and what might come next, both for Cage and for movies.

But to understand where we're heading, we first have to understand how we got there.

AGE OF
CAGE

1

The Origins of Cage

To understand Nicolas Cage, you first have to understand Nicolas Coppola. And to understand Nicolas Coppola, you first have to know a bit about the Coppola family, which, since arriving in America from Italy at the turn of the century, has produced multiple generations of artists whose lofty ambitions have collided, sometimes violently, with the commercial expectations and financial realities of the country that welcomed them. And while it might be easy to dwell on the Coppola side of the family, with its rich history and famous members, it's best to keep going. The Coppola name loomed large over Nicolas Cage's childhood and young adulthood—so large that he felt the need to shed it before he could move on. But his early days were defined just as much by his mother—sometimes by her presence, sometimes by her absence.

Family may not be destiny, but recurring patterns can be tough to ignore, particularly when they take the form of irrepressible artistic instincts. Cage's great-grandfather Francesco Pennino, a first-generation Italian immigrant, played music, wrote songs, helped import Italian films to the United States, and even served as Enrico Caruso's pianist. Another great-grandfather, Augustino Coppola, produced two musician sons, Anton and Carmine. Carmine Coppola, Cage's grandfather, played flute, a talent that earned him a scholarship to Juilliard and brought the family to Detroit for a job with the Detroit Symphony that included work for the *Ford Sunday Evening Hour*. In 1939, the show's corporate sponsor would provide a middle name for one of Carmine's sons, Francis.

Francis Ford Coppola wasn't the first child born to Carmine and Italia Coppola, however. He was preceded by five years by his older brother, August, born in Hartford, Connecticut, in 1934. To August, Francis would become both sidekick and acolyte.

"As a younger man, the words I'd use of Augie are a purity, and a kindness," Francis told biographer Peter Cowie. "A lot of brothers would dump a kid five years younger, but he would always take me everywhere. At one point we even lived in the same room, and you'd think he'd be dying to get rid of me even more. I was very charmed by him and very much wanted to imitate him." With their sister, Talia, who'd follow Francis in 1946, the Coppola boys lived a peripatetic existence, moving from one New York neighborhood to another as Carmine's jobs changed and his fortunes rose and fell.

A gifted but less-than-dedicated student, August would frequently skip school to take Francis to the movies, where they took in everything, from Disney films to Abbott and Costello comedies. August's mentorship didn't stop with movies. He'd later introduce his younger brother to other forms of art and literature as August developed into a talented writer. August also became something of a local legend, described by Francis years later as "the hero in the neighborhood ... the one the girls liked and the other fellows were afraid of." The relationship proved central to Francis's development, and intense fraternal relationships would find their way into many of his films.

In these early days, August always seemed a few steps ahead of his younger brother, including in his choice to trade the East Coast for the West. August earned a philosophy degree from UCLA; returned to New York by way of Hofstra, where he picked up a master's degree in English; then went west again, earning a doctorate in comparative literature via an unusual program designed—as the author bio for his sole published novel, *The Intimacy*, notes—"for Renaissance men and women" that involved work at Occidental, Claremont, Whittier, Redlands, and Pomona. (That it was sponsored by the Ford Foundation seems like another cosmic coincidence. It wouldn't be the last such coincidence to play a role in Nicolas Cage's origin story.) Upon graduation, August took a job teaching comparative literature at Cal State Long Beach.

It was in Los Angeles that August met dancer and choreographer Joy Vogelsang, who, like August, had roots in another part of the country. The daughter of Bob and Louise "Divi" Vogelsang, Joy had moved with her family to Los Angeles from Chicago, where they'd run a grocery on the city's South Side. In LA, they'd picked up where they'd left off, opening a market on Melrose Avenue. Bob and Louise purchased a home in Hollywood, where Louise would remain for more than sixty years, continuing to call it home after Bob's 1988 death until shortly before her own death in 2010, at the age of ninety-five. Cage would be a frequent visitor, and sometime resident, during his childhood and through the early days of his career. Occasionally, he'd need a place to which he could escape.

❑ ❑ ❑

Nicolas Kim Coppola was born on January 7, 1964. The third son of August and Joy, he followed his brothers, Marc (born in 1958) and Christopher (born in 1962). Theirs was not always a settled home. Early in Cage's career, he'd say little about his family. As time passed, he revealed more about an upbringing troubled by his mother's struggles with mental illness. Joy first entered an institution in 1970, when Cage was six. "She would go away for years at a time," he told the *New York Times* in 1994. "When she got too erratic, she went to the—she went away. Then my childhood consisted of going to see her. And that hallway was a long hallway, let me tell you, going in there with the crazy people who would be touching and—it was very arresting."

Cage responded in part by retreating into a fantasy world, looking first to television as a way out. "I was six years old. I was sitting on the living room carpet watching our old round, oval-shaped Zenith TV," he told NPR's Terry Gross in 2002, "and I just remember, I wanted to be inside that TV so bad. I just wanted to get out of there and get in that TV. And I think that's my first real cognizant recollection of wanting to act." (The particular Zenith he remembered seems to have belonged to his grandmother Louise. Years later, he'd ask her for it and install it in one of his homes.) Yet even as he tried to retreat from the world and his mother's condition, they became a part of him.

"It obviously, when I look at some of the characters,

impacted the work," he told *Rolling Stone* in 1995. "If it wasn't for her, I don't think I would have been able to act. I was just lucky that whatever was looking out for me gave me the ability to be a catalyst and to convert it into something productive." That future use didn't assuage fears of inheriting his mother's condition. "I used to freak out that it was going to happen to me," he said, "but everybody who I asked about it said that if it was going to happen, it would have happened when you were in your teens."

In interviews, Cage sometimes recalls happy memories of making plays, sketches, radio shows, and Super 8 movies with older brothers Marc (who'd become an actor and radio personality) and Christopher (who'd become a director and producer). These would prove to be formative experiences, as would his father's cultural education, a habit August carried over from his childhood with Francis. Guided by August, Cage watched Fellini and Kurosawa films as a preteen. "When I was a kid, the other kids were seeing Disney, and he was showing us movies like Fellini's *Juliet of the Spirits*," Cage would later tell *Playboy*'s David Sheff. Jean Marais's rumbly, leonine work in Cocteau's *Beauty and the Beast* made a deep impression, as did films from the German Expressionist school, like *Nosferatu*, *The Cabinet of Dr. Caligari*, and *The Golem*, for both their atmosphere and their stars' performance style, which often sought to channel extreme emotion through gestures and facial contortions that held nothing back.

In early interviews, Cage often mentioned a more dramatic childhood incident: his expulsion from school at the age of ten for a prank in which he brought egg salad sandwiches to school after lacing them with fried grasshoppers. This landed him in what he describes as a school for juvenile delinquents. After being bullied by a trio of older kids, he decided to take matters into his own hands. "One day," he told the *LA Times*'s Michael Wilmington in a 1990 profile, "I went home and I'd had enough. I disguised myself as this character—you know, chewing gum, wearing sunglasses, cowboy boots—and I got on the bus and said, 'Yeah, I'm Roy Richards, Nicky Coppola's cousin, and if you screw with him again, I'm gonna kick your ass!' They *bought* it. That was really my first experience in acting."

Cage's parents divorced in 1976, when he was twelve. By fifteen, he knew he wanted to act, inspired in particular by James Dean's work in *East of Eden*. In that inspiration he's hardly alone among young actors, but Cage has also mentioned performers as far afield as Jerry Lewis and Bill Bixby—the latter the mild-mannered star of *The Courtship of Eddie's Father*, *My Favorite Martian*, and *The Incredible Hulk* (in which Bixby played the Hulk's meek alter ego)—as influential favorites. But wanting to act is one thing, and making it happen is another, and Cage would encounter distractions and obstacles along the way. One such distraction involved moving in with one of the titans of 1970s filmmaking, his uncle Francis, as a high school freshman while his father traveled. And it's here, at Francis's Napa Valley home, miles away from Los Angeles, that the story of Nicolas Cage first hit the ever-changing tides of Hollywood filmmaking.

❑ ❑ ❑

There's a simple, two-part story about what happened in Hollywood between 1969 and the early '80s, one that makes Francis Ford Coppola a hero in the first half and a victim in the second. It goes like this . . .

By the end of the 1960s, Hollywood had started to spin its wheels, releasing flop after flop that failed to lure moviegoers to the theaters, especially younger moviegoers. Enter Peter Fonda and Dennis Hopper's *Easy Rider*, an innovative road movie that became a runaway hit and constituted a shot across the bow to the Hollywood Old Guard that a new generation of filmmakers had arrived. From film schools like NYU, USC, and UCLA (Coppola's alma mater), a generation of movie-mad filmmakers steeped in the influence of Bergman, Kurosawa, and the French New Wave and informed by the break-the-rules sensibility of the counterculture began to remake Hollywood in their own image. Coppola found great success in this environment, penning the Academy Award–winning screenplay to the 1970 film *Patton* and releasing a string of unimpeachable masterpieces: *The Godfather* in 1972, both *The Conversation* and *The Godfather: Part II* in 1974, and *Apocalypse Now* in 1979. He thrived in the world he helped create.

In the middle of the 1970s, however, that world had started to fall apart thanks to greed and changing tastes. Steven Spielberg's *Jaws* created the modern summer blockbuster, and studios' goals shifted from turning a profit by way of many small and medium-size films to making a *lot* of money with fewer bigger, and inevitably less personal, productions. George Lucas's *Star Wars* confirmed the wisdom of this approach. Soon, quirk and character gave way to space epics and sequel after sequel. What's more, some of the era's best and brightest spent too much money on movies no one wanted to see, like Michael Cimino's *Heaven's Gate* and Coppola's *One from the Heart*. If New Hollywood can be said to have begun with the premiere of *Easy Rider* in the summer of '69, then *One from the Heart*'s less-than-rapturously received Radio City Music Hall premiere in January 1982 serves as convenient end point.

Though true in broad strokes, this version of the story leaves out some important details, Coppola's role not least among them. In truth, Coppola's first attempt to find a new, more personal way of making movies virtually collapsed before the decade had even begun. In August 1969, he released *The Rain People*, an unusual road movie he made on his own terms that earned strong reviews but never found an audience. In December he founded American Zoetrope, a still-active, if much-changed, production company based in San Francisco, in an attempt to put some symbolically significant and practically useful miles between himself and Hollywood.

But it was Hollywood that still paid the bills, and less than two years into its existence, American Zoetrope experienced the first of many existential threats. In 1971, its first feature, *THX 1138*, directed by Coppola's close friend, and American Zoetrope vice president, George Lucas, met with a frosty critical reception and commercial indifference. Its failure led Warner Bros., whose meager investment in American Zoetrope had helped keep it afloat, to sever ties, bringing in-the-works projects to a halt. These included what would have been the debut film of *Black Stallion* director Carroll Ballard, Coppola's *The Conversation*, and an unusual project entitled *Apocalypse Now*—an adaptation of Joseph Conrad's *Heart of Darkness*, written by John Milius and originally envisioned as a project for Lucas to shoot documentary style with 16 mm cameras. Coppola made *The Godfather*, his first masterpiece, out of economic necessity, reluctantly agreeing to adapt Mario

Puzo's lurid best seller while lamenting to his father that Paramount wanted him to direct a "hunk of trash."

Out of a work-for-hire job adapting a much-read potboiler for famously temperamental producer Robert Evans, Coppola made one of the landmark films of the 1970s. *The Godfather*—which went on to win an Academy Award for Best Picture, Best Actor, and Best Adapted Screenplay—didn't begin as a distinctive artistic statement. Coppola wrestled with it until it became one. Between its even-better sequel, Coppola sandwiched the smaller, thornier classic *The Conversation*, becoming, in the process, the first director to see two films nominated for Best Picture in the same year. *The Godfather: Part II* walked away with the prize, earning Coppola awards for Best Director and, with Puzo, Best Adapted Screenplay. Also picking up Oscars: Robert De Niro, for Best Supporting Actor (his first), and a Dean Tavoularis–led team for Best Art Direction. This wasn't the independent future Coppola envisioned for himself and those around him when he founded American Zoetrope, but he was making it work anyway.

Success brought money, but Coppola was never good at holding on to money. He poured it, along with his energy, into American Zoetrope, particularly the newly revived *Apocalypse Now*, a film he now planned to direct and whose agonizing production could easily have ended the company (to say nothing of Coppola's career, marriage, and possibly life). Though some speculated that the film would never see completion, as its release date changed first by months and then years, Coppola pulled it off, to tremendous acclaim and surprising financial success.

Then, either his luck ran out, hubris caught up with him,

audiences abandoned him for shinier projects, or some combination of the above took place. Determined to make an
old-fashioned film using cutting-edge technology—and to
work on soundstages after the dangerous location shooting of
Apocalypse Now—Coppola created expensive, elaborate sets for
the bittersweet musical *One from the Heart* while directing the
action from inside a trailer filled with fresh-from-the-factory
video equipment. As his vision expanded, so did American
Zoetrope's debt, one intensified by the underperformance of
projects like *Hammett* (directed by Wim Wenders) and *The
Escape Artist* (directed by another longtime Coppola associate,
cinematographer Caleb Deschanel). In 1983, Coppola would
declare bankruptcy and then spend the rest of the '80s attempting to eliminate that debt, sometimes making payments of over
a million dollars per week as he took on jobs he would have
eschewed just a few years earlier.

Coppola's story both confirms the accepted New Hollywood narrative and complicates it. His career illustrates that
a trend can be true on a macro level but made fuzzy by individual examples. Coppola was part of a wave of 1970s auteurs
who thrived in that decade's more relaxed, less risk-averse
atmosphere, and in some ways his path mirrors that of Robert Altman, Hal Ashby, Cimino, Peter Bogdanovich, Michael
Ritchie, and others. Yet American Zoetrope nearly collapsed
in the early 1970s, at the height of the film industry's supposed
openness to daring new filmmakers. Coppola and his peers
found success within the Hollywood system, but even before
the success of *Jaws*, signs abounded that the changes they
introduced wouldn't last. In 1974, the year Coppola earned
two Best Picture Oscar nominations, the top-grossing films

included studio disaster movies like *The Towering Inferno*, *Earthquake*, *Airport 1975*, and *The Trial of Billy Jack*, *The Life and Times of Grizzly Adams*, and *Benji*, a mix of oversize Hollywood productions and independent films that no one would mistake for the work of paradigm-shifting visionaries.

Coppola, for his part, took on the role of paradigm-shifting visionary as a burden and tried to carry it as far as he could. At its height, American Zoetrope's empire included an LA studio, multiple production facilities, a magazine, a traditional theater, a radio station, and a production and distribution wing whose output included original projects and films by Coppola idols like Akira Kurosawa and Jean-Luc Godard. Coppola's undoing came less because he tried to separate from Hollywood and more from his attempt to become his own Hollywood. With *One from the Heart*, he even tried to tap into the spirit of classic Hollywood using new techniques. The film's out-of-control costs had little to do with its modest story and much to do with its grandiose scale and Coppola's commitment to pursuing a lifelong interest in cutting-edge technology.

Even as this dream fell apart, however, New Hollywood's grasp on the movie world didn't loosen all at once. Lucas helped spread the studios' mania for blockbuster-size hits, but *Star Wars* remained the result of an independent-spirited filmmaker pushing hard for a vision that nobody else could see and a film that (at first, at least) nobody wanted to make—and one inspired in part by the images of American military might clashing with the Vietcong. Lucas didn't so much abandon the Zoetrope dream with *Star Wars* as repackage it. And the moviegoing public's taste for the thornier, more intimate filmmaking that helped define the decade didn't dissipate at the first sight of Darth Vader. The top-grossing film of 1979, two years after *Star Wars*, wasn't *Rocky II* or *Alien*, but *Kramer vs. Kramer*.

In the end, Coppola built a kingdom on a foundation of sand, one shored only temporarily by the miraculous success of *Apocalypse Now*. But while it lasted, it still felt like an empire, one at its height when Coppola welcomed Nicolas Cage into his home for a year.

❑ ❑ ❑

In the years after August and Joy's divorce, both Marc and Christopher grew old enough to move out of their father's house, leaving only Nicolas behind. Early in Cage's high school career, August told his son he'd be spending the next year in Napa Valley with his uncle Francis and aunt Eleanor. The move would produce unintended consequences, removing Cage from what had become a comfortable environment in LA and sending his grades plummeting.

"I was in ninth grade, getting straight A's, really excited about school," Cage told the *New York Times* in 1994. "Then I was put into this little country school. I went suddenly from being the cool guy to the geek. My grades went from straight A's to straight F's." He also found himself exposed to wealth of the sort he'd never experienced back in Long Beach.

Cage was presumably unaware that, at the time, United Artists had only recently considered repossessing Coppola's property and evicting his family from their home to recoup the company's investment in *Apocalypse Now*, and he couldn't foresee the money troubles that would dog Francis in the years to come. But he *could* see what he didn't have, and despite describing living in "a wonderful house with wonderfully generous people," he found himself overwhelmed with envy, drawing parallels between his situation and that of the orphan Heathcliff in *Wuthering Heights*, telling himself, "I am going to get even somehow." Later, he'd reflect that it was "sort of unfortunate that it was revenge that fueled much of my ambition."

This didn't interfere with his plans to pursue that ambition as far as it would take him, even if he'd yet to discover a channel for it. He'd soon find one, however. Cage's time in Northern California also brought him to San Francisco's American Conservatory Theater, which had already served as a training ground for Danny Glover and would later produce alums including Annette Bening, Anna Deavere Smith, and Chris Pine. Beyond high school productions, this would be the extent of Cage's formal acting training.

But Beverly Hills High, to which he returned after his time with Francis's family, offered advantages unavailable at other schools. Among them, acting teacher John Ingle, who'd find steady, high-profile work after his retirement from the school in 1985 thanks to his supporting turns in films like *True Stories* and *Heathers* and a nine-year run on TV's *General Hospital*. If a teacher's achievements can be measured by his students' accomplishments, then Ingle's are considerable; his former students include Albert Brooks, Richard Dreyfuss, Barbara Hershey, David Schwimmer, and Crispin Glover, a friend of Cage's who'd soon costar in his first paying job.

❑ ❑ ❑

By 1981, the cameras beckoned. Now seventeen, Cage, who'd grown up making 8 mm films with his brothers, appeared in the Super 8 short *The Sniper*, directed by a classmate. His other project, the ABC-TV pilot *The Best of Times*, reached a wider audience. A hybrid of sitcom, sketch show, and after-school special, it was executive-produced by George Schlatter, who'd enjoyed great success with *Laugh-In* in the late 1960s and early '70s and had launched the hit human interest show *Real People* in 1979. *Laugh-In* had connected with audiences by repackaging the era's youth culture in a format safe for mainstream audiences. *The Best of Times* plays like a similar attempt to tap into the interests of early '80s kids drawn to video games and New Wave music.

Billed as a show in which "seven energetic teenage performers express their views on parents, peers and politics through song, dance and comedic vignettes," the *Best of Times* pilot yielded strange, though sometimes charming, results. Crispin Glover stars as a normal, everyday teen—it's pretty much the last time the famously eccentric actor would play it straight—who serves as the central figure in a group of kids cast to represent different types: the nerd, the popular girl, etc. (Jackie Mason rounds out the cast as an easily annoyed convenience store owner, the only adult with a significant role.) As "Nicolas"—the show's conceit had the cast sharing first names with their characters—Cage plays the resident jock, a Stallone-worshipping, usually shirtless beach rat who spends most of his time lifting weights (when not dancing in overalls during a car wash musical sequence set to the recent Dolly Parton hit "9 to 5").

It's a window into how Cage's career might have gone. Towering over the rest of the cast and already appearing too mature for high school, he could look the part of a dumb jock and might easily have gotten slotted into such roles. To the show's credit, *The Best of Times* does give him a chance to show off some dramatic chops, via a monologue in which his character worries about global tensions and his future. The script could never be mistaken for Eugene O'Neill ("I just hope we don't have a war! It'd kind of spoil things, you know what I mean?"), but Cage sells it.

Writer Carol Hatfield recalls the teenage Cage as being "very cute." "He had a ton of energy and a lot of ambition," she says. "When the auditions were held, he ran from his high school to Beverly Boulevard, where George's studios were located.... [W]e knew right away that he was destined for greatness." The pilot drew mixed reviews when it aired in July. In the *Sacramento Bee*, critic Dean Huber called it a "teenage world in wild caricature," but the *New York Daily News*'s Kay Gardella dubbed it "a blessed relief from specials about teenagers on drugs." There would be no further installments, however. "I would have been surprised if it was picked up," Hatfield says. "It looked pretty cute when I saw it recently. But at the time, the writers were disappointed, to say the least."

Though *The Best of Times* went nowhere, it still pointed Cage toward his future. He washed his hands of high school before finishing his senior year. Completing a proficiency exam allowed him to pursue acting full time, and he next appeared—billed, as in *The Best of Times*, as "Nicolas Coppola"—in *Fast Times at Ridgemont High*. Directed by Amy Heckerling, *Fast Times* functioned like a magnet for actors of Cage's generation, providing breakout roles for some (Sean Penn, Jennifer Jason Leigh, Phoebe Cates, Judge Reinhold) while drawing an unusual number of future stars to small roles, including Eric Stoltz, Forest Whitaker, and Anthony Edwards. Cage falls into the second category, appearing only fleetingly in the role of "Brad's Bud." (You can see him wearing a fast-food uniform and watching, stone-faced, as Judge Reinhold gets fired for talking back to an obnoxious customer. The most notable experience on the film for Cage seems to have been other cast members' teasing him about his famous last name.) He wouldn't have to wait long for his first significant role, however. But he would have to turn to his uncle to provide it.

❑ ❑ ❑

After *One from the Heart*, Francis Ford Coppola needed a hit. In search of one, he followed the advice of some elementary school kids from Fresno. In 1980, the librarian of Fresno's Lone Star School (which then boasted a student body of 324) sent Coppola a copy of S. E. Hinton's classic 1967 young adult novel *The Outsiders*, and her students' plea for him to turn it into a movie. Coppola decided to take them up on the idea, and in 1982 he set up shop in Tulsa, Oklahoma. Like *Fast Times*, *The Outsiders* features a remarkable cast of young actors, including Tom Cruise, C. Thomas Howell, Diane Lane, Emilio Estevez, Rob Lowe, Patrick Swayze, and Matt Dillon. It did not include Cage, but he'd play a major part in Coppola's next film, *Rumble Fish*, another Tulsa-set S. E. Hinton adaptation that works both as a companion piece to *The Outsiders* and as a study in contrasts.

In an unusual arrangement, Coppola stuck around Tulsa to film *Rumble Fish*. Some outside factors helped keep the momentum going. He'd been working alongside Hinton for a while, collaborating with her on the script for the novel's adaptation. Already on the set of *The Outsiders*, Hinton began cowriting *Rumble Fish* with Coppola during their downtime. Hinton, who'd grown close to the cast, wanted Dillon to play Rusty-James, *Rumble Fish*'s protagonist. What's more, Coppola already had a crew in place in Tulsa, far from Hollywood, as he liked it. He suspected he could film the black-and-white *Rumble Fish*, which he described as "an art film for teenagers," quickly and relatively cheaply. He even shot a kind of rough draft version of the film on videotape as a form of rehearsal.

The complicated fraternal relationship of Hinton's novel, an element it shares with *The Outsiders*, drew Coppola to making the film. In *Rumble Fish*, Dillon plays Rusty-James, a sensitive Tulsa teen who lives in the shadow of his older brother, Motorcycle Boy (Mickey Rourke), the leader of the wrong-side-of-the-tracks gang that doubles as his social circle. As the film opens, Motorcycle Boy has absented himself from Tulsa for California, leaving Rusty-James at loose ends as he hangs out with the old gang, daydreams his way through classes thinking of his girlfriend, Patty (Lane), and suffers through a home life made tempestuous by his alcoholic father (Dennis Hopper). In Rusty-James and Motorcycle Boy, Coppola saw an echo of his relationship with August, to whom he dedicated the film. "Everything I aspired to be, the desire to be in the arts, to know about literature, to be the kind of a person to whom knowledge and learning were important, it was all taken from my brother, August," Coppola revealed on an audio commentary recorded for the film's DVD release.

Coppola cast Cage as Smokey, a rival to Rusty-James's tenuous hold on the gang. The family connection undoubtedly made Cage top of mind. Coppola even costumed his nephew in the satin jacket that August—who'd tried to steer his son away from acting and toward writing—had once worn to symbolize his membership in the teenage social club the Wild Deuces. Reflecting on the film later, Francis would speak of Cage's inventiveness and the creative choices he brought to the performance, calling it the result of "his talent and his intelligence," words that suggest Cage more than earned his spot.

Others saw it differently. Cage would frequently allude to unpleasantness on the set resulting from his relationship to the director. "That was a hard experience for me because I was still Nicolas Coppola," he'd later tell *Rolling Stone*. "I felt the pressure from the other actors like 'He's just here because Francis is his uncle.'" (He named no names at the time. Recalling similar incidents on the *Fast Times* set, he'd later single out costar Eric Stoltz.) Yet there's no nervousness in the seventeen-year-old Cage's performance, nor any evidence of the fact that Coppola treated it as a kind of trial-by-fire, requiring his nephew to perform forty-two takes of a scene in which his character looks at a watch. In Cage's most memorable moment, Smokey reveals he's taken Rusty-James's place in the gang and has started dating Patty. Cage convincingly stares down the more experienced Dillon, who had a considerable head start playing moody teens thanks to a career that stretched back to *Over the Edge* in 1979.

Still, the Coppola name hung on Cage, weighing him down, causing others to think they knew him before they met him and to form assumptions about why he was meeting them in the first place—as if he had been born lucky, as if opportunity came to him without effort, as if he weren't the kid who took the bus to Beverly Hills High while others drove gleaming Porsches. He knew something had to change. Late in production, a caller from California would ask *Rumble Fish*'s puzzled production manager about coordinating the schedule of an actor wanted for a role in a film soon to enter production, an actor with a name the production manager had never heard before: "Nicolas Cage."

2

Valley of the Cage

Martha Coolidge was having trouble getting started, and it was partly Francis Ford Coppola's fault. Not that Coppola had meant to stand in her way. In fact, he'd tried his best to help her. Nor was working with Coppola the first stumbling block Coolidge had encountered on her winding path to directing Hollywood movies, a path that would lead to her casting Nicolas Cage in his first starring role—even though she had no idea who he was.

Coolidge arrived at that career after cultivating interests in acting (which she studied with Lee Strasberg and Stella Adler), singing, and woodcutting, the last her intended focus when she enrolled into the Rhode Island School of Design in the 1960s. The daughter of architects, Coolidge grew up around Alexander Calder and Josef and Anni Albers, and *some* kind of career in the arts seemed inevitable. When she started making films at RISD, she knew what form that career would take. She also knew it wouldn't be easy.

Coolidge enrolled in Columbia University's film program shortly before protests shut the school down in 1968. From there, she became showrunner and jack-of-all trades at the Canadian kids' show *Magic Tom*, sometimes directing when the assigned directors went AWOL. After Canada, she returned to New York, enrolled at NYU, and won acclaim making personal documentaries and her first feature, the experimental, autobiographical rape drama *Not a Pretty Picture*. These caught the attention of Coppola and producer Fred Roos. Looking for a female director to champion, they invited Coolidge to Zoetrope to make a film called *Photoplay*, the story of a woman who falls for a rock star in the vibrant world of the early 1980s LA rock scene. Coolidge threw herself into the project, extensively researching LA nightlife as she prepared to make what would be her breakout film.

Except, it didn't happen. Blame *One from the Heart*, the failure of which rippled out to touch other Zoetrope films. After *Photoplay* collapsed, Coolidge shot what would become *City Girl*, a film she completed with the financial help of another then-struggling 1970s auteur, Peter Bogdanovich, after trouble with the original production. The film would remain unreleased for years. While assembling it, she had dinner with a producer friend, Andrew Lane, who'd cowritten a script with his writing partner Wayne Crawford inspired by the sudden interest in the teen culture of the San Fernando Valley. They felt it would benefit from a female director and wanted to offer her the job. "I was so afraid it was going to be a porno film or something," Coolidge says. "But, in fact, it was *Valley Girl*."

❑ ❑ ❑

A pair of converging trends helped make *Valley Girl* possible, most immediately the faddish fascination with Valley culture that took over the American imagination in 1982. It's not hard to find a patient zero for the fad's spread. Released in the summer of 1982 and billed as a collaboration between Frank Zappa and his then fourteen-year-old daughter, Moon Unit, the song "Valley Girl" never climbed higher than No. 32 on *Billboard*'s Top 40 chart, but it helped spread the region's distinctive "Valspeak"—with its always vaguely affronted cadences and catchphrases like "Gag me with a spoon!" and "Fer shure!"—from coast to coast. Bookstore shelves filled with titles like *How to Deprogram Your Valley Girl* (written by a speech therapist whose offerings included an attempt to eliminate Valspeak) and *The Valley Girl's Guide to Life*. Fashion inspired by Valley culture—and its shopping mall nexus, the Sherman Oaks Galleria—spread well beyond its original California confines, even to a pop-up boutique at New York's Bloomingdale's. The Valley Girl gave the decade one of its first new stereotypes. That her emergence coincided with another trend made a movie essentially inevitable.

In 1979, *Animal House* nudged open a door that allowed teen-appealing comedies, filled with rude humor and strategically deployed nude scenes, to make their way from the drive-ins to the mainstream. In 1981, *Porky's* kicked the door open the rest of the way. Nineteen eighty-three saw one teen sex comedy follow another, films with titles like *Screwballs*, *Private School*, *Spring Break*, and *Joysticks*. The opening allowed films that could pass as teen sex comedies to slip through as well, as long as they checked all the boxes necessary for them to be marketed as part of the genre. *Risky Business*, for instance, delivered sex and hijinks alongside a stylish, quietly despairing exploration of materialistic excess and the commodification of desire. Audiences showed up for the former; the latter made the film an enduring classic.

Like *Risky Business*, *Valley Girl* isn't, at heart, a sex comedy. But it *could* be marketed as one. Coolidge recalls having a great deal of creative freedom in making the film, but also being reminded by producers that they needed to see "nude breasts four times." Even here, she had some leeway. "We don't care how you do it," Coolidge recalls being told. "We just want you to do it." By delivering the requisite number of breasts, and securing an R rating in the process, she could fill in most of the other blanks as she saw fit.

Coolidge's creative say extended to the casting. She'd initially wanted Judd Nelson for the role of Randy, the wrong-side-of-the-tracks Hollywood kid who romances Julie Richman (Deborah Foreman). A Valley resident, Julie enters into a romance with Randy that makes her realize she wants more from life than to be on the arm of her handsome jock boyfriend Tommy (Michael Bowen)—despite pressure from her Valley Girl friends. Frustrated by her inability to find an actor who fit the part, Coolidge told her casting director, "Don't bring me any more pretty boys." Then she made what would be a fateful gesture. "I looked over at the discard pile," Coolidge says, "and this is absolutely true. On top of the discard pile was this guy. I pulled the picture up. And I said, 'Bring me somebody who looks like this,' and it was Nic Cage. First time he'd used that name to submit a picture."

Despite Coolidge's connection to Zoetrope, she didn't recognize Cage. "He was the only Coppola I didn't know," she says. "I knew his father. I knew everybody, but I didn't know him." She brought him in and liked what she saw. "He was *incredibly* shy, wouldn't talk to me. But that's not a bad sign in an actor. That's actually a pretty good sign," she remembers. "When he did the reading, I just thought, That's it. This guy is it." She moved to cast him, only to learn that he still had some pickup work to do on the film he'd just been working on, *Rumble Fish*. Regarding Coppola as "like family," Coolidge assumed that arranging an agreement to share Cage's time would be no problem. One phone call later, she learned that, until recently, her new star had gone by another name: "Nicolas Coppola."

❑ ❑ ❑

"When I first started going to auditions and was still using my real name, it was obvious that people were thinking about 20 years of someone else's history," Cage told the *Los Angeles Times* in 1988. "I wanted to be able to go into an office and just do what I had to do, so I took the name Cage, and the first audition I did under that name was the best audition I'd ever had. That told me I'd done the right thing."

The new name had two disparate sources of inspiration, one from the world of comics, the other from twentieth-century classical music's avant-garde. Introduced in 1972 in the pages of *Luke Cage, Hero for Hire*, Luke Cage began as Marvel Comics' attempt to cash in on the popularity of blaxploitation films like *Shaft*. Like Nicolas Cage, Luke Cage also shed his birth name. Born Carl Lucas, he adopts the name "Luke Cage" after a prison experiment leaves him with super strength and impenetrable skin. Setting up shop in Harlem, he uses those powers to perform tasks for whoever can pay his fee. Despite his well-meaning white creators' tendency to indulge in stereotypes, Luke Cage, who also used the name "Power Man," found an appreciative audience. Cage's choice of name would provide the first sign of the actor's comic book fandom, but hardly the last.

The other source dates back farther, and bears the stamp of August's influence. Composer John Cage helped reshape classical music in the middle years of the twentieth century by building on the ideas of teachers such as Henry Cowell and Arnold Schoenberg, drawing on Eastern influences, inventing the prepared piano by placing objects within the instrument to alter its sound, and otherwise looking beyond the traditional rules of composition. John Cage's "4'33"" asked musicians to sit silently for four minutes and thirty-three seconds and let audiences treat the sound of their environment as a kind of sound composition. It would become his most famous piece, but his innovations go well beyond this one radical idea.

The name feels, in light of Cage's later career, carefully chosen, reflecting both the actor's love of pop culture and larger-than-life characters and his desire to ignore convention. But even if it had been selected at random—if he'd gone with, say, "Nicolas Smith"—it would still have accomplished its main goal of freeing him from the expectations of the Coppola name.

Now he just had to live up to the new one.

❑ ❑ ❑

Though alternately living in his car and in his maternal grandmother's house at the time, Cage came to *Valley Girl* prepared, helping Coolidge make the film on a small budget and within a two-week shooting schedule. He also found ways to bring inventiveness to the performance, as in a string of reaction shots in a scene in which Randy hangs out in a bathroom waiting for a chance to talk to Julie again. Introduced shirtless on a beach, Randy could easily have been a stock '80s beefcake character with a rebellious side, one not that far removed from the musclebound beach rat of *The Best of Times*. (Albeit one with his chest hair shaved into a peculiar, Superman-inspired triangle pattern, a Cage contribution.) Cage never lets this happen. His performance keeps a light touch, but it's also clearly the work of an actor who'd been inspired by *East of Eden*, a funny turn deepened by the suggestion that it could easily slide into despair, particularly in a long, drunken scene after Randy seemingly loses Julie for good.

Valley Girl hit theaters as the fad that spawned it had started to cool (and after a failed trademark infringement lawsuit from Zappa), but critics and audiences greeted the film, and its new star, warmly. That's undoubtedly in part because the film feels at once specific to a particular time and place and universal. *Valley Girl* features no shortage of Valspeak and Valley Girl–friendly fashions, but Coolidge doesn't overplay those elements. Julie and her friends quickly emerge as ordinary teenagers and the Valley as the site of a classic conflict between peer pressure and individual expression and between the haves and have-nots—both echoing Cage's own experiences in Hollywood and at Beverly Hills High.

The film also reflected a generational divide that would play out over the course of the decade. Julie's interests have nothing to do with those of her ex-hippie parents (Frederic Forrest and Colleen Camp), whose health food restaurant looks like one of the last vestiges of a 1960s Los Angeles fast being swallowed up by the '80s. They'd dreamed of a better world, but their kids want nothing to do with those dreams. Equally of the moment is the film's soundtrack, filled with the New Wave hits popularized by the left-of-center LA station KROQ. Coolidge even makes the club research she conducted for *Photoplay* pay off in a pair off concert sequences featuring the cult-favorite band the Plimsouls.

This strong sense of place helps set the film apart from other teen comedies, as does Coolidge's choice to rely more on character and atmosphere than plot. She's more interested in the worlds in which Randy and Julie live and the culture clash created by the *Romeo and Juliet*–inspired mismatched couple. *Valley Girl* looks back to *The Graduate* (which Coolidge directly references at a couple of points) and forward to Cameron Crowe's *Say Anything*, a film similarly adept at capturing a particular moment while depicting outsize teen passion.

Reviews praised the cast as a whole while often singling out Cage. Even those lukewarm on the film, like Steven Rea in the *Philadelphia Inquirer*, praised the actor as "endearingly goonish." Like other critics, Rea didn't quite know what to make of Cage's offbeat appearance, describing him as "goofily handsome" and noting his "furry eyebrows" and "big nose." In a positive review, the *Cincinnati Enquirer* remarked upon his "sleepy eyelids" and noted a resemblance to Prince Charles.

In spite of the good press, those wanting to know more about the emerging star were left wanting. As August turned to September, the *Los Angeles Times* ran a weeklong series profiling the "Summer's Hot Faces," which included Tom Cruise, Jennifer Beals, Matthew Broderick, Rob Lowe, and

Ally Sheedy, all of whom agreed to speak to the paper. Not Cage, who let agent Ilene Feldman field the inquiry. "He just wants to work," Feldman told the *Times*. "He just wants to do his best. If people want to write about his work on-screen, he thinks that's fine. He just doesn't want to exploit himself." Cage did volunteer to journalist Deborah Caulfield one personal detail via Feldman: "He said to mention that he has a 2½ foot monitor lizard named Smokey."

Smokey's name came from Cage's character in *Rumble Fish*, which premiered that October. Critics, most of whom dismissed the film as an exercise in style over substance, made little note of Cage's work, and moviegoers paid little attention. Where *The Outsiders* gave Coppola a much-needed hit, *Rumble Fish* underperformed at the box office. Time has been kind to it, however, and the film has since earned reappraisals and found an appreciative audience that missed it the first time around, but caught up with its striking imagery and heartfelt depiction of teen alienation and troubled fraternal bonds via home video and cable. That was years ahead, however. In the meantime, Coppola needed to work, a need that would lead him to take on a project already teetering into disaster.

❑ ❑ ❑

As *Rumble Fish* arrived in theaters, Cage had already completed his next movie and started work on another. The first, *Racing with the Moon*, cast him alongside another rising star, Sean Penn, as a pair of Northern California kids trying to figure out how to spend their last days before reporting for military service at the height of World War II. Penn plays Henry "Hopper" Nash, who whiles his days away working as a bowling alley pinsetter alongside Cage's Nicky, his self-destructive friend from, once again, the wrong side of the tracks.

It's not hard to see what attracted Cage to the film. Its screenplay, the first effort from up-and-coming writer Steve Kloves (later to script all but one of the *Harry Potter* films and write and direct *The Fabulous Baker Boys*), keeps the focus squarely on the central characters. Richard Benjamin, an actor turned director, had enjoyed success with *My Favorite Year*, his directorial debut, released two years before. Benjamin appeared poised for a career helming small-scale, actor-friendly films that wouldn't have felt out of place in the preceding decade.

Though a bit too sleepily paced for its own good, *Racing with the Moon* fits that mold and allows Cage to play desperation verging on mania as he tries to secure enough money to pay for his girlfriend's abortion, most memorably in a sequence in which Henry and Nicky try to hustle some sailors at pool. Both Cage and Penn give performances of an intensity Benjamin has no interest in matching. Both would also soon find projects that would take all the intensity they could deliver. Respectful reviews failed to turn *Racing with the Moon* into a hit in the spring of 1984, when it struggled to be noticed amid competition that included the much bigger movies *Police Academy*, *Splash*, and *Footloose*. In the changing market, a sweet character study could work if, like *Valley Girl*, it almost looked like a different sort of film. More straightforward efforts, however, found themselves hitting walls. (That the stars did no publicity probably hurt the film as well. Cage explained a few years later that he wasn't "a great fan of that film.")

Racing with the Moon appeared shortly after Cage wound

down work on a film that had taken up more of his time than he'd expected. Reunited with Coppola again, he had taken the role of an even more self-destructive character in *The Cotton Club*, in which he plays Vincent "Mad Dog" Dwyer, the younger brother of protagonist "Dixie" Dwyer (Richard Gere), a cornetist reluctantly drawn into the criminal underworld of 1920s and '30s New York City when he saves the life of gangster Dutch Schultz. Vincent, for his part, enthusiastically plunges into the world. His sanity starts to slip away as his crimes escalate, and the role allows Cage to attempt a fresh spin on classic gangster film performances from James Cagney and Edward G. Robinson.

If the idea had been to show up, deliver a memorable supporting turn, then move on to the next movie, it didn't quite work out as planned. As with previous Coppola films, the shoot proved rocky. Originated by Coppola's *Godfather* producer Robert Evans, with whom Coppola already had a tumultuous relationship, and with a story conceived by *Godfather* author Mario Puzo, the film looked on paper like the reunion of a powerhouse team. In reality, the team didn't mesh particularly well this time, thanks in part to outside drama. *The Cotton Club* went through multiple rewrites and reconceptualizations over the course of a troubled production involving Las Vegas casino owners, a Middle Eastern arms dealer, and the murder of a financier.

"I was slated for three weeks' work," Cage later said of the experience. "I was there for six months, in costume, in makeup, on the set." In response, he acted out. He trashed his trailer in frustration and used destructive techniques to get into character, like crushing a street vendor's toy car to work himself into a frenzy. "'I had to do it to learn that I didn't have to do it," he told the *Los Angeles Daily News* in 1990, "but it got pretty dark." This unhappy period remained on his mind nearly a decade later, when he told *Rolling Stone*, "My name in Manhattan was really worth mud. I really made quite a little reputation for myself on that set, trying to live the part. It took me years to get to a point where New Yorkers in the film industry would want to work with me again. I have to say, both my uncle and my father seemed amazingly patient with my shenanigans, so to speak, as an actor." The less indulgent Gere, however, found such shenanigans alarming. "You keep going like this," he said, "and you're only going to have about five more movies in you."

The torturous process resulted in a film that flatlined at the box office despite sharing so much DNA with *The Godfather*. Comparisons to that classic proved unflattering—as they would with most any film. *The Cotton Club* doesn't approach *The Godfather*, but it has much to recommend it, from the musical and dance sequences to the rich period detail. It's an imperfect movie, but also a movie out of time, dominated by a '70s sensibility deeply at odds with competition like *Beverly Hills Cop*, the top film the week *The Cotton Club* arrived in theaters. As with *Rumble Fish*, it would benefit from a rehabilitation effort in later decades. In 2019, Coppola released a self-financed cut of the film that restored the balance in screen time between Gere and Gregory Hines, whose dancer character was conceived as a co-protagonist. Cuts to the film prior to its theatrical release had reduced Hines's role, and with it, the importance of many of the film's Black characters and some remarkable musical numbers. In both cuts, however, Cage makes a strong impression playing the unhinged, doomed Mad Dog.

It wouldn't be *The Cotton Club* that earned Cage attention when it finally arrived in theaters on December 14, 1984, but a film that entered limited release a week later—one whose production involved a different sort of torture.

❑ ❑ ❑

"Earlier in my career I was very specific in my concept of who I wanted to be," Cage told the *New York Times*'s David Marchese in 2019. "I saw myself as a surrealist. This is going to sound pretentious, but I was, quote, trying to invent my own mythology, unquote, around myself." That sort of mythology gets built brick by brick, with stories like this: to prepare for his role in *Birdy*, Cage voluntarily had four teeth pulled, a detail that would turn up in virtually every Cage profile for years to come. That they were impacted baby teeth that needed to be extracted anyway sometimes got lost in the telling.

Baby teeth or not, it still seemed like an extreme measure to take to prepare for the role of Al, a wounded Vietnam veteran, in Alan Parker's *Birdy*, though perhaps not as extreme as another choice. During the five weeks spent filming the scenes set after Al returns from Vietnam, Cage remained covered in the bandages worn by his character and refused to look at his face. "Once the bandages were on, he wanted to forget what his face looked like," Parker recalled on the film's audio commentary track, released in 2019. "It was his way of dealing with the acting. So, even when fresh bandages were put on each morning for continuity, he would close his eyes. So, for the whole period that we shot with him, which was continuous, with the bandages on, he wanted to forget exactly how his face looked." Cage lost fifteen pounds in the process. It wasn't the first time he had taken extraordinary steps to stay in character—he'd slashed his arm filming one *Racing with the Moon* scene—and it wouldn't be the last step he'd take to stay in character that could double as myth-burnishing anecdote.

Cage was, by birth, associated with the school of filmmaking that dominated the 1970s. By working with Parker, he connected to an equally distinct group in the process of defining the 1980s, though their story begins much sooner. Where Roger Corman productions doubled as a kind of film grad school for up-and-coming directors in Hollywood, starting the 1960s crop that included Coppola, the advertising world played a similar role in '60s London. Drawing on the French New Wave and other influences, directors like Adrian Lyne, Hugh Hudson, brothers Ridley and Tony Scott, and American transplant Michael Mann broke with the staid tradition of previous advertisements, bringing in striking visuals and disarming gags to sell less-than-sexy products like Hovis Bread and Birds Eye frozen burgers. And because many of them had larger ambitions, the ads also served as both experiments and calling cards.

Known for his humor and habit of populating his ads with characters that reflected his working-class background, Parker became the first to make the leap to features with the 1976 film *Bugsy Malone*. A musical inspired by classic gangster films and starring a cast of children (most notably, Jodie Foster and Scott Baio), the film became a hit at Cannes and in the United Kingdom, where it earned a handful of BAFTAs. Parker followed it with *Midnight Express*, a fact-based film exploring an

American college student's experiences in a Turkish prison, in 1978. With its diffuse lighting, electronic Giorgio Moroder score, and moody atmosphere, it helped define a look and feel that would dominate '80s filmmaking, alongside the work of others from the British ad school.

By 1984, this group's influence was inescapable, thanks to projects like *Alien* and *Blade Runner* (both directed by Ridley Scott), *The Hunger* (Tony Scott), *Thief* and the TV series *Miami Vice* (Mann), *Chariots of Fire* (Hudson), *Foxes* and *Flashdance* (Lyne), and Parker's *Midnight Express* follow-ups *Fame*, *Shoot the Moon*, and *Pink Floyd: The Wall*. It could also be felt outside movie theaters, putting a deep stamp on early '80s music videos, whose aesthetic, in turn, influenced the era's movies—a kind of ouroboros of influence spinning out of thirty-second spots made for British television decades before. (And even after transitioning to features, many kept a toe in the ad world, most famously Ridley Scott, via his Orwell-inspired 1984 Super Bowl ad introducing Apple's Macintosh.)

Like his contemporaries, Parker had to fight accusations of prioritizing style over substance, but the charge doesn't stick to *Birdy*, which effectively lets one element serve the other. Adapted from the 1978 debut novel of William Wharton (the pen name of painter Albert William Du Aime), it's the story of the unlikely friendship between two Philadelphia teens in the 1960s. Cage plays the confident Al, who spends his time chasing girls but develops a fascination with his next-door neighbor, an odd kid whose obsessive interest in birds has earned him the nickname "Birdy" (Matthew Modine). The film flashes back and forth between their high school misadventures, including Birdy's attempt to fly while wearing a homemade bird suit, and the aftermath of their Vietnam service. While recovering from his wounds, Al travels to a mental hospital where Birdy spends his days speechless, perched on the edge of his bed, behaving more like bird than man.

Parker shot the prewar scenes in the early part of the production, following them with the hospital scenes. Cage similarly divides his performance in two. He's a suave neighborhood kid in Philadelphia and a broken man in ways not evident by his bandaged face and missing teeth in the hospital scenes. Both halves presented acting challenges Cage had never really faced before, but he rises to them, particularly when asked to suggest Al's mounting desperation as his attempts to get Birdy to open up repeatedly fail, raising the possibility that his friend will be institutionalized for life. The intensity hinted at in *Racing with the Moon* and glimpsed in *The Cotton Club* finds full expression here in disturbingly raw scenes that find Cage playing Al as a man who may have slipped beyond repair. Where Birdy has retreated into fantasy, Al has no such means of escape. He's a weeping, rageful mess, unable to find comfort even when it's offered to him unconditionally by a compassionate nurse (Karen Young).

Parker brings his trademark visual style to *Birdy*, particularly in flying sequences using the then-new SkyCam (a kind of Steadicam for aerial scenes) and in the film's most famous shot, in which a nude Birdy, drenched in blue light, stares up at the night sky through the bars of a cell. Yet the film relies just as heavily on the performances of its leads, a study in contrasts that brings out the best in both Modine and Cage. Just a few years later, the casting would seem counterintuitive, with Cage naturally being slotted into the role of the "crazy" character. In the more grounded role, his performance grows more affecting as the film progresses and as Al transforms from a confident kid to a weeping mess. The two styles—Modine's gentle oddness and Cage's nervy energy—complement each other beautifully, indirectly conveying Wharton's suggestion that the two characters might actually be aspects of one person. (And, indeed, both Al's and Birdy's stories bear traces of Wharton's own.)

Birdy received an awards-qualifying release in a few theaters at the end of 1984 and then never played more than a handful of American theaters at a time over the next few months. Parker may have helped define the look of commercial '80s movies, but that didn't mean all his movies found commercial success. Those who saw the film remembered it, however, earning Parker some of the best reviews of his career (though the influential *Variety*'s mixed review likely depressed its commercial chances). The cast drew particular praise, with the *Chicago Sun-Times*'s Roger Ebert noting that Cage's inability to use much of his face to emote for a bulk of the film increased the difficulty of his performance.

What worked for others, however, didn't work for Cage, who, speaking to the *Louisville Courier-Journal* in 1990, said, "I like the film itself, but my performance is hard for me to watch. It's almost as if I'm embarrassed by it because it's so bare. There's very little choreography or thought behind it. It's just this very stripped, very wounded character, and for me it's so personal that I feel uncomfortable watching it." Asked if his later turn toward more expressionistic performances stemmed from that dissatisfaction, he replied, "Somewhat. I just felt my own naturalistic style had reached a dead end and I was getting bored with it. I was neglecting this whole other part of my psyche that wanted to get out." An opportunity to release it would soon present itself.

But not immediately. Cage next traveled to Canada to play Ned Hanlan, a famous Canadian sculler (insofar as a Canadian sculler can be famous), in *The Boy in Blue*. Cage has rarely talked about the film, though the press notes include a quote of him stating, "One of the reasons I really wanted to do it was that I needed a crash course to get me off that guy in *Birdy*." Whatever improvements the project might have made to his mental state, it had a visible impact on his physique: Cage trained extensively in order to perform the rowing scenes. But the film's virtues don't really extend much farther than whatever health benefits it might have had for its star. Dully directed by British veteran Charles Jarrott (*Anne of the Thousand Days*), it's a by-the-numbers biopic that would sit on the shelf until receiving a small release in 1986 and the first film that even Cage didn't know how to liven up.

This would rarely be the case, but *The Boy in Blue* did provide an early example of Cage struggling with a project that didn't play to his strengths. The material was weak, but for another actor—one comfortable coasting on easy charm, a handsome face, and a sculpted torso—it might have been an easy layup. Instead, Cage appears to struggle in an undemanding role, one resistant to any attempts to put an interesting spin on the clichéd hunky bad boy. It wasn't his part to play, or at least his to play well. Taking on such roles wouldn't get him noticed, at least not in the ways he wanted to be noticed; nor would it provide a path to stardom. Getting there would mean clearing his own, strange path—and making some wonder if he'd lost his mind along the way.

3

Cage Unchained

They wanted a prom king. He gave them a claymation horse.

All acting involves choices, but some actors make choices that wouldn't occur to anyone else. For his role as Charlie Bodell in the 1986 romantic fantasy *Peggy Sue Got Married*, Nicolas Cage made unusual, borderline ridiculous decisions that might have proven disastrous (and did prove divisive): bleached-out, brushed-back hair; big, fake teeth; and a voice borrowed from Pokey, the equine best friend of the stop-motion animation hero Gumby. But they also, weirdly, worked, turning what could have been a stock character (the high school stud gone to seed) into a memorably vulnerable creation, cartoon voice and all. Sometimes the weird choice is the right choice—even if not everyone sees it that way.

The film stars Kathleen Turner as Peggy Sue Bodell, a bakery owner and mother of two in her early forties who, once upon a time in 1960, was Peggy Sue Kelcher, a high school senior with her whole life ahead of her. A class school reunion doubles as a reminder that life hasn't turned out quite as she planned. She's watched her marriage to Charlie, her high school sweetheart, hit the rocks due to his infidelity and has come to realize she has little to call her own, having wrapped her life so tightly around Charlie's as he fell into an unsatisfying career selling electronics. The universe responds with the apparent offer of a second chance. After passing out at the reunion, Peggy Sue awakens in the spring of her senior year. The clock has rewound for her and only her. She carries with her the wisdom of adulthood while everyone else around her remains the kids they were in the final year of the Eisenhower administration, including Charlie, the future prom king to her queen.

Peggy Sue Got Married is, in many respects, Turner's movie. She's rarely off-screen, and the film—scripted by the married writing team of Arlene Sarner and Jerry Leichtling—never strays from her emotional journey through the past. Turner rises to the challenge with a remarkable performance. Early scenes ring with such raw emotion that they become almost hard to watch, as she tells her sister Nancy, still just a ponytailed Girl Scout (played by Cage's cousin Sofia Coppola), that she wants them to be closer and finds herself unable to talk on the phone to her long-dead grandparents.

Peggy Sue's time in 1960 becomes a progression of existential roller-coaster dips that make her question the choices she's made and her memories of the past, which rarely square with the world in which she now finds herself. How, for instance, given that her classmates included a fiery, handsome beatnik and a future billionaire, could she have ended up with such a dork?

Turner must have asked herself the same questions about Cage. She found herself unable to contain her skepticism, warning Cage, "Remember, film is a permanent record." But later, she allowed that he might have been on to something, telling *Vulture* in 2018 that "[i]f anything, it [Cage's portrayal] only further illustrated my character's disillusionment with the past."

She hadn't always been so kind. In her 2008 memoir, *Send Yourself Roses*, Turner attributes Cage's choice to a single motivation: an urge to rebel. When he shot *Peggy Sue Got Married* in July 1985, it would be the third film in his eight-film career that found him taking advantage of his family's film connections while trying to distance himself from them. He had changed his name to "Cage" partly to avoid charges of line jumping, yet he kept taking roles in Coppola's films, none more substantial than Charlie. Turner recalled:

> The problem was that once Nicolas got the role, he wanted to prove that he wasn't there as the result of nepotism. And so everything Francis wanted him to do, he just went against—just to show he wasn't under Francis's wing. Which was ridiculous, because Francis's instincts and direction were excellent. But Nicolas had to do the opposite to everything: that stupid voice and the fake teeth—oh, honestly. I cringe to think of it.

So was Cage's Charlie the result of an urge to assert himself against Coppola or a thoughtful interpretation of the character? Sometimes two things can be true at once. Cage's history with Coppola had been complicated, but Turner also pinpoints what makes the performance work. In Peggy Sue's mind, the Charlie of 1960 remains a romantic ideal. The *real* Charlie of 1960, however, is nobody's dreamboat. He's a boy with a boy's voice and a boy's attitudes, telling her they should see other people after graduation but get back together in three years, when he's become a big singing star like his hero, Fabian.

What Charlie can't realize is that, also like Fabian, he's already peaked. A teen idol who helped fill the void during Elvis's army years, Fabian shot to stardom after appearing on *American Bandstand* and became inescapable in 1959. By the spring of 1960, he'd still have diehard fans like Charlie, but the hits had all but dried up. Though Fabian would enjoy some success as an actor in the years that followed, his music career hit a dead end. Charlie, Peggy Sue now knows—though she can't explain how she knows—won't get even that far.

In the film's pivotal scene, the two have it out in the basement of Peggy Sue's parents' house. She's fooled around on him, and now Charlie, the kid who wanted to see other people, wants only Peggy Sue. She can't help but hear him out, even knowing it will end badly. Barely containing himself, he demands her love while moonlight beams in behind them. "There's this window in my heart," she tells him, "and every time I leave it open, you climb in. Unless I close it now, nothing's ever going to be different." Charlie replies with rage and tears, baffled at her change of heart and vowing never to sell appliances or chase women like his father. The voice doesn't change. It's still Pokey. The fussed-over pompadour, though a little messier, doesn't change, either. And the teeth don't look any realer. The Charlie of this scene remains the misguided goofball he's been throughout the movie. And in that moment, your heart breaks for the goofball, and every seemingly absurd choice Cage has made in crafting the character seems like the *only* choice he could have made to bring Charlie to life and to make that heartbreak sting.

By doing everything wrong, Cage had done everything right.

❑ ❑ ❑

It nearly got him fired.

For Coppola, *Peggy Sue Got Married* was far from a passion project. Yet, as usual, the future of his career depended on its success. When he joined the film at the behest of independent producer Ray Stark, for whom Coppola worked as a screenwriter in the 1960s, the film had already lost two directors (Jonathan Demme and Penny Marshall) to creative differences and would soon lose original star Debra Winger to back problems. The tension didn't end there, thanks to long hours and a tight shooting schedule and skepticism about Cage's performance.

Cage would recall Stark traveling to the set, via Learjet, with the intention of firing him until Coppola talked him down. Where Turner wrote of an actor rebelling against his director, Cage remembered it as a case of compatible sensibilities making for a happy collaboration. "[Coppola's] philosophy is that if you're going to gamble, then gamble with everything you've got," Cage told the *Los Angeles Times* as the film hit theaters. "He loves taking chances and so do I."

In this instance, both men's gambles paid off. Released on October 10, 1986, *Peggy Sue Got Married* became an undeniable hit. Joined the next week by Martin Scorsese's *The Color of Money*, a film by another director seeking a comeback by way of a mainstream work-for-hire job, it suggested that 1970s auteurs could still be formidable at the box office. Neither could unseat the season's reigning champ, *Crocodile Dundee*, from the top spot, but both had legs that kept them in theaters through December, and both benefited from the fall return of moviegoers seeking more restrained fare after a blockbuster summer dominated by *Top Gun*, *Aliens*, and *The Fly*.

Not all the reviews glowed with appreciation, particularly not those of the *New York Times*'s Vincent Canby ("a small, amiable, sort of sloppy comedy-fantasy") or the *New Yorker*'s Pauline Kael ("no depth . . . groggy"), but it won over many others. Most compared it to the previous summer's hit *Back to the Future*, such as *Time*'s Richard Corliss, who called it a "sweeter, slower spin on the time machine."

Cage's performance provoked strong responses on both ends of the critical spectrum. In *People*, Peter Travers dubbed Cage "a dud as a romantic hero for any decade." Others, however, singled him out for praise, such as the *Detroit Free Press*'s Catharine Rambeau, who noted, "Nicolas Cage is a startling choice for a leading man, but his selection was one of the film's better moves. Cage isn't conventionally attractive—he's a jerk in a lot of ways, too—but the way Cage emphasizes Charlie's single-minded devotion to Peggy Sue—and we're talking serious love-is-eternal emotion here—makes him irresistible."

Peggy Sue Got Married set a pattern that would repeat itself throughout Cage's career, particularly with his more outré performances. What resonated with some repelled others. Some saw his choices as artful and innovative. Others couldn't see past the teeth or hear any music in the funny voice. Where Cage's more naturalistic performance in *Birdy* was easy to grasp, and just as easy to praise, this new, riskier approach found him ranging into unknown territory. His efforts earned him attention and helped land him work, but he'd soon find that not everyone was interested in racing to the edge along with him.

❑ ❑ ❑

The studio chief took a break from spitting out sunflower seed shells to ask Joel and Ethan Coen a question: "Why is *Revenge of the Nerds* making so much money?" The Coens had traveled to LA in 1983 in an attempt to sell their debut feature, a stylish neo-noir named *Blood Simple*, and hadn't met with much luck. Recounting the trip to *Rolling Stone* in 1987, they recalled it as a string of frustrating encounters with Hollywood, but none more puzzling than this one. As they left, Ethan told the never-named executive, "If there's anything else you want to know about the movie business, feel free to call me." The unnamed chief laughed, but he didn't buy the movie.

Blood Simple found success anyway, on the modest scale by which success for an independently financed film was measured in the 1980s before the breakout success of *sex, lies, and videotape* in 1989. Directors of such films were now mentioned in the same breath as John Sayles, Alex Cox, and Jim Jarmusch, which was nice, but it didn't solve the problem of what to do next or how to stay true to their artistic impulses while also making a movie they could sell.

The question of *Revenge of the Nerds*'s success, however bizarre a non sequitur it must have seemed at the time, wasn't *entirely* irrelevant to the Coen brothers' future, given their aspirations to make comedies (and an unmistakable streak of dark humor runs through even the brutal *Blood Simple*). While they shopped *Blood Simple* around, mainstream movie comedies had entered a period of transition.

As little as they have in common, both *Valley Girl* and *Revenge of the Nerds* owe their existence to a demand for R-rated teen comedies. Yet, for as much success as *Revenge of the Nerds* enjoyed in the summer of 1984, that year also saw the premiere of John Hughes's directorial debut, *Sixteen Candles*, which mixed rowdy antics with sensitive drama and squeezed both into a PG-rated package, widening the potential audience. Hughes's influence would be felt through the rest of the decade's teen films as heavily as the influence of *Porky's* could be felt in the first half of the 1980s. Elsewhere, comedies went big and merged with other genres, as evidenced by two of the year's biggest hits, *Ghostbusters* and *Beverly Hills Cop*.

So where did a couple of inventive, eccentric brothers from Minnesota by way of New York fit into this changing landscape? For their second film, the Coens found a spot next to some successful, superficially similar films. As critic Adam Nayman observed, the mid-1980s saw a small explosion of comedies featuring "protagonists unexpectedly thrust into caregiver roles," a trend that stretched from *Mr. Mom* in 1983 through the *Look Who's Talking* films of the late 1980s and early '90s. Nineteen eighty-seven became its high-water mark thanks to the release of *Baby Boom*, *Three Men and a Baby*, and the Coens' *Raising Arizona*.

While *Raising Arizona*'s premise might have borne a resemblance to other '80s comedies, that resemblance doesn't extend much farther than the broad details of its plot. Working with a larger budget and on a bigger scale than *Blood Simple*, the Coens took the opportunity to construct a comedy reflecting the deepening Reagan-era divide between haves and have-nots, one that often resembles a live-action cartoon as it erupts into long, unpredictable action set pieces. Between such moments, the film clearly treasures the humanity of its flawed, occasionally dim-witted, but soulful central couple: H. I. McDunnough, a small-time Arizona criminal forever blowing his attempts to go straight, and Edwina (better known as "Ed"), the police officer whose heart he captures over the course of several mug shot sessions. Devastated by Ed's infertility and their inability to have "critters" of their own, they take the extreme step of stealing one of the quintuplets born to Nathan Arizona, the wealthy owner of a big-box furniture store.

To embody such characters would require finding actors capable of walking the divide between the absurd and the heartfelt. For Ed, the Coens didn't have to look too far. They were friends with Holly Hunter, an emerging actress they'd tried to cast as the lead for *Blood Simple*—instead settling for Hunter's roommate (later, Joel Coen's wife), Frances McDormand—and wrote *Raising Arizona* with her in mind. The role of H.I., however, would prove more challenging.

Cage immediately saw himself in the part. "When I read *Raising Arizona*, I knew it was a film I really wanted to do," he told the *Los Angeles Times* the fall before its release. "But after I met with Ethan and Joel Coen they told my agent they couldn't see me in the role at all. I was very disheartened." The Coens took some convincing via multiple auditions, and even after Cage won the role, the collaboration wasn't without its bumps. The same *Rolling Stone* profile of the Coens alludes to Cage feeling "stymied," unhappy that the Coens wouldn't take his suggestions or, initially, let him watch dailies of his performance. In 1990, speaking to *American Film* magazine, the actor would use the word *autocratic* to describe their directorial style. Speaking to *GQ* in 2018, he recalled Joel telling him, "You know, I could have cast Kevin Costner in this part." Cage's reply: "Well, then why did you cast me?"

The answer is evident in the film itself. With just one movie under their belt, the Coens were not yet well known as the makers of carefully choreographed films that share an unmistakable tone, whether exploring the gothic underside of golden age Hollywood in *Barton Fink* or the story of a 1960s radical turned full-time slacker whose name puts him at the center of a labyrinthine mystery in *The Big Lebowski*. Their Swiss-watch precision works better for some actors—they often recycle cast members from film to film—than others. The Coens make films that demand a shared vision of their cast, and that vision often involves deferring to the filmmakers' wishes. Yet, while Cage may not always have enjoyed serving as a cog in the Coens' machine, the film would play radically differently without him at its center.

Cage frequently cites the cartoon character Woody Woodpecker as a source of inspiration for his performance, and his character even sports a woodpecker tattoo (though it bears a closer resemblance to the angry auto parts mascot "Mr. Horsepower" than the mischievous cartoon bird). That's evident in the rubber-like contortions the physically demanding role asks of him in scenes that find him running from the police through a grocery store and across the lawns of unsuspecting suburban homeowners and engaging in several intense fights. Yet beneath the unruly head of hair that underscores the cartoon connection, H.I. possesses worried eyes and a reflective temperament. However wild the movie around him becomes, Cage never lets viewers forget that his character is acting out of love and desperation and that his responsibility to Ed weighs heavily on him. He lives to make her happy. He knows he might end up dying to do so.

The Coens' ambition extends beyond pratfalls and diaper gags, though *Raising Arizona* has both in abundance. H.I.'s recidivism has less to do with a faulty character than an absence of other options. "I tried to stand up and fly straight, but it wasn't easy with that sumbitch Reagan in the White House," he says in a voiceover. But because he's a fundamentally gentle soul, he adds, "They say he's a decent man, so maybe his advisors are confused." This innate kindness extends to a moving final scene, also narrated by H.I., in which he imagines a future where he and Ed find the happiness they want and share it across generations of children and grandchildren at a Thanksgiving feast that seems to stretch on forever. It might be just a dream, but who can live believing that dreams never come true?

Picked up by 20th Century Fox and released gradually in the spring of 1987, *Raising Arizona* became a warmly embraced hit. At the box office, the film never cracked a top five dominated by *The Secret of My Success* and *Police Academy 4: Citizens on Patrol*, but it earned steadily and charmed critics as it rolled across the country. One voice of dissent came from the *Arizona Republic*'s Marsha McCreadie, who objected to Arizonans being portrayed as "materialistic, good-natured and simple minded . . . well-meaning buffoons" while raising the charge of condescension that would dog the Coens throughout their career.

Raising Arizona's reputation would only grow over the years, however, and any tension that existed on the set can't be sensed in the final film. Cage's recollection of being penned in has also seemed to soften with the passage of time. In 2018, he described the shoot as "a terrific experience," elaborating, "That's where I coined the phrase 'I'm getting that Super 8 feeling.' I used to make movies in the backyard when we were children and we had a Super 8 camera that my father gave us and we would make movies. That Super 8 feeling is that feeling where you're making a movie simply because you love the movie. You're not doing it for money. You're not doing it for awards. You're doing it simply because you love the story you're telling and the filmmaking feeling itself."

It's not a feeling he'd find with every film.

4

The Rage of Cage

Sometime after making *The Boy in Blue*, Nicolas Cage acquired his first tattoo, the image of a lizard wearing a top hat. It was, he told *Rolling Stone*'s Debby Bull, because he felt his soul was leaking out of his body and he hoped the tattoo would burn it back in. The *Boy in Blue* experience had not been a pleasant one, and the film's dead-on-arrival limited release in 1986 only confirmed his impulse to follow his instincts in choosing jobs going forward. That, however, did not apply to a movie originally known as *The Bride and the Wolf* and written by John Patrick Shanley, an acclaimed playwright making his first forays into screenwriting.

"I was only 21 when I made *Moonstruck*," Cage told the *Dallas Morning News* in 1992. "I was angry and rebellious. I wanted to make the kind of movies that are essentially punk gestures. I read the screenplay to *Moonstruck* and thought, 'I would never pay money to see this film!' But my agent insisted I do it, practically forced me to do it." So he did it. The film became a tremendous financial and critical success, raised Cage's profile by introducing him to his widest-yet audience, won him acclaim, and opened up new opportunities. All this confused him. "When I saw the finished film," Cage continued in the same interview, "I didn't know what in the world to make of it. That was my era of wanting to make new-wave alternative films."

These would have to wait for Cage to veer away from the mainstream, and *Moonstruck* was as mainstream as he'd ever gotten. Shanley's warm, clever, beautifully crafted script about the many types and stages of love and the difficulty of finding and hanging on to it—as experienced by multiple generations of an Italian American family in Brooklyn—landed in the practiced hands of director Norman Jewison. Jewison had a long track record of success with a variety of movies, including *In the Heat of the Night, The Thomas Crown Affair, Fiddler on the Roof,* and most recently *Agnes of God.* He therefore inspired trust among both producers and actors. (Mostly, anyway, as *Moonstruck*'s production would reveal.) The project also won the notice of Cher, who agreed to star, a bit of casting that guaranteed the film attention. This didn't make *Moonstruck* look like a sure thing in the days leading up to its release, however. "And we're just all so happy. And we don't think it's going to make very much money, but we are proud," Cher recalled to Caity Weaver in a 2020 *New York Times Magazine* interview before noting that MGM was less fond of the movie (using what Weaver describes as "Technicolor language"). "So they just shelve it," she continued. "And then a movie comes out for Christmas, but it just isn't good." (On a 2011 audio commentary recorded for the film's Blu-ray release, Cher was less reluctant to name the film in question; it was the Kurt Russell/ Goldie Hawn comedy *Overboard*.) This created a window for *Moonstruck*, which opened in two New York theaters and then spread, in Cher's words, "like wildfire." *Moonstruck*'s commercial prospects soon became apparent, and in retrospect, the film seems like the obvious winner. But this was harder to predict in 1987. The Hollywood that Cage entered in 1982 had changed significantly in the half decade that followed. In 1987, who knew what would work?

❑ ❑ ❑

The movies had gotten bigger. To study the charts of top-grossing films released between 1982, the year of Cage's debut, and 1987 is to watch the ascent of the modern blockbuster, as genre films, star-driven comedies, and sequels to these started to edge out films that didn't lend themselves to concise elevator pitches. It's a lot easier to sum up, say, *The Terminator* ("Killer robot from the future time-travels to Los Angeles") than *Children of a Lesser God* ("A teacher at a school for the deaf struggles to break through to a young woman working as janitor with whom he falls into a romantic relationship complicated by . . ." etc.). Nonetheless, in the top-grossing films of 1982, *The Verdict*, *Gandhi*, *Tootsie*, and *Das Boot* coexisted peacefully alongside *E.T.*, *Rocky III*, and *Conan the Barbarian*.

Nineteen eighty-seven still had room for films that fell outside the blockbuster mold, but success had gotten less predictable. The year's surest-fire hit, *Beverly Hills Cop II*, a Tony Scott–directed sequel released at the height of Eddie

Murphy's stardom, easily nabbed the number two slot. Sandwiching it, however, were the year's biggest hit, *Fatal Attraction*, and its biggest sleeper surprise, *Dirty Dancing*.

Directed by Adrian Lyne, a product of the same London ad world as Alan Parker, *Fatal Attraction* struck a cultural nerve by using a violent erotic thriller to raise questions about sex and fidelity. *Dirty Dancing* was a nostalgic period piece set in the Catskills of the early 1960s that found a young audience via a combination of oldies music, elaborate choreography, and Patrick Swayze's tank top. Rounding out the top ten: *3 Men and a Baby* (which featured all the adorableness and bumbling of *Raising Arizona*, without the weirdness), *The Living Daylights* (from the reliable James Bond franchise), *Lethal Weapon*, *Predator*, and *The Untouchables*, but also less predictable fare including *Good Morning, Vietnam* and *Moonstruck*.

Though its grip had yet to fully tighten, the event film had started to take hold, in part because of the success of slick, high-concept, star-driven movies ranging from *Ghostbusters* to *Top Gun* and in part because of shifts within the business, in which power had drifted away from studios and into the hands of agencies. With CAA, Michael Ovitz had imported from television to films the concept of the package deal, by which an agency would assemble much of the talent involved in a project from the ranks of its clients. The studio system had collapsed, but the idea of vertical integration had survived via agencies that could supply concepts, writers, directors, and actors for a project.

When the approach worked, it could work spectacularly. *Rain Man* churned through cast members, writers, and directors as CAA tried one combination of in-house talent after another. The end result, however, became a huge hit when it arrived in theaters in 1988, in addition to winning Oscars for Best Picture, Best Actor, Best Original Screenplay, and Best Director. The system also resulted in a swelling of salaries, a welcome development for talent and agencies but one that kept much of the financial risk with the studios—and a trend that would continue to reshape the industry in decades to come.

As studios' financial investment increased, their willingness to take chances decreased. For *Rain Man*, star power served as a hedge against risk that allowed room for artistic expression. Another 1988 film, *Twins*, provides a better example of the package deal in action. A comedy about mismatched siblings seemingly tailored to accommodate the contrasting visuals of CAA clients Arnold Schwarzenegger and Danny DeVito (and directed by CAA's Ivan Reitman), it could have been created from the poster out. Even better: properties with built-in name recognition, be they sequels or remakes of old TV shows. Yet, for all their advantages, package deals had a way of making talent feel like, well, part of a package, a feeling that could chafe an actor in the habit of treating films as "punk gestures."

❏ ❏ ❏

It also helped create a movie marketplace in which a film like *Moonstruck* seemed less of a safe bet than *Overboard*, which featured a pair of recognizable stars and an easily summarized premise ("Snob gets amnesia and falls for slob"). Even Cher couldn't guarantee a film's success. Just four years earlier, audiences had snickered when she turned up in the trailer for *Silkwood*, her first high-profile role as an actress since the 1969 flop

Chastity. Nonetheless, that film earned her a Best Supporting Actress nomination, and she'd proven herself in subsequent films. But moviegoers can be fickle, and Cher still served as the butt of talk show jokes. (Less than a year before *Moonstruck*'s release, she'd used an appearance on *Late Night with David Letterman* as an opportunity to call its host an "asshole" on air.)

In *Moonstruck*, Cher plays Loretta Castorini, a Brooklyn Heights widow who keeps the books for neighborhood businesses and lives with her mother, father, and grandfather in an expansive home that's been in family hands for generations. After making the sensible, passionless choice of accepting a proposal from her boyfriend, Johnny (Danny Aiello), she agrees to try to mend fences with Johnny's brother, Ronny (Cage), a baker, while Johnny tends to their ailing mother in Italy.

Loretta enters the situation at a disadvantage, knowing nothing about Ronny or the bizarre circumstances of his estrangement from Johnny. Distracted by his brother, Ronny lost part of his hand in a bread slicer and hasn't been the same since. Within moments of meeting Loretta, he's threatening to kill himself as a kind of wedding present and shouting, "I lost my hand! I lost by bride! Johnny has his hand! Johnny has his bride!"

He's a character of outsize, readily expressed passions—and, appropriately, an opera lover, we'll soon learn—in a film filled with characters prone to keeping secrets, suppressing their dissatisfaction, or talking around their problems. Soon, he'll direct that passion toward Loretta, whom he quickly recognizes as the love of his life, whatever her commitment to Johnny. Loretta, however, takes some convincing, and as with *Birdy*, Cage again finds an effective complement by working opposite an actor prone to well-deployed understatement. Much of the credit for the pairing belongs to Cher, who, taken with Cage's *Peggy Sue Got Married* work, threatened to leave the film before playing opposite anyone else. "In my mind, when I read the script," she noted on the film's audio commentary, "I always saw Nicky doing those words."

Cage's performance stands out in other ways as well. Much of the excellent cast had reached the far side of middle age and play Shanley's clever lines with a wry wistfulness. All youthful energy, Cage bellows and entreats, sometimes seeming as bestial as the wolf Loretta likens him to. He was almost more bestial still. Early in production, Cage modeled his performance after Jean Marais's work in Jean Cocteau's *Beauty and the Beast*, a film he'd loved since childhood. In the film, Marais's leonine Beast speaks in raspy tones as close to growls as human speech can approach. Two weeks into production, Jewison told Cage "the dailies weren't working" and directed him to change his approach.

With *Peggy Sue Got Married*, Cage had made daring choices that would have lost him his job without Francis Ford Coppola's intervention. Jewison, however, didn't want him to persist in an approach he felt didn't work for the film. Not only didn't he give Cage free rein, but he fundamentally didn't agree with the choices Cage had made. It didn't always make for a happy collaboration.

"From the beginning I thought that Nicolas Cage, at that point in his life," Jewison recalled later, "was the most tormented soul I had ever met. I just thought he was a tormented person. And I told Cher that, and she agreed with me."

The tension came to a head while they were filming the

climactic scene, a warm, all-cast gathering around a kitchen
table in which the truth of Ronny and Loretta's relationship
comes out alongside other secrets and in which the characters'
conflicts melt away in a happy ending. The film depended on
the scene's working—and on everyone contributing to make it
work. Cage, as Jewison remembers on the audio commentary,
decided he didn't want to appear in it. On the same commentary, Cher backs up that memory and goes farther, recalling:

> Nicky walks in and goes, "I don't want to be in it. I don't
> think I can do it. I think it's silly. I don't want to be
> in it. I don't know how it's gonna work. I just think I
> shouldn't be in it." So of course everybody just, like, fell
> apart. And so Norman caused this fight. He kind of got
> everybody . . . He just caused all this energy. And Nicky
> was really cranky and pissed off. And then [costar] Julie
> [Bovasso], who was an acting teacher and a director in
> her own right, she said something to Nicky that really got
> him so crazy that he threw a chair across the living room.
> People were just going insane. It was so weird! And that's
> when we started shooting it.

Yet there's no evidence of that turmoil in the finished film,
even that final scene, which sends audiences out on a happy
note that affirms the power of love even in the midst of a life
shaped by messiness and disappointment. Perhaps it's fitting
that a film about the messy drama that comes with simply
being human would have a bit of tumult in its making.

One of the few critics to treat the film dismissively, the *New
York Times*'s Janet Maslin, praised Cher but called the part of

Ronny "so awful it's hard to know whom to blame." By contrast, the *New York Daily News*'s Chris Chase penned an unabashed rave, noting that "*Everybody's* good here" and singling out Cage as "hilariously moving," adding, "People keep being surprised that Cage, who's only 23, is such a terrific actor. Maybe you have to be 23 to have that combination of wildness and earnestness work for you." Most critics would align themselves with Chase, in their opinions both of the film as a whole and of Cage in particular.

Moonstruck opened in a few theaters just before Christmas, expanded in January, and then kept playing through June, well past the awards season that culminated in six Academy Award nominations and three wins: a Best Actress trophy for Cher, a Best Supporting Actress award for Olympia Dukakis, and a Best Original Screenplay prize for Shanley.

Yet, despite the acclaim, Cage went without a nomination. If it bothered him, he didn't let it show. Besides, he'd already made another movie he was eager to discuss.

❑ ❑ ❑

If a picture is worth a thousand words, sometimes two pictures can tell an even bigger story. In February 1988, Nicolas Cage sat for a *Los Angeles Times* profile inspired by his *Moonstruck* success.

"I feel like there's a big, wet fish slapping itself against the inside of my head right now," Cage told journalist Kristine McKenna. "Things have changed quite a bit in the past three weeks and I don't know what to make of all the attention the film is receiving." *Moonstruck* had conferred on Cage the status of a sex symbol, and he didn't know what to do with it. He had fought his representatives' pressure to make the film, disagreed with Jewison on his approach to his character, watched as some of his scenes disappeared from the movie, and then headed for the exit. But others loved the film and loved him in it, even if he wanted to spend his time making different sorts of movies. The photos accompanying the article capture the split. Up top, Cage looks like a tortured heartthrob as he runs his fingers through his hair. Below, mouth agape, he prepares to eat a cockroach.

The second image comes from *Vampire's Kiss*, a film Cage had shot in New York on the heels of *Moonstruck*. It wouldn't make it to theaters until June 2, 1989, and then just barely. At the height of its release, it could be found on just forty-five screens, playing to sparse crowds opposite *Batman*. It wouldn't even make it to video store shelves until August of the following year. Few saw it, but those who did witnessed a side of Cage not evidenced in even his most bizarre work to date. If *Moonstruck* was the work of an actor being told "no," *Vampire's Kiss* plays like the work of someone being allowed, even encouraged, to follow every crazy whim. Yet, as with *Peggy Sue Got Married*, it somehow adds up to a complete performance, a portrait of a man already operating at the edge of sanity as the film begins and who quickly teeters over the brink.

Cage plays Peter Loew, a literary agent with an active nightlife and a yearning to find true love that's led him to seek treatment with a sympathetic but no-nonsense psychiatrist, Dr. Glaser (Elizabeth Ashley). A habitué of 1980s downtown New York City landmarks like the Tunnel and Mondo Cane, Peter finds himself troubled when a bat flies in his window, interrupting his lovemaking with his girlfriend of the moment, Jackie (future *Eve's Bayou* director Kasi Lemmons). Fighting it off, he finds himself sexually aroused. The next night, he chats up Rachel (Jennifer Beals), a woman drinking alone, who uses an intimate moment to reveal herself as a vampire and suck his blood.

Maybe. Or maybe it's all just in his head, along with his subsequent delusions of becoming a vampire himself, delusions that feed into his mistreatment of his secretary, Alva (Maria Conchita Alonso), whom he's charged with the nearly impossible task of retrieving a decades-old contract from deep within the company's archives. As Peter's conviction that he's become a vampire deepens, so does his abuse of Alva. At one point, he chases her into the women's room, an incident he later laughs about in a roomful of fellow executives, all white men in expensive suits. As Peter reaches bottom, he sexually assaults Alva and then, while wearing cheap plastic fangs, kills a clubgoer before making his tortured way home, a wooden plank in hand, convinced that he's destined to die in direct sunlight. Once there, he instead meets his fate at the hands of Alva's brother, who stabs him with the plank. The question of whether he was actually a vampire remains unanswered to the end.

The mere plot description of *Vampire's Kiss* doesn't begin to convey the sense of a film defined at every moment by Cage's eccentric performance. For starters, there's the voice. In professional settings, Cage has Loew speak in a high-toned, vaguely British accent, an affectation he drops outside the workplace. Then there are the eyes. Berating Alva, Cage bugs his eyes out to a grotesque degree. Peter might not actually be a vampire, but he doesn't seem quite human, either. Finally, there's the alphabet, which Peter, recalling his frustration with Alva's inability to find the contract, recites in full for Dr. Glaser while gesticulating wildly. It looks less like someone playing a madman than a madman who happened to be caught on film.

In reality, Cage had choreographed the gestures the night before, working on them in his hotel room for an audience of one, his cat. For the accent, he drew on his father. On the film's commentary track, recorded over a decade later, in conversation with the film's director, Robert Bierman, Cage notes that his father, August Coppola, "made a decision at some point to speak with distinction. And to me it always sounded absurd, although now I understand." The extreme poses, bizarre body language, and tortured gait had a different source: the German Expressionist silent films Cage would frequently cite as inspiration, with a touch of Mick Jagger's preening stage poses thrown in for good measure. (A clip from F. W. Murnau's *Nosferatu* even plays in one scene. Touches of star Max Schreck's work as a vampire found their way into *Vampire's Kiss* as well, and years later Schreck would turn up in a different Cage production.)

Yet for all the thought Cage put into the performance, his Method-inspired habit of trying to inhabit characters spilled over off-screen as well. In a profile for *Spin* magazine, Lynn Geller revealed that Cage asked for warm yogurt to be poured over his toes to enhance a love scene. Over the years, more details of the shoot would emerge. Feeling the film needed a real bat, Cage demanded that one be chased down, a demand Bierman defused by suggesting the actor might die if bitten. "I wasn't the most pleasant person to be around while shooting this film," Cage later admitted on the audio commentary, on which he also alludes to a "love/hate" relationship with Beals.

And, of course, there's the cockroach, which Cage consumed live. Or, more accurately, *cockroaches*. Bierman asked for two takes, which means two bugs had to die for Cage's art.

The cockroach eating, however, was Cage's only major change to Joseph Minion's screenplay, which called for Peter to eat raw eggs. However wildly, Cage colored within the lines. The movie was weird before he got there. In fact, that was much of the attraction. Financed by Hemdale, an independent company that had enjoyed great success via a mix of genre films like *The Terminator* and *Return of the Living Dead* and such award-winning fare as *Platoon* and *The Last Emperor*, *Vampire's Kiss* was shot on a shoestring budget and earned its star a mere forty thousand dollars (which he used to buy a sports car). Cage signed on against the advice of his agent, then dropped out, then came back, drawn by the intensity of Minion's writing.

Cage wasn't the first to be attracted to Minion. A few years earlier, Martin Scorsese chose to make Minion's *After Hours* as a fast, loose, small-scale film after the collapse of the director's first attempt to make *The Last Temptation of Christ*. A journey through the strange heart of 1980s New York City, populated by a cross section of characters representing the crazies, criminals, and oddballs who inhabited its nightlife, it allowed Scorsese to reconnect with his scrappy roots while exploring a darkly comic mode he'd never attempted before. He might not have had the financial difficulties of Coppola, a friend, but Scorsese, too, was finding the new realities of studio filmmaking tough to negotiate. Well received by critics, *After Hours* became a cult classic almost upon release.

Vampire's Kiss emerged from a dark period in Minion's

life, in spite of the tropical surroundings in which it was created. Minion and girlfriend Barbara Zitwer, a film producer, took off for Barbados, where Minion remained for weeks to work on a script at Zitwer's request. "I was just alone with my demons," he told *The Ringer*'s Zach Schonfeld in 2019. "I rented a typewriter. I pounded it out." For inspiration, he looked to his relationship with Zitwer, which he described as toxic. Zitwer saw herself in the script as well, much to her displeasure. Nonetheless, she agreed to produce the film.

To direct, she hired Bierman, an up-and-coming British director best known for his HBO thriller *Apology*. Where a more experienced director might have balked at the conditions, Bierman dove in. Filled with striking images of the Manhattan skyline and hauntingly lighted location photography, the film never looks cheap. It meshes well with Minion's screenplay, a darker return to *After Hours* territory that doubles as a depiction of yuppie entitlement and how everyday misogyny can mask the presence of a madman intent on victimizing women. (Loew anticipates *American Psycho*'s Patrick Bateman in ways beyond the two characters' shared interest in bloodshed and sharp suits.) As Peter loses more of his mind, and as the alphabet recitations and wild-eyed rants give way to threats and violence, much of the humor gets leached away. The film's funny until it's not.

That's true as well of Cage's performance. Years later, *Vampire's Kiss*'s strangest moments would serve as fodder for YouTube users, GIF enthusiasts, and meme makers, but they play differently in context, as part of an increasingly queasy depiction of a troubled man losing his grip. The film's key scene—and the one that best captures the scope of Cage's bizarre, amusing, but ultimately disturbing performance—never went viral. It arrives late in the film, when Peter, having lost all semblance of sanity and donned plastic teeth to make up for the vampire fangs he never developed, approaches a woman in a club. She's amused by his undead appearance and bizarre mannerisms, which he's taken to extremes beyond even those of earlier scenes, and she can't help but laugh. Then he sinks his teeth into her neck until she dies. Her killer's absurd, but that doesn't make him any less deadly.

Filming wrapped in the fall of 1987. Hemdale first insisted on some trims and then shelved the film. When it finally escaped to theaters, critics largely got it. "What *Vampire's Kiss* is about," Patrick Taggart wrote in the *Austin American-Statesman*, "is a particularly sick set of attitudes toward women.... While individual men can get away with their poor treatment of women, the movie says such behavior hurts society." In the *Dallas Morning News*, Philip Wuntch saw in Peter's conviction that he's become infected an echo of AIDS and praised Cage's "vaguely simian" performance, calling it "the male equivalent of Bette Davis' Halloween charade in *Whatever Happened to Baby Jane?*" In the *Philadelphia Inquirer*, Carrie Rickey noted the performance's Expressionist origins and wrote that "only twice in recent memory has an actor dared as much as Cage does here." (The other two: Robert De Niro in *Brazil* and Jack Nicholson in *The Shining*.)

The film would have a lasting effect on Cage's work, reminding him of the extremes he could reach while still keeping control of his performance. In 2018, he'd call it his favorite of his movies, a "laboratory" whose experiments cleared the way for later performances. If they also made him vulnerable for mockery—even in those pre-internet days, before an actor's work could be reduced to a few strange seconds for the casual amusement of others—so what? "Over the top is one of those things that doesn't work with me," Cage told Bierman while recording their commentary, "because I don't believe in such a thing. I feel that it's just stylistic choices. And this was obviously a choice to use grand gesture and go bigger." Bierman goes even farther, suggesting that Cage was less out of step than ahead of his time. "The day will come," the director says, "when naturalism will die."

❑ ❑ ❑

Cage almost seemed as if he were trying to kill naturalism single-handedly with his next appearance, a one-minute cameo in the little-seen comedy *Never on Tuesday*, directed by Adam Rifkin. Cage plays a character credited only as "Man in Red Sports Car." Outfitted in a huge prosthetic nose, he drives up to a trio of protagonists stranded in the jungle, asks in a ghostly rasp if they need a lift, throws back his head and cackles, then drives away. "I had a whole character worked out for that one scene, a whole subtext, a complete unspoken backstory," Cage told *Vulture*'s Charles Bramesco in 2019. "I'd come out of wanting to be a Surrealist. I was interested in André Breton and [Luis] Buñuel. I liked all the otherworldly imagery, and I wanted to find a way to embody that through performance."

The final Cage film to see release in the 1980s would be one of his least seen. Adapted from a novel by Ennio Flaiano, a frequent writing partner of Federico Fellini, *Time to Kill* cast Cage as Enrico Silvestri, an Italian lieutenant serving in Ethiopia during Italy's occupation of that country in the 1930s.

Suffering from a toothache, Silvestri seeks a shortcut to a nearby doctor, only to get lost along the way. After meeting a young Ethiopian woman bathing in a pond, he rapes her, after which she stays by his side only to die from a ricocheting bullet when Silvestri attempts to shoot a menacing panther. Later, convinced he's contracted leprosy from the encounter, Silvestri tries to sneak aboard a ship back to Italy. Helmed by veteran Italian director Giuliano Montaldo, the dreary film stretches an unsubtle, if effective, metaphor for colonialism to the breaking point. Cage, however, delivers an unexpectedly understated and unmistakably naturalistic performance. The film made its American premiere in video stores, where few sought it out.

Cage ended the decade on an unexpectedly quiet note, though not entirely by choice. Elia Kazan cast him as the lead in a sequel to his landmark *America America*, which would have allowed Cage to work with the director of *East of Eden*, which had made such a deep impression on him as a teenager. Unable to secure its budget, the film went unmade, and Kazan returned to retirement. Inescapable in 1987, Cage had suddenly become hard to find.

This wasn't an accident. Though Cage's no-interviews policy didn't survive for long, he didn't relish talking to the press in the 1980s. When he did grant interviews, they were usually headlined with variations on "Nicolas Cage Opens Up" or "Nicolas Cage Allows a Peek Under His Veil of Privacy." Speaking to *Newsday*'s Joseph Gelmis shortly before *Peggy Sue Got Married*, he likened himself to the Wizard of Oz, saying, "I'm the man behind the curtain and I don't want you to look behind the curtain." He did pull it back a bit, however, offering glimpses of a life dedicated to art and literature, referencing Dostoyevsky and opera: "I try to cultivate my imagination. I think that's the most important tool for any artist. So I look at paintings and read and try to do what Goethe said: to get on the saddle of life and ride it."

Cage cultivated the image of a loner who spent his days wandering art museums and his nights reading by the fireside. "I have a ceiling that I stare at an awful lot," he told the *Atlanta Journal-Constitution* in 1987. "I rent videos and watch movies now and then. I bought a cappuccino machine recently and now I never have to leave my house." In this pre-internet era, it was easier, with a little discretion, to create and maintain a reclusive image, and it seems likely Cage devoted more time to intellectual pursuits than the average Hollywood twenty-something. Still, it wasn't an entirely monkish existence. His circle of friends included Chris Penn and Charlie Sheen. Photos from the era capture him hitting the town with Johnny Depp, whom he'd met while Depp was an aspiring musician and whom he encouraged to try acting, even introducing him to his agent. Cage took Brooke Shields to the *Moonstruck* premiere and dated actress Ami Dolenz, daughter of the Monkees' Mickey Dolenz. By the fall of 1988, he'd begun a relationship with actress Christina Fulton. In 1990, she would give birth to their child, Weston Coppola Cage (who would later transpose his middle and surname).

Cage began the decade in high school. He ended it as star living in a kind of temporary exile. As part of his habit of keeping a low profile, the public saw him only when he had a movie to promote, however reluctantly. But with no movies coming beyond the limited release of *Vampire's Kiss* and the never-seen

Time to Kill, Cage effectively disappeared from the public eye. It was a strange way to end the '80s, but the end of the '80s was a strange time to be a movie star. Some actors were learning they had to pivot to stay afloat. Tom Hanks and Michael Keaton both started out as amiable, wisecracking comedic leading men. With 1988's *Big*, Hanks started to transition toward more complex material. The following year, Keaton became Batman.

Many of Cage's contemporaries struggled. Cage rarely got lumped in with the Brat Pack, the group of young actors who emerged in the early '80s, often by way of John Hughes movies, but he emerged alongside them. By 1989, most had already peaked in their popularity. Demi Moore would become an even bigger box-office draw in the '90s, and Rob Lowe would find a second act as a television star at that decade's end, but Emilio Estevez, Anthony Michael Hall, Molly Ringwald, Andrew McCarthy, Judd Nelson, C. Thomas Howell, Ally Sheedy, and others would soon segue into lower-profile projects and supporting roles. For many, the journey from appearing on magazine covers to appearing in *Weekend at Bernie's II* would prove alarmingly short.

Others made the transition more smoothly. Cage's costar and sometime friend Sean Penn established himself as an actor of rare gravity in the mid-1980s, leaving stoned surfer roles behind him for good. John Cusack enjoyed a similarly smooth transition by way of thoughtful projects that took him from *Better Off Dead* to *Eight Men Out*, *Say Anything*, and *The Grifters* without missing a step. Robert Downey Jr. made similarly deft choices, earning a Best Actor nomination for the 1992 film *Chaplin*, while Downey's *Less Than Zero* costar James Spader discovered a new gear by appearing in Steven

Soderbergh's *sex, lies, and videotape*, a breakout success in 1989 that heralded American independent filmmaking's '90s boom years.

Soderbergh's debut and other maverick works, including Spike Lee's *Do the Right Thing*, looked like outliers in 1989, however. Mammoth efforts dominated the box office, with *Batman* joined by sequels such as *Indiana Jones and the Last Crusade*, *Lethal Weapon 2*, *Back to the Future II*, and *Ghostbusters II*. Films outside the blockbuster mold could still find a toehold, but they tended to be star-driven vehicles like *Rain Man* and *Field of Dreams*. More intimate stories, like *Beaches* and *When Harry Met Sally*, emerged from well-oiled marketing machines, arriving in theaters accompanied by assaultive publicity campaigns and synergistic-minded tie-in soundtracks. Visionaries still found ways to work, but carefully packaged big-budget movies had become the primary concern of a Hollywood dominated more than ever by a corporate mind-set.

Where could Cage call home in this altered landscape? Most immediately, he'd find work at both extremes by way of a film that let him collaborate with a singular director eager to let him experiment and a would-be blockbuster in which he took to the sky. It would be an odd way to start the 1990s. The years that followed would be odder still.

5

Wandering Cage

He started with a handspring. It got weirder from there. Clad in a black leather jacket, tight black jeans, and a matching T-shirt, Nicolas Cage entered the set of the popular BBC One talk show *Wogan* tumbling and grinning. From there he launched into a karate kick before digging a wad of cash out of his pocket and throwing the bills to the crowd. All the while, host Terry Wogan's band played staid, upbeat music that didn't come close to matching the energy of the guest, who would perform one more karate kick before taking a seat on the couch. It was August 1990, and after appearing to sit out the last years of the 1980s, Nicolas Cage was back.

A veteran broadcaster, the Irish-born Wogan typically greeted eccentricity with wry amusement, but tonight's guest would test those skills. As Cage reattached a microphone that had fallen off during his entrance, Wogan tried to get him back on topic. "You did a bit of that in *Wild at Heart*, all those karate kicks," he said, bringing up the movie Cage was promoting. "Sure did," Cage said, before apologizing for his entrance and saying he had "to get it off my chest" because he was "a bit wound up back there." But any hopes for a return to business as usual quickly evaporated. First, Cage compared Wogan to Patrick Macnee, the dapper star of the 1960s spy series *The Avengers*—only, he couldn't remember Macnee's name, so he asked the crowd to "give it up for the Avenger!" Then he listened politely as Wogan praised both *Wild at Heart* and Cage's performance in it.

"Well, thanks," Cage replied before continuing, "You know, this leather's really hot," after which he removed both jacket and T-shirt (a *Wild at Heart* shirt he presented to Wogan) and punched the air, his hair flopping from side to side with every blow.

From there, Cage and Wogan settled into a groove as Cage told several stories from previous interviews: the desire to climb inside the television, the "cousin" he created to ward off bullies, the teasing that led him to change his name from "Coppola" to "Cage." If anything, it felt a bit rehearsed. But it's the first part of the interview that viewers would remember (even if it was no less choreographed in its own way). A live show that served as the much-watched lead-in to the long-running British soap *EastEnders*, then at the height of its popularity, *Wogan* beamed Cage's high-kicking, nude-to-the-waist appearance into homes across the United Kingdom. They saw a wild man, but maybe also a wild man who knew what he was doing. Is there a better way to get attention for a strange movie than to bring some of its strangeness out into the real world? They also saw a man they hadn't seen in a while, one trying to pick up where he'd left off after *Moonstruck* over two years before. It was a new decade filled with new possibilities. Who knew where it would take him?

Who knew where it would take anyone?

❑ ❑ ❑

It's tempting, when considering the past, to search for neat divisions, particularly when looking at decades. One ten-year stretch ends, and the next begins, and what exists on one side of the line has no place on the other. But history rarely works that way. Changes don't respect the calendar. They move at their own pace, sometimes arriving seemingly out of nowhere, other times taking years to manifest.

In music critic Alfred Soto's words, "Decades aren't walls of mortar." To discuss the pop music that roughly coincided with the presidency of George H. W. Bush, Soto coined the term "Poppy Bush Interzone," an apt name for the fuzzy, culturally ill-defined post-Reagan/pre-Clinton years that found cult tastes and previously fringe artists redefining the mainstream. Some of this came as a result of slow but unstoppable ascents. Hip-hop, once dismissed as a novelty, became impossible to ignore, and acts first popularized on college radio, from R.E.M. to Depeche Mode, found larger audiences than ever before. Some of it came in the form of jarring disruptions, like the sudden ascent of grunge in the fall of 1991. New faces appeared out of nowhere. Some older acts weathered the change. Others never made it to the other side. The corporate machinery running the industry kept humming along, but some of the products emerging from it looked like nothing that that machinery had produced before.

As with music, so with movies. As the 1980s ended and

the '90s began, the margins separating the mainstream from the underground had started to get blurrier. *Vampire's Kiss* may not have had much of a chance against *Batman* in the summer of 1989, but *Batman*'s success wasn't *just* a case of a studio blockbuster steamrolling its way there by exploiting a universally recognized character and engaging in relentless marketing. It was that, but it was also owing to the film's being an unusual, unmistakably personal work directed by Tim Burton, who, just five years earlier, had lost his job at Disney after making the macabre (but heartwarming) short film *Frankenweenie*. If the culture wasn't ready for Burton in 1984, 1989 was another story. So it was for other filmmakers as well—such as Spike Lee, who attracted acclaim and debate with *Do the Right Thing*, and Steven Soderbergh, whose *sex, lies, and videotape* bounced from Sundance to Cannes to art houses to the multiplexes, playing alongside films like *Ghostbusters II* and *Star Trek V* and setting the table for the golden age of American independent filmmaking in the 1990s.

It was a strange time and a time newly open to strangeness. But where did Nicolas Cage fit in? Between 1989 and 1990, Cage shot three strikingly different films back to back to back, in a seeming attempt to find out. He arrived at no firm answer.

Maybe it was as a mainstream action star, an idea that seems less bizarre now, on the other side of *The Rock* and other action blockbusters, than it did in 1990. Then, moviegoers roundly rejected *Fire Birds* (aka *Wings of the Apache*), which placed Cage, as hotshot pilot Jake Preston, in the pilot seat of an Apache helicopter to do battle with South American drug lords. It was, by all accounts, an unpleasant experience.

Speaking of the shoot from the distance of over a decade, with polite reserve and what sounds like carefully worded under-statement, British director David Green made allusions to a triangle of tensions between Cage and his costars Tommy Lee Jones ("They never really got close") and Sean Young ("I had to ask Sean Young to leave the set. She didn't mind doing so. And it wasn't an issue. But it made me realize that sometimes separating the actors, when they're not actually working on a scene, can work well").

The tension did little to improve a film concisely, and accu-rately, described by many reviewers as "*Top Gun* with helicop-ters." Opening with a saber-rattling war-on-drugs quote from President George H. W. Bush, it boosts *Top Gun*'s fetishiza-tion of military hardware, borderline hostile romantic subplot, and cocky-hero-learns-to-grow-up structure. But it makes the puzzling decision of focusing on Jake's struggle with his left-eye dominance, a hindrance while using the Apache's state-of-the-art targeting system. It's far from the most cinematic of choices in a movie with little more to offer than some striking shots of helicopters framed against sunsets and Cage trying his best to play it straight as an all-American hero.

Few bought it. Released over Memorial Day weekend, *Fire Birds* not only got buried by *Back to the Future Part III*, but also finished behind films that had been in theaters for weeks. Speaking to the press a few months later, Cage didn't disagree with the assessment, telling the *Los Angeles Daily News*, "I was at a place where I was starting to think that maybe I should try to do something a bit more mainstream just to ensure that I could get another job. It wasn't really true to any instincts, so the whole thing blew up in my face." Cage could play charismatic outsiders and tormented weirdos. Macho, all-American heroes in crowd-pleasing action movies, however, remained outside his range. When he returned to action movies, he'd play different sorts of protagonists, in films with new takes on the genre.

◻ ◻ ◻

Yet, even as *Fire Birds* bombed in American theaters, Cage triumphed elsewhere. Before stepping into the Apache cockpit, he'd spent nine weeks on the road in a snakeskin jacket with director David Lynch and costar Laura Dern. The jacket was Cage's own, picked up because it reminded him of Marlon Brando's costume in *The Fugitive Kind* and kept in his wardrobe for later use. The film would be a collaborative effort, one that Lynch and the cast filled with images of fire, sex, murder, and spontaneous bits of experimentation—the polar opposite of a carefully choreographed action film filled with heavy machinery. And where *Fire Birds* would inspire only indifference, the results of their trip would inspire both admiration and disgust.

A loose adaptation of a Barry Gifford novel of the same name, *Wild at Heart* premiered at Cannes in 1990, where it beat out new films from Jean-Luc Godard, Clint Eastwood, Zhang Yimou, *Birdy* director Alan Parker, and others to win the Palme d'Or, the festival's highest honor. Its success arrived in the midst of a heady period of productivity and recognition for Lynch.

A month earlier, ABC aired the pilot to *Twin Peaks*, a television series Lynch had created with Mark Frost. Another product of the same cultural moment that drew into the spotlight what had previously been on the fringes, *Twin Peaks*

gave an unlikely home on prime-time television to the sensibility Lynch had honed since his first student films. Mixing
images of postcard-ready Americana with sex and violence
and resting self-conscious strangeness atop an undercurrent
of emotional earnestness, the show became a critical hit and
a ratings sensation—briefly. By the end of its short first season, ratings had dropped, and *Twin Peaks* narrowly avoided
cancellation (a fate it would succumb to at the end of season
two). It wouldn't be the last evidence of Lynch's unexpected
rise to prominence, or the last project to experience a back-
lash.

Lynch's ascent didn't happen overnight. After a peripatetic
childhood thanks to his father's job with the U.S. Department of Agriculture, he set out to study painting, incorpo-
rating filmmaking only gradually into his repertoire during
his studies at the Pennsylvania Academy of the Fine Arts. In
Philadelphia, he lived in the Fairmount neighborhood, a section then filled with crime and industrial noise. His time there
would inspire his first feature, *Eraserhead*, a surreal expression
of urban anxiety and parental fears shot over the course of five
years. After quietly debuting at the Los Angeles–based Filmex
festival in 1977, *Eraserhead* became a midnight movie staple.
Lynch's next feature, *The Elephant Man*, found him incorpo-
rating his stylistic trademarks into an empathetic biopic of
Joseph Merrick, a deformed Victorian man rescued from life
as a circus freak by a compassionate surgeon. The film earned
Lynch acclaim and his first Best Director nomination at the
Academy Awards.

After turning down the chance to direct *Return of the Jedi*,
suspecting he would not be able to reshape it to fit his sensibility,

Lynch took on the mammoth project of adapting Frank Herbert's landmark science-fiction novel *Dune*. Forced to compromise—never a comfortable experience for the director—he didn't care for the final product. Audiences and critics agreed, and the film was a high-profile flop when released in the waning days of 1984. His smaller-scale follow-up, however, attracted both praise and controversy. *Blue Velvet* follows an innocent-seeming college kid through the shady underworld of his bucolic Pacific North-west hometown, where his attempts to solve a mystery lead to some uncomfortable realizations about the ways sex, violence, desire, and innocence can become entwined. An art house hit in 1986, it earned Lynch another Best Director nod and helped set the template for his later work, which frequently begins in the familiar worlds of crime and film noir before setting off for even murkier psychological and cultural terrain.

Blue Velvet also helped Lynch find firmer footing in Holly-wood, though not so firm that he didn't see several long-gestating projects collapse. And it was in the rush to fill the vacuum in his schedule this created that *Wild at Heart* was born. He began work on the film shortly after completing the *Twin Peaks* pilot. Given Gifford's still-unfinished novel by producer Monty Montgomery, Lynch recognized the raw material for a fevered vision of an America permeated by vio-lence. From Gifford's story of two young lovers on a desperate cross-country road trip, Lynch sculpted a disorienting, often funny, sometimes upsetting film rich in pop-cultural refer-ences ranging from *The Wizard of Oz* (which serves as a kind of blueprint for the story) to Marilyn Monroe to Elvis Presley, whose spirit Cage would channel as Sailor Ripley, a convict whose love of loud music and free-spirited living is matched only by his devotion to his one true love, Lula Fortune (Dern).

In the film's best scene, Sailor dozes in the backseat as Lula drives their 1965 Ford Thunderbird across a desolate Texas landscape listening to increasingly apocalyptic news broadcasts about murder, necrophilia, and environmental disaster. On the verge of panic, she stops the car, demanding that Sailor find "some music on that radio this instant, I mean it!" He tunes into some of the thrash metal they both adore, and Lula dances as Sailor kicks the air, but the power chords give way to romantic Richard Strauss music. The couple embraces as the camera frames them against a perfect sunset. They're two people who've found solace in each other in the midst of chaos and destruction—and in the midst of a film that asks again and again whether that solace will be enough to sustain them.

Lynch works in broad strokes and inspired details. For his take on the road movie, the director looked to the most obvious signifiers of twentieth-century America, but he treated them largely as points of departure. Dern's Lula has hints of Monroe, but she's her own fully developed character, a spirited, sexually confident woman whose habit of freely expressing her unusual perspective on the world bears little resemblance to Monroe's breathy provocations. Cage's performance, however, remains tightly tethered to the spirit of the King, from Sailor's accent to his courtly manners to his physical carriage to his karate kicks.

It wouldn't be the last time Cage's life brushed up against Presley's, and *Wild at Heart* is clearly the work of an actor in deep conversation with Elvis. Cage would later claim to have chosen an Elvis impression in an attempt to flout Method pioneer Konstantin Stanislavski's admonition that performances should avoid imitations, but he also looked to Andy Warhol for inspiration when playing Sailor. "I believe in art synthesis," Cage told critic Rene Rodriguez in 2012. "Warhol used to do that. He would take Mick Jagger or Elvis Presley and use them in his paintings. So I decided to take Presley and embody his aura while playing Sailor Ripley. It was an overlay of performance over performance."

Yet if Cage set out simply to drop an Elvis impression onto Lynch's canvas, he failed in the best way possible. As an actor, Elvis had a strong screen presence, but he often read as cryptic and distant, always Elvis, never the character he was playing. Apart from his snakeskin jacket—which he describes as "a symbol of my individuality and my belief in personal freedom"—Sailor is a man without any armor, an open, beating heart who freely expresses his emotions and desires and who has found in Lula the only person who can soothe his restless spirit. Dead thirteen years at the time of the film's release, Elvis had become a T-shirt icon, a punch line, and a symbol of a lost age. Cage's performance as Sailor helps make him seem human again, a nice kid whose wild side both threatens to envelop him in darkness and provides a means of escape.

Cage and his *Wild at Heart* costars spoke glowingly of the experience of making the film, which took them from California to New Orleans to Texas. "A *lot* of it was intuition because I was working with people that I really trusted—David Lynch and Laura Dern," Cage told an interviewer. "So I could allow the more spontaneous side of what I do to come out. I just let it all flow of its own accord and let David pick and choose what he needed that made poetic sense to him." Over the years, intriguing references to deleted scenes in which Sailor sings opera have surfaced alongside mentions of scenes too sexually explicit to make the final cut. And though Cage treated the film as an attempt to flout the rules of Method acting, this didn't prevent him from applying Method touches, including taking an in-character road trip to Las Vegas with Dern.

"Around the time that *Wild at Heart* came out, there were lots of interviews and journalists doing pieces on actors being Method *really* getting into their parts and all of that," Dern reflected years later in a short documentary about the making of the film. "I think there are actors who think you *need* to do that and then there actors who just want to do it for fun. I think Nic and I fell in the category of wanting to do it for fun. And I think David sort of encouraged it and liked that for those nine weeks we just *were* Sailor and Lula."

Even at Cannes, *Wild at Heart* proved divisive. Roger Ebert's dispatches from the festival expressed dismay and hostility at the film's embrace there, questioning the sincerity of the Cannes audience's reaction and comparing Lynch to an emperor without clothes. Then a Lynch skeptic (he'd write admiringly of the director's later work), Ebert had famously given a one-star review to *Blue Velvet*, turned off by the director's combination of sexual violence and the film's borderline parodic depiction of small-town America. Though it eventually earned one and a half more stars than its predecessor, *Wild at Heart* did little to quell the critic's misgivings about the director or his unease at Lynch's ascent.

When *Wild at Heart* reached American shores in August, Ebert was far from alone in his distaste. Lynch's film earned puzzled-to-dismissive reviews from the *New York Times*, the *Washington Post*, *Time*, and the other major outlets. What's more, though *Wild at Heart* recouped its modest budget, audiences proved slow to show up, in spite of an ad campaign that emphasized its *Twin Peaks* connection. If anything, the connection may have hurt *Wild at Heart* through a combination of *Peaks's* flagging ratings and content that didn't match some of the expectations of the series' fans. ("I will never see another film by David Lynch!" one moviegoer, lured by the connection to the ABC show, told the *Los Angeles Times*.)

Nonetheless, the film and its (occasionally gymnastics-filled) publicity tour helped restore Cage's profile in ways the calculated commercial choice of *Fire Birds* didn't, confirming him as an exciting actor who brought an element of unpredictability. *Wild at Heart* and *Fire Birds* may have both underperformed at the box office, but at least one offered artistic fulfillment. In the struggle between creative instincts and commercial canniness, Cage seemed better off going with his instincts. Those instincts would next steer him, again, toward New Orleans—and toward sex and disaster.

□ □ □

The cultural disruptions of the late 1980s and early '90s briefly suggested that movies might be entering a new era of cinematic frankness. Lynch was contractually obligated to deliver an R-rated film, and anyone who saw the cut screened at Cannes knew *Wild at Heart* wouldn't meet the MPAA's nebulous standards without some trims. Lynch made the necessary cuts, mostly to the film's violence, but its situation became part of a larger story that played out over the year as films like *The Cook, the Thief, His Wife & Her Lover*, *Henry: Portrait of a Serial Killer*, and *Tie Me Up! Tie Me Down!* played in theaters without ratings, skirting the dreaded X rating that had become synonymous with pornography. None fits that description, but all contain moments that wouldn't easily fit into an R-rated film, ranging from graphic violence to casual graphic nudity to haute cuisine cannibalism. On TV and in their respective newspapers, Gene Siskel and Roger Ebert led a charge to create an adults-only rating for such films. With the introduction of the NC-17 rating in September 1990, it seemed like a moment of broadened horizons.

It didn't last. Though the first film rated NC-17, *Henry & June*, performed reasonably well, the new rating essentially picked up where the X left off, becoming a "must avoid" for any film hoping to play widely. By 1992, *Basic Instinct* had resumed a game of walking up to the edge of what an R rating could show without crossing over into NC-17 turf. The window closed almost as soon as it opened, but a few stray items from that moment continued to surface here and there, including one that would find Cage stripping to his underwear, covering himself in black paint, and grunting like an animal.

"The movie everyone's talking about is *Zandalee*, and it won't even open until next spring," entertainment writer Diana Maychick cooed in a May 1991 column. "They're not actually talking, just whispering, really," she continued, before noting, "*Zandalee* probably holds the dubious distinction of including more graphic sex scenes than any non-pornographic movie ever released." She was only half right. Cage shot *Zandalee* in

New Orleans—a city that would come to play major roles in both his career and his personal life—on the heels of *Wild at Heart*, and it does contain an astounding amount of graphic sex scenes, even by the standards of a more permissive moment. But Maychick's estimation that "everyone" was talking about what would end up being one of the least-seen entries in Cage's filmography would prove unfounded. So would her assertion that the movie would be released next spring, or much noticed when it did see release.

A tale of obsession set amid one of the sweatiest depictions of New Orleans ever put to film, *Zandalee* stars Judge Reinhold as Thierry, an affluent young businessman whose chronic impotence threatens his marriage to the eponymous Zandalee (Erika Anderson, another Lynch veteran, having played twin sisters in *Twin Peaks*'s show-within-the-show, *Invitation to Love*). Enter Johnny Collins (Cage), Thierry's childhood friend, a lusty painter with a carefully groomed goatee who takes a day job with Thierry's cable company to support his art and then sticks around to have sex with Zandalee in a series of increasingly inappropriate locations, including atop a washing machine (with others in a nearby room) and inside a church. Meanwhile, a supporting cast that includes Steve Buscemi, Marisa Tomei, Joe Pantoliano, and Aaron Neville breezes in and out of the movie.

Born in Massachusetts, *Zandalee* director Sam Pillsbury came of age in New Zealand, working extensively in the Kiwi film industry, first as a documentarian and then as a director and producer of narrative features. He came to his first American production with an outsider's eye—evident both in his avoidance of clichéd New Orleans locations (a tough feat for a film shot extensively in the French Quarter) and in *Zandalee*'s unusually graphic sex scenes. "Before I did the movie," Pillsbury says, "I told the actors, 'Listen, I can't stand it when I see a sex scene in an American movie and they're wearing bra and panties.'" The film reflects this distaste in scene after scene.

A sincere, if ultimately doomed, attempt to make the cinematic equivalent of literary erotica on a comfortable budget with name stars, *Zandalee* might have been the sort of film everyone talked about if it hadn't been deemed unreleasable after troubling audience reactions. "When we screened the first test screening, half the theater got up and walked out," Pillsbury recalls. "I've mostly been really successful in my life. I've made a few mistakes, and *Zandalee* was one of them, and I got to tell you something, you learn a hell of a lot more from your mistakes than you do from your successes."

Though it ultimately feels both shapeless and overheated, the film has laudable elements, from the rich atmosphere to a strong sense of style to a bunch of go-for-broke performances sure to please connoisseurs of unusual cinema. None is more go-for-broke than Cage's, a collection of lecherous glances and explosive gestures that recall *Vampire's Kiss* and that climax in a shower of paint, a Cage invention that Pillsbury approved.

"He arrived on the set like a bomb about to go off, and that never stopped," Pillsbury says of Cage, by way of a compliment. "People think he must be a lunatic to work with. He was totally professional. Lots of fun. As funny as shit. We would drive at night to restaurants and stand on top of tables and sing to the audiences."

The bonhomie didn't stop the film from sinking, however. Though *Zandalee* played a few theaters overseas, it quietly made its American debut on video store shelves in the summer of 1991. A film seemingly tailor-made to push the boundaries of a more permissive era disappeared as the era drew to a close, a troubling development for a career that had started to hit choppy waters. Cage had handsprung his way into the '90s only to be greeted by failure as an action star and indifference as the leading man of an erotic drama. It was enough to make even the most assured actor feel adrift.

"I've been in one place too long. I'm just sitting here in Los Angeles getting soft. Twenty-seven years old, balding, and without a shred of inspiration," Cage wrote in "On the Road with Nicolas Cage," a cross-country travel diary published in the July 1991 issue of *Details*, inspired by Jack Kerouac in both subject and style. Recounting a Los Angeles–to–New Orleans road trip with his friend Jeff Levine, who later become a producing partner, Cage free-associates about Lynyrd Skynyrd, having sex at the intersection of La Brea and Melrose, the color purple ("I am purple. I have become that color in recent years"), getting rejected in high school because he didn't have a car, and observations about the state of the country circa 1991. ("I wonder if there's a hole in the soul of my generation. We've inherited the American Dream, but where do we take it? It's not about cars and wealth. It is always been freedom, but are we free in our thoughts or are we paralyzed by our dreams of consumption? The country's arteries are coagulating into muteness, and we have to inject them with a thinner to get thoughts spurting again.")

"I am not a demon," one especially purple passage begins, "I am a lizard, a shark, and a heat-seeking panther. I am one watt above darkness. I am a glow-in-the-dark rollercoaster. I am a hard-on. I want to be John Denver on acid playing the accordion; I want to drink Jack Daniel's while driving my Corvette off the Grand Canyon. I am the frog you never kissed. I am a sinner looking for some peace. I believe in the sword that gives life. I am a family man and a bachelor. I don't believe in God but I'm afraid of Him. So I'll pray." The article alternately reads like the prose equivalent of the *Wogan* appearance (a self-consciously wild, attention-getting provocation) and a boozy cri de coeur inspired by professional and personal malaise, new fatherhood, and encounters with locals met along the way. It ends with Cage returning to Los Angeles, missing his son, and troubled by his own inability to settle down.

The article is franker than Cage ever let himself be in interviews, and not always flattering in what it reveals. Most of Cage's observations are trite, to put it politely. (On the fundamental dynamic between men and women: "Most men want sex. They need to make money to have sex. Most women want money. They need money to feather their nesting instincts, to raise a comfortable family. A rich man is as attractive to a woman as a beautiful woman is to a man.") Yet for all its celebration of the open road as a symbol of freedom, it reads like the work of someone who'd reached a cul-de-sac, personally and creatively, offering up random thoughts in the hope that one might lead him in the right direction and not finding much inspiration in spite of the effort.

While he'd won acclaim for *Wild at Heart*, even from critics who didn't care for the film, there was only one David Lynch, and it would be hard to make a career out of Lynch movies. Cage's next step seemed unclear, particularly after he'd watched one artistically ambitious project after another collapse around him, such as the Kazan film and a proposed remake of the surreal Italian political thriller *Investigation of a Citizen Above Suspicion*, scripted by Paul Schrader. "I'd *like* to do a movie that was politically oriented next," he said at the time. "I'd like to rip the mask off American politics."

That would have to wait. Instead, he opted for another reinvention, as shocking in its own way as any shirtless talk show appearance. He came back as a nice guy.

6

The Softer Side of Cage

By 1987, Tom Hanks was already weary of the James Stewart comparisons. "It's Jimmy Stewart this, Jimmy Stewart that," Hanks told *Parade*. "It's as big a compliment as you can get, but it's not anywhere near accurate." At any given point, Hollywood has only a limited number of well-defined slots, but Hanks had no interest in playing the role of the Nice Guy Everyman, at least not in 1987. He responded by frequently taking big steps outside his comfort zone, playing a troubled stand-up comic in *Punchline* and a symbol of everything wrong with the '80s in *The Bonfire of the Vanities*, and starring in *Joe Versus the Volcano*, the strange, charming directorial debut of *Moonstruck* writer John Patrick Shanley. The films largely left audiences cold—though *Joe Versus the Volcano* would pick up a well-deserved cult following years later—but even Hanks's hits from the era have an element of risk. He turned on the nice-guy charm for *Sleepless in Seattle*, but *Big* (in which he plays a child in a man's body), *Philadelphia* (for which he took on the part of a gay lawyer dying of

AIDS at a time when many actors feared their careers would suffer if they played gay characters), *A League of Their Own* (which asked him to make an alcoholic, borderline abusive baseball manager likable), and *Forrest Gump* (which required him to play a developmentally disabled man) look like sure things only in retrospect. Ordinary Joes? Let others play them.

It was Cage who unexpectedly stepped up to the challenge. Here was an actor so disturbed by the experience of making the humane, romantic *Moonstruck* that he responded by taking the lead in *Vampire's Kiss*, turning an already strange movie into a kind of proving ground for his most extreme acting instincts. In the restless years that followed, he tried a bit of everything, with mixed results. In the road trip diary he penned for *Details*, Cage complains about "never reading a good script." The one true bright spot, *Wild at Heart*, won the top prize at Cannes, only to disappear when it reached American shores. So he made the weirdest choice he could possibly make: he stopped playing weird.

In what Cage would later dub his "Sunshine Trilogy"— *Honeymoon in Vegas*, *Guarding Tess*, and *It Could Happen to You*—he plays characters who go beyond being good guys. They practically glow with virtue, each a little brighter than the one before. It's these roles that would define his early '90s work. With one wild exception, even the outliers of this era find him playing unexceptional men trying to do what's right in a world defined by greed and corruption. The body swapping of *Face/Off* lay a few years in the future, but for a strange, short stretch, it seemed like Hanks and Cage might have traded careers.

What's more, it worked. Cage will undoubtedly be remembered for his more colorful performances, but watch his eyes and his sincerely downturned mouth when he says "a promise is a promise" in *It Could Happen to You*. Look at the way concern washes over his face when he believes the former First Lady he's in charge of protecting might be in danger in *Guarding Tess*. Study—to choose a performance from a slightly different movie from this period—the way his desperate character considers and then rejects, and then considers and rejects again, the urge to take an unguarded stack of cash in *Red Rock West*. In each of these moments, Cage wears a face of absolute sincerity. After venturing to the extremes, he's retreated to a style that appears to have no artifice. He's simply inhabiting these men and quietly working through their hard choices and inner conflicts.

The change in direction started, per Cage, while he was watching an old interview with Jim Morrison in which the Doors front man mused, "I don't think we've done a song yet that conveys pure happiness." Not wanting to find himself in the same position, Cage decided to pursue a different path. It's a good story, one that squares with other changes in his life in the years after the birth of his son Weston. Cage's relationship with on-again, off-again girlfriend Christina Fulton wouldn't last, but Cage, by all reports, remained closely involved in Weston's life.

It changed the way he presented himself to the public as well. "Sex is where it's at!" Cage told British interviewer Terry Christian on the 1990 press tour that produced his kickboxing *Wogan* entrance. Six years later, speaking to *Playboy* journalist David Sheff, he noted that "One of the amazing things about children is that they automatically cut out any debauchery or decadence left over from your youth. As soon as Weston was born I stopped smoking and started buckling my seat belt." He also claimed that fatherhood had changed him, and possibly his craft, noting, "It brings a new kind of emotion, a depth that wasn't there before."

In the same interview, however, Cage suggested that the changes in his personal life and artistic ambition coincided with a need to reinvent himself. "It was 'Nic Cage? He's the guy with the snakeskin jacket and the wooden hand in *Moonstruck*, and he eats cockroaches. He's not right for that role, you know,'" he told Sheff. "You can intense yourself right out of the business; I've seen it happen."

He didn't name names, but his immediate orbit contained examples. Cage's friend Crispin Glover, costar of Cage's in the *Best of Times* pilot and a supporting player in *Wild at Heart*, had become forever associated with a bizarre 1987 appearance on *Late Night with David Letterman* that ended abruptly after Glover launched a karate kick in the host's general direction. A career playing weirdos awaited him (one Glover seemingly welcomed). Cage's *Rumble Fish* costar Mickey Rourke saw the conversation shift from his skills as an actor to stories of on-set difficulties and personal turmoil. In 1991, Rourke would temporarily put acting aside to pursue professional boxing. What made an actor intriguing one day could make him a joke the next. Even the most promising talent could steer into a wall.

One alternative: jump out of an airplane with a bunch of Elvis impersonators.

❑ ❑ ❑

Andrew Bergman never really fit in in Hollywood, but he made not fitting in work for him. Most of the time, anyway. The son of Jewish immigrants who'd fled Nazi Germany, Bergman grew up in New York City surrounded by comedy. His father wrote about radio and television for the *New York Daily News*, a job that would bring him into the orbit of comics like Ernie Kovacs and Bob and Ray. Bergman opted to study history rather than show business, but ended up pursuing both. He earned a PhD at the University of Wisconsin–Madison and penned *We're in the Money: Depression America and Its Films*, a dissertation later published as a widely respected book. Ordinarily a bucolic college town, the Madison of the late 1960s was in the full grip of the era's political turmoil, turmoil that inspired Bergman's first screenplay, *Tex X*, a comedy Western about race relations. Attracting the attention of Mel Brooks, who kept Bergman around to join a team of writers to revise it, *Tex X* evolved into *Blazing Saddles*.

Success hit Bergman fast and unexpectedly—and it mostly stuck. His next screenwriting credit, for the Arthur Hiller–directed *The In-Laws*, starring Peter Falk and Alan Arkin, became a hit in the summer of 1979. It also established a set of elements Bergman would revisit in future projects: dropping a hapless straight man into a dangerous underworld filled with colorfully named comic characters and farcical gags, neither of which would have felt out of place in the screwball classics Bergman studied as a grad student. Bergman's first stab at directing, *So Fine*, stumbled at the box office, and he abandoned his second, *Big Trouble*, in progress. (John Cassavetes would step in as director. It would be his final film.) But Bergman still had writing opportunities aplenty, including the 1985 hit *Fletch*. That same year, *New York* magazine dubbed him "the unknown King of Comedy." When Bergman tried directing again, he found success with *The Freshman*, which cast Matthew Broderick as an unsuspecting college student drawn into performing "totally legitimate" favors for a mobster named Jimmy the Toucan (Marlon Brando), whose uncanny resemblance to *The Godfather*'s Vito Corleone serves as the film's running gag.

For *Honeymoon in Vegas*, Bergman didn't so much start over as reshuffle the deck, bringing in Brando's *Godfather* son James Caan to play another gangster (well, professional gambler, but the line seems pretty thin), named Tommy Korman, and dropping Cage into the role of the over-his-head ordinary guy sucked into his orbit. Cast only after agreeing to a screen test that assured Bergman he could do comedy, Cage plays Jack Singer, a private eye with a habit of attracting eccentric clients (like a middle-aged man convinced his dowdy wife is having an affair with Mike Tyson). Jack's romantic life is hamstrung by his mother's (Anne Bancroft) deathbed attempt to extract a promise that he'll never marry. Deciding to risk her disapproval from beyond the grave, Jack takes his schoolteacher girlfriend, Betsy (Sarah Jessica Parker), to Vegas for a quickie wedding. Her resemblance to Korman's late wife leads him to sucker Jack into a card game he can't win and exchange a weekend with Betsy to pay off the debt, a decision Jack regrets when he realizes how this diminishes him in Betsy's eyes—and that she might not be immune to Korman's wealth and charm.

The pleasure of Cage's performance comes from watching him crack, but not quite break, under pressure. Already living in the shadow of his mother's dying wish, Jack seemingly frees himself, but ultimately he finds he hasn't escaped at all. His mother has filled him with doubts about marriage. His job chasing cheating spouses has only confirmed her suspicions. Korman's machinations make those doubts manifest, until Jack appears to be on the verge of melting down, a process Cage depicts as a slow progression that turns him into a sputtering mess as he chases his would-be bride from Vegas to Hawaii and back again, until making a literal leap of faith by parachuting into Vegas in the company of Elvis impersonators just in time to rescue Betsy, who now sees Korman as the schemer he's been all along.

It's a sweet ending to an unapologetically old-fashioned movie that, like Bergman's best films, layers silliness on top of sophistication. Bergman finds room for characters like Sally Molars, a bookie/dentist who describes his patients' conditions in terms of odds ("eight to five, you need a root canal"), while also taking Jack's fears seriously, allowing Cage to deliver a heartfelt performance that lets the comedy come from his character's distress. Bergman also gives Caan space to humanize Korman, turning what could have been a stock villain into a man motivated by real loss and pain. Sure, he's a slimeball, but slimeballs have feelings, too.

It's also, even with its climactic spectacle, a film content to work small. Bergman may have seemed like a filmmaker out of time, but he also understood the tradition of comedies driven more by characters and gags than wild concepts and special effects. In 1992, that tradition still had a place, despite a decade in which comedies kept getting bigger, with box-office expectations that grew to match them in scale. A stunt-filled spectacular as big and expensive as any action film, John

Landis's *The Blues Brothers* helped set the tone at the beginning of the 1980s, which would find big business in expensive hybrids, joining jokes to action (*48 Hours, Beverly Hills Cop*) and to special effects (*Ghostbusters, Back to the Future*).

A human-scaled comedy could still find a place, however, be it a sophisticated romantic comedy like *Bull Durham* or one of the many teen comedies that dominated the decade, whether the crass *Porky's* clones of its first half or the John Hughes knock-offs of its second. A modestly budgeted film—a *Hairspray* or *Can't Buy Me Love*—could appear in a dead month or serve as low-key counter-programming in a summer overrun with action movies, and turn an impressive profit if it caught on (and often one that wouldn't send anyone home crying even if the movie didn't become a huge hit).

That would change later, in the 1990s, but not quite yet. Released in the fall of 1990, *Home Alone* topped the box office for twelve straight weeks. By mid-decade, Cage's *Peggy Sue Got Married* costar Jim Carrey had begun commanding record-breaking salaries for starring in comedies treated as event films on a blockbuster scale. But in 1992, box-office success still accounted for relativity. The Disney offshoot Touchstone, for instance, could release a string of mid-budget comedies like *Betsy's Wedding* and *Green Card*, and the success of a hit like *Pretty Woman* or, earlier in 1992, *Sister Act* could erase any disappointments and then some, justifying the whole strategy. *Honeymoon in Vegas* arrived at the end of a long summer dominated by a contentious presidential race and the disastrous arrival of Hurricane Andrew and charmed its way to box-office success in spite of mixed reviews. It debuted at number one as August came to a close and drew even more viewers in its second weekend, enough to qualify as a solid success. It also established Cage as an actor who could play everyday guys, and he threw himself into the task, at least for a little while.

❑ ❑ ❑

Hugh Wilson never really fit into Hollywood, either, but that didn't stop him from staying busy. A veteran of the advertising world who found his way into MTM Enterprises in the 1970s, an era that saw the company turning out the classic sitcoms *The Mary Tyler Moore Show* and *The Bob Newhart Show*, Wilson had a habit of creating TV series beloved by critics but largely ignored by audiences, most famously *WKRP in Cincinnati*, which regularly turns up on lists of TV's greatest comedies but which limped its way through four low-rated seasons before its cancellation in 1982. Post-*WKRP*, he'd found tremendous success rewriting and directing the unexpected 1984 hit *Police Academy*, which he disliked, and then traveled freely between film and TV, where he ran into the same problems he'd had before, watching as critically embraced projects like *The Famous Teddy Z* and the innovative *Frank's Place* vanished after single seasons. "I'm doing movies that I can't stand, that I think are completely stupid," Wilson told an interviewer from the Television Academy Foundation a few years before his death in 2018. "But on television I'm full of artistic starch."

Cowritten with *WKRP*'s head writer, PJ Torkovei, the 1994 film *Guarding Tess* plays like an attempt to bring some of that artistic starch to Wilson's film work. A cozy but occasionally acidic comedy, it casts Cage as Doug Chesnic, a by-the-book Secret Service agent who, as the film opens, is about to punch out on the frustrating assignment of protecting the impossible-to-manage former First Lady Tess Carlisle (Shirley MacLaine), who treats him like a member of the help and forces him to leave his gun behind whenever he enters her bedroom. After bidding her farewell and relaxing for the first time in years on the plane ride home, he reaches Washington only to learn that Tess has requested his return and that he doesn't have much choice in the matter, thanks to her influence on the current president (voiced by an unseen Wilson, whose phone calls provide some of the film's funniest moments).

Though the film suffers from a final act that threatens to turn a clever comedy into a straightforward thriller, it mostly coasts along on a charming script and the fractious chemistry of Cage and MacLaine. She's all pursed-lip tartness. He plays Doug as a man whose professionalism and sense of duty just barely act as a restraint on his mounting frustration. It's a fun dynamic and another in a string of films in which Cage generates tremendous chemistry working opposite an older leading lady (though *Guarding Tess* is absent the romantic elements of *Moonstruck* or *Peggy Sue Got Married*).

Going even farther than *Honeymoon in Vegas*, the film finds Cage playing a character shorn of all oddness, a fundamentally good man tested by an extraordinary situation. And, also like *Honeymoon in Vegas*, it earned largely approving reviews and found an appreciative audience, debuting atop the weekend box office. But the movie it displaced, the Jim Carrey–starring *Ace Ventura: Pet Detective*, doubled as an omen for changing times that would soon have less room for comedies so modest in scale.

For the moment, however, Cage could call them home. This made a reunion with Andrew Bergman, for a film to be released later that summer, a logical next step. Where *Honeymoon in Vegas* found Bergman looking to the classic era's screwball comedies, *It Could Happen to You* borrowed from Frank Capra for a story that pits greed and materialism against virtue and honesty. Working from a script by playwright and TV veteran Jane Anderson loosely inspired by a true story, Bergman essentially erases the distance between the New York of the 1990s and the one found in old Hollywood movies. Cage plays Charlie Lang, a friendly beat cop who takes time to play ball with the neighborhood kids at the end of each shift. He's content with his lot in life, but his wife, Muriel (Rosie Perez), has bigger dreams. When Charlie buys a winning lottery ticket, it looks like her dreams will come true. The only problem: earlier in the day, a short-of-cash Charlie offered half the ticket to Yvonne (Bridget Fonda), a down-on-her-luck waitress, in lieu of a tip, and now feels obligated to give her half the winnings.

Cage doesn't just play a nice guy; he plays the *nicest* guy, and he looked to Capra's go-to nice guy for inspiration. Later, Bergman would recall offering Cage only "More Jimmy!" by way of direction. But Cage is not simply doing Stewart. There's nothing studied about his disarmingly earnest work here. In *Vampire's Kiss*, he twisted his face into paroxysms of unhinged malevolence. Here, he looks like a man who's never had an unkind thought in his life, albeit one not immune to temptation. Given the chance to keep Yvonne in the dark, he hesitates. Later, when he realizes he's falling for her in spite of the commitment he's made to the increasingly avaricious Muriel (a descent into materialistic madness Perez realizes to comic perfection), he plays it as a state of silent torment.

Cage's filmography is loaded with far showier roles, but few as heartrendingly understated. Paired with Fonda (then in a relationship with Cage's onetime bête noire Eric Stoltz), who delivers a similarly heartfelt performance, he anchors a bewitching big-city fantasy in real emotions. He was good at this, and if Tom Hanks had no interest in the Jimmy Stewart slot, then Cage seemed happy to fill it. The film found an audience, too. Bolstered by largely positive reviews (the *Washington Post*: "Simply and without pandering or insults to your intelligence, the movie delivers more of the old-style pleasures of moviegoing than any other picture in a long while"), it finished sixth at the box office following its July 29 release. Though that may not sound all that impressive by today's standards, in 1994 an intimate comedy like *It Could Happen to You* could stick around as counter-programming, playing for weeks as an alternative to louder, more expensive fair while turning a satisfying profit before heading to video stores and cable.

That moment wouldn't last much longer. Carrey again topped the box office that weekend, this time with *The Mask*, the second of the three 1994 hits that would make him an in-demand superstar and prompt Hollywood to reconsider the scale of its comedies. Cage himself came *this* close to costarring in Carrey's third 1994 hit. "We talked at length about trying to do a movie together," Cage told *Huffington Post* reporter Mike Ryan in 2012. "In fact, he wanted me to be in *Dumb and Dumber* with him. And then I wanted to do a much smaller movie instead, called *Leaving Las Vegas*." That decision would soon put Cage on a different path.

Even rom-coms would start to think big. When Hanks and

Meg Ryan reunited for *You've Got Mail* in 1998, after the success of *Sleepless in Seattle*, the film cost $65 million, three times the budget of either *Sleepless* or *It Could Happen to You*. Also of note: as a quasi-remake of Ernst Lubitsch's *The Shop Around the Corner*, it would see Hanks stepping into a role originated by James Stewart. Maybe Hanks didn't mind the comparisons so much anymore. By then, Cage would have long since vacated the Stewart slot. It didn't take long after the end of the Sunshine Trilogy for darkness to set in.

❑ ❑ ❑

There's more to Cage's early '90s work than the Sunshine Trilogy, yet even the films outside it, which include broad comedies and a modern film noir, feel like part of the same phase, an exploration of the difficulty of doing good in a world that seldom rewards it. In a pair of broad comedies, Cage plays career criminals who discover their better natures.

In *Amos & Andrew*, he costars opposite Samuel L. Jackson as Amos, a seemingly incorrigible thief enlisted to provide cover for an upscale resort community's police chief (Dabney Coleman) when cops surround the home of Andrew (Jackson), a renowned writer they mistake for a burglar when neighbors jump to conclusions after seeing him. In time, Amos and Andrew find common cause against the racist, upper-class locals, even forming a kind of friendship. The setup suggests a film concerned with social issues. It even anticipates Henry Louis Gates's 2009 arrest outside his own home, but the few who saw it the spring of 1993 largely ended up agreeing with Roger Ebert's summation that any humor ends up "undermined by the sadness of the basic situation." When Amos gets

Andrew to admit that he's too sensitive about race, it's hard not to cringe, though Cage seems to be having fun playing a reprobate.

The same can't be said for 1994's *Trapped in Paradise*, in which Cage stars as the unlikely brother to characters played by Jon Lovitz and Dana Carvey. Both alums of *Saturday Night Live*, Lovitz and Carvey appear to be in a slightly cartoonier movie than the rest of the cast—not that there's much to be said about the more grounded elements of the George Gallo–directed film. Cage plays a New York restaurant manager who's trying to leave a life of crime behind him but who keeps getting sucked into his brothers' schemes. The setup is almost as Capraesque as *It Could Happen to You*. Over Christmas, the trio finds themselves stuck in the small Pennsylvania town whose bank they've just robbed, only to be overwhelmed by the natives' kindness. But Cage struggles to figure out what to do in the sort of film that mistakes car crashes and wacky voices for high comedy. If this is what playing a nice guy in funny movies got him, it's no wonder he would soon opt out.

❑ ❑ ❑

The most daring film Cage made during this stretch almost didn't see release at all. Shot on a low budget in Arizona in the winter of 1992, *Red Rock West* seemed for a while in danger of falling through the cracks. A modern noir set in the eponymous desert town, a dusty little spot on the map filled with characters of bad intent, it was deemed too mainstream for the art house crowd but too tough a sell for a wide audience. Tough times had come to genre filmmaking. Where even ten years earlier, knotty little movies—even knotty little movies with artistic aspirations—could find a home in drive-ins, grindhouses, and on multiplexes' smaller screens, home video had eroded these outlets. (It's easy to imagine even a film like *Zandalee* finding its way to unsuspecting moviegoers in an earlier era.) What's more, major studios had edged into the territory that less well-heeled genre filmmakers had once occupied, pushing largely low-budget thrillers, science fiction, and horror movies out of theaters in favor of their big-budget equivalents. Though *Red Rock West* successfully played Europe in the summer of 1993, in North America it made a quiet debut on HBO before shuffling off to video stores—or, it would have, if not for a theater owner with a little distribution company who liked the film too much to let it go.

Impressed by the film, Bill Banning secured it for the movie theater he owned, San Francisco's Roxie, where it broke records. From there it spread, making its way across the city, and then down to Los Angeles, and then to New York, and then to art houses across the country. It worked as a testament to Banning's savvy; Roxie Releasing, the distribution company he ran in conjunction with the theater, didn't release *that* many movies, but the films it did release had an impact: the controversial and prescient *Man Bites Dog*, Nick Broomfield's twisty doc *Kurt & Courtney*, Michael Haneke's breakthrough *Benny's Video*. Movie studios didn't know there was an audience for such misfit movies, but Banning did. "The film doesn't fall neatly into any marketable category," marketing consultant Peter Graves told Ann Hornaday in the *New York Times*. "A western film noir isn't something people can immediately spark to." But by then, people were already sparking to it.

Featuring corruption, a femme fatale, a hired killer, and more than a couple of double crosses, *Red Rock West* at first seems a world away from the lighter fare Cage made for major studios at the time. But the conflict at the heart of it remains much the same. Cage plays Michael Williams, an honest man trying to ride out a long streak of bad luck without losing his soul. A former marine injured in the 1983 Beirut barracks bombing, he's spent the better part of a decade drifting in search of jobs that will take him on, in spite of the lingering effects of a leg injury sustained during the attack. That he refuses to cover up his limitations costs him a job on an oil rig as the film opens, setting him drifting again. When an easy, but immoral, solution presents itself in the form of an open, unattended cash register, Michael's eyes dance with a temptation he just barely manages to tamp down. He's just not that sort of person.

He's also not "Lyle from Dallas," the hit man he's mistaken for when he walks into the Red Rock bar owned by Wayne (J. T. Walsh). Wayne would like to dispose of his unfaithful wife, Suzanne (Lara Flynn Boyle), and while Michael has no intention of doing that, he decides to take the money, warn Suzanne, and get out of town before anyone's the wiser. His plan hits a series of snags, however, the arrival of the real Lyle from Dallas (Dennis Hopper) not the least of them.

Though John Dahl had watched his first film and first attempt at a modern noir, 1989's *Kill Me Again*, fall through the cracks, he decided to stick with the genre. Cowritten by Dahl and his brother Rick, *Red Rock West* plays like the work of creators who know the style inside and out. They also know how to play against expectations. Film noir historian Eddie Muller popularized the phrase "the noir moment" to describe that point when a noir protagonist makes a decision that will take him into the shadows and into a darkness from which he's unlikely to emerge. (When Fred MacMurray locks eyes with Barbara Stanwyck in *Double Indemnity*, for instance, his fate is already sealed. It's just a matter of filling in the details.) In *Red Rock West*, Michael struggles to fight off the noir moment, to do what's right even when it's easier to do what's wrong. Unaware of what Wayne has hired Lyle from Dallas to do when he agrees to a private meeting, he has little choice *but* to take the money if he wants to get out of the man's office alive.

"The amusement in that film, and in Cage's performance," Muller says, "is in the character's resistance to *being in a noir*. He knows better at every turn, and can't believe that it keeps getting worse no matter what he does." Michael ultimately leaves the film empty-handed but alive, and in full possession of his integrity. Through it all, Cage plays it as the story of a man struggling to survive while listening to his better angels.

"How do you cook a frog in boiling water? Really slowly. That was the idea," Dahl says of the film, adding, "when you have somebody as appealing as Nicolas Cage, it's a little bit easier to pull that off." Michael could be one of Cage's Sunshine Trilogy protagonists who's just been beaten up by life a bit. In a period that found Cage playing different varieties of straight-arrow ordinary Joes, he's no less an Everyman. Only, the genre has changed. Though he first attracted attention for his deft handling of oddballs, Cage had reinvented himself as an expert in normality.

Most of the time. He couldn't neglect all the experiments cooked up in the *Vampire's Kiss* lab forever, and the 1993 film *Deadfall*, directed by Cage's brother Christopher Coppola, gave him license to let his wilder instincts come roaring to the surface. The film's a star-packed mess filled with Coppola family and friends (its cast includes James Coburn, Peter Fonda, Charlie Sheen, and Talia Shire), a con artist tale with one foot planted in parody. Often that foot belongs to Eddie King, the mustachioed, bewigged tough guy played by Nicolas Cage in an unrestrained performance filled with screaming, leering, weird verbal tics, strangely pronounced words, and bizarre gesticulations. Dismissed as a vanity project, *Deadfall* barely saw release, but it picked up a reputation among those drawn to Cage's stranger performances over the years. For much of the early '90s, watching Cage meant watching an actor trying to master the art of playing it straight. But the wilder side was still there, just waiting to escape.

7

The Year of Cage

Nineteen ninety-five was supposed to be David Caruso's year, one that had been a long time coming. A child of divorce, Caruso grew up idolizing Humphrey Bogart, Edward G. Robinson, James Cagney, and other classic Hollywood tough guys, watching their movies and learning their moves during lonely hours as a kid in Queens. When he got a bit older, Caruso worked as a movie usher. He kept his eyes open, and when he watched *The Godfather* on opening night, he knew he had to be an actor. Hollywood beckoned, and Caruso spent the 1980s and early '90s taking on a string of increasingly high-profile supporting roles in films like *First Blood* and *King of New York* and memorable guest turns on the series *Hill Street Blues*. Each provided a spotlight for the sort of characters he played best: flinty tough guys with sensitive eyes who seemed perpetually on the verge of exploding into a violent rage. He found success without really achieving stardom, at least at the movies.

In 1993, however, he found stardom elsewhere. Reuniting with *Hill Street Blues* creator Steven Bochco, Caruso took the part of Det. John Kelly on *NYPD Blue*, a series destined to change television by pushing the boundaries of what network TV allowed via episodes filled with harsh language, violence, and glimpses of bare flesh. At thirty-seven, Caruso became something of an overnight sensation and sought to capitalize on his increased profile by pursuing his dream of becoming a movie star. During the summer hiatus that followed the end of *NYPD Blue*'s first season, he took the lead in *Kiss of Death*, a loose remake of a 1947 film noir classic about an ex-con drawn back into a life of crime.

Intended as the next chapter in the story of Caruso's ascent, it should have cemented the actor's future in movies. When the film arrived in theaters in April 1995, however, the story had shifted. The previous fall, Caruso had acrimoniously departed *NYPD Blue*, a high-profile split that disappointed fans of the show and later led Bochco to liken the actor to a "cancerous" presence empowered by the discontent he created. Bad press followed, as did a swell of schadenfreude. *Kiss of Death* became not just an attempt to branch out into movies but also a referendum on Caruso's career. He left TV to do *this*? Let's see if it was worth it.

The verdict would be both immediate and unkind. It was also unfair, to both Caruso and the film, which earned largely positive reviews but debuted at number three at the box office before quickly leaving theaters. Written by Richard Price and directed by Barbet Schroeder, the French auteur who'd directed Jeremy Irons to a Best Actor win in *Reversal of Fortune* and cultivated a talent for florid thrillers like *Single White*

Female, it throws out much of the original's plot but otherwise feels like a modernization of its grimy setting and themes, depicting a world in which honesty can be deadly. Caruso's performance fits into that world snugly.

It also offers few surprises. Though playing a character on the other side of the law, Caruso doesn't veer too far from his *NYPD Blue* persona. If he wanted his performance to be one moviegoers talked about later, he chose his first star vehicle poorly. And anyone who did see *Kiss of Death* left the theater talking about Nicolas Cage.

After a few years playing good guys, Cage decided to go bad. Or, more accurately: BAD. As Little Junior Brown, a man whose diminutive nickname belies his hulking physique, Cage plays a violent criminal with a philosophical bent who, in one memorable scene, explains to Caruso's Jimmy Kilmartin the need to have a personal acronym to "help you visualize your goals," his being BAD: "balls, attitude, direction." With a crew cut and goatee, and sporting a gym-sculpted body, Cage looks every inch the tough guy. But it's the look of absolute sincerity that sells the scene and the performance as a whole. He plays Little Junior as a man as vulnerable as he is volatile, one who lashes out at henchmen with only the slightest provocation, but who breaks down in tears as he half-dances on the floor of his family's strip club after the death of his father. He's a monster but also a man in pain.

Critics took note. In the *Los Angeles Times*, Kenneth Turan called Cage "one of the few American actors who gets more interesting from film to film." Now, over a decade into his career, Cage hadn't lost the ability to surprise, here joining the madness of his *Vampire's Kiss* work to the searching earnestness of his nice-guy phase, a potent combination that invited both repulsion and sympathy. Though the film was largely overlooked at the time, those who caught it had a hard time shaking Cage's performance, a big, bravura turn that overshadowed his costar's.

Again, this isn't entirely Caruso's fault. Great stars, from John Wayne to Tom Cruise, can build whole careers around offering subtle variations on the same persona. Time and familiarity make those variations feel all the more potent. The older, slower, more pensive Wayne of *The Man Who Shot Liberty Valance* and the misguided cockiness of Cruise as the doomed protagonist in the overlooked *American Made*, for instance, draw some of their power from the actors' on- and off-screen histories. With time and better choices, Caruso might have had a similar film career. But 1995 wasn't the time to start it. That year belonged to someone else.

❑ ❑ ❑

Leaving Las Vegas was the sort of movie that just didn't get made, not even in 1995, a year in which the definition of what could and couldn't get made seemed to change by the day. A slow-building wave had crested the previous October with the release of *Pulp Fiction*, the zeitgeist-resetting Quentin Tarantino film that synthesized a lifelong film nerd's passions into a time-bending collection of crime stories. A Palme d'Or winner at Cannes that spring, it upended notions of what sort of film could become a hit. Star John Travolta was so synonymous with has-beendom that he served as a punch line on an episode of *The Simpsons* that aired mere days before *Pulp Fiction*'s release, and though Miramax had already established itself as the decade's premier indie studio, it wasn't in the habit of releasing box-office smashes. What's more, *Pulp Fiction* mixed moments of shocking violence with dark humor, floating on a sea of cinematic references to everyone from Anna Karina, a Danish-French film actress and French New Wave icon, to pop cinema's Roger Corman, and expecting audiences to keep up. What a few years earlier might have been confined to the art houses that gave *Red Rock West* a second life instead found its way into malls.

Pulp Fiction's success confirmed the growing commercial power of the American independent film scene, which had been building since the unexpected success of Steven Soderbergh's *sex, lies, and videotape* in 1989. Tarantino first made a name for himself, like Soderbergh, at the Sundance Film Festival, when his first film, *Reservoir Dogs*, premiered there in 1992. In the same era, the festival became a conduit for Black, LGBTQ, Latinx, and female filmmakers looking for ways to skirt both Hollywood and the executives who'd never take a meeting for films like *Go Fish*, *El Mariachi*, *Gas Food Lodging*, or *Just Another Girl on the I.R.T.* If none would enjoy success on the scale of *Pulp Fiction*, Tarantino's film still helped bring a swath of smaller films out of the shadows. It played roughly the same role as Nirvana's *Nevermind* did for music in 1991, a product of the underground that, with the help of industry money, tunneled up into the mainstream and left a path that others could try to follow.

Pulp Fiction would be much imitated, and its stars recruited for the cachet they lent to other projects. (It's no accident that *Pulp Fiction*'s Samuel L. Jackson and Ving Rhames both found their way into *Kiss of Death*.) But change was all around in 1995. Pixar made its feature debut with *Toy Story*, and though its computer animation then seemed like a novelty, it would soon become the norm for American animation. In Paris that spring, Danish directors Lars von Trier and Thomas Vinterberg unveiled the tenets of a movement they called "Dogme 95," an attempt to "purify" filmmaking through a set of ten limitations, including the requirement that filmmakers use handheld cameras, employ location shooting, and avoid using any genre elements. While such developments hardly signaled a global rejection of the old ways—the Joel Schumacher–directed *Batman Forever* would top the year's box office—they collectively suggested a yearning for new visions and new ways of creating movies.

Dogme 95's influence wouldn't be directly felt until its first products, starting with Vinterberg's acclaimed *The Celebration*, started to appear in theaters in 1998, but some of its same impulses can be felt in *Leaving Las Vegas*, even if they originated more from necessity than design. Director Mike Figgis was no stranger to Hollywood. He was also, by the time he started shooting *Leaving Las Vegas* in the fall of 1994, no fan. After working for years as a musician, he branched out into photography and theater and then found a way to combine all his interests. In 1988 he made his feature directing debut with *Stormy Monday*, a moody, noir-inflected thriller with political undertones starring Tommy Lee Jones, Melanie Griffith, Sean Bean, and Sting and set in Newcastle upon Tyne, the port city in the North of England in which Figgis grew up after spending his earliest years in Kenya. He found success in America with his second film, the tough, complex cop thriller *Internal Affairs*, starring Richard Gere. His subsequent efforts had been less pleasant, however, particularly *Mr. Jones*, a second collaboration with Gere taken out of Figgis's hands and given to another director to finish. It was enough to make anyone consider a change in career.

Instead, Figgis went small. While in a used-book store, his friend the actor turned producer Stuart Regen had happened upon *Leaving Las Vegas*, a short, sad 1990 novel about an alcoholic trying to hasten an end he felt inevitable. Regen reached out to its author, John O'Brien. After assuring O'Brien that the film he hoped to make of the novel would follow the story to its bleak ending, he brought in Figgis. Together, Regen and Figgis found financing via a French production company. They moved forward, but the $3.5 million budget necessitated a tight shooting schedule and other constraints, including the use of 16 mm cameras and a guerrilla approach to shooting on location where permits might have eaten into the budget.

Figgis would attempt to turn these potential problems into advantages, shooting on found locations, treating the limited palette and washed-out look of the 16 mm film as an aesthetic choice, and finding in the lightweight cameras improvisatory opportunities the 35 mm equipment he was used to working with wouldn't allow. But to make it work, he'd need a cast willing both to go along for the ride and to tackle the film's tough material.

As Ben Sanderson, a screenwriter who, in the film's opening scenes, loses his grip on the professional ladder and opts to use a large severance check to fund a fatal drinking binge in Las Vegas, he found an eager star in Cage, who read the script during the unhappy *Trapped in Paradise* shoot. For the part of Sera, he made the unlikely choice of Elisabeth Shue, then best known for her wholesome roles in much-loved '80s films like *Adventures in Babysitting* and *The Karate Kid*.

The film offered none of the luxuries of a Hollywood production and demanded a draining investment on the part of its leads. Shue's performance required her to perform a type of material she'd never played before, including explicit sex scenes, depictions of abuse at the hands of Sera's pimp, Yuri (Julian Sands), and a gang rape scene staged with disturbing intensity (but, Figgis would later clarify, shot with an attention to safety that was accomplished in part by his threatening to fire any of the actors playing Sera's rapists should they cross any lines). Cage had to play a character who remained drunk in every scene, apart from a handful of sober moments in which Ben suffers from delirium tremens.

Cage initially wanted to achieve the effect just as Ben would. When first discussing the role with Figgis, he proposed playing the part drunk and borrowing Marlon Brando's late-career habit of having an assistant feed him his lines via an earpiece. Though Cage would ultimately play a few scenes intoxicated, Figgis talked him out of taking this approach for the whole film, arguing that it would make him less nimble and less able to improvise, as well as being unfair to Shue. Instead, Cage studied great drunk performances from the past, like Ray Milland's in *The Lost Weekend*, Kris Kristofferson's in *A Star Is Born* (from whom he borrowed Ben's habit of smiling even as he destroys himself), and, especially, Albert Finney's in John Huston's *Under the Volcano*. (Via Figgis, Finney advised Cage to rub his lips with a small amount of alcohol before scenes, to get the taste of it in his mouth.) At cousin Roman Coppola's suggestion, he also brought in the alcoholic poet Tony Dingman, a friend of Francis's who'd worked on his films in various capacities since the late 1960s, as a kind of on-set "drinking coach" during the shoot.

It could have gone horribly wrong. Handled differently, *Leaving Las Vegas* might have played like a fantasy glamorizing self-destruction, one that turned Ben into a martyr and Sera into a one-dimensional creation present only to ease him into death. Ben could have been treated as the sort of meaty, showy role other actors would have torn into like a three-course meal, throwing subtlety out the window in search of acclaim and awards. Cage would later claim he had nothing of the sort on his mind, believing he was acting in a movie nobody wanted to make and that might never see the light of day—not a far-fetched assumption at the time. Instead, he makes Ben an object, first of pity, and then of horror, and ultimately of empathy, demanding that viewers see the humanity in a man determined to make himself into a wretch. In that, he's in lockstep with Figgis, who resists any impulse to glorify Ben's drinking by repeatedly depicting its horrific consequences, and with Shue, who makes Sera a three-dimensional character with an open heart and a spine made of steel.

Shue would later recall a meeting at Figgis's Los Angeles home, during which he performed some of the music he'd composed for the film's score, as a turning point for the collaboration. "I looked over at Nic, and we kind of looked at each other and went, 'Ahh,'" she told the *Ottawa Citizen*'s Jay Stone in 1996. "It was just this feeling of 'I understand, I understand this movie.' It was weird, just a momentary thing, but it all made sense to me. The innocence. The innocence of our love for each other made sense to me when I heard the innocence of that melody."

Innocence might seem an odd choice of word, but *Leaving Las Vegas* supports it. We learn little of Ben and Sera beyond how they live their lives as Ben attempts to wind his down. Yuri makes some allusions to a past life with Sera in Los Angeles, and shortly before burning his possessions, including a family photo, Ben says, "I can't remember if my wife left me because I started drinking or if I started drinking because my wife left me," an admission that seems less writerly overstatement than a genuine side effect of his habit. We do, however, see Ben and Sera together and witness the ways their vulnerabilities complement each other. They form a bond as strong as it is doomed, one predicated on Sera's willingness to let Ben die.

Death hung over the film even before the cameras rolled. As *Leaving Las Vegas* entered preproduction, O'Brien took his own life at the age of thirty-three. He'd written the novel during a sober stretch, but the demons he depicted in its pages ultimately claimed him. Cage brings darkly comic touches to the performance, but remains locked into the material's funereal tone. When he laughs, it's usually at some joke only he understands, one in which he serves as the punch line.

He's raw in his vulnerability, sometimes frighteningly so. Dismissed from his job by an understanding boss who feels he has no choice, Ben exclaims, "I'm sorry!" and it sounds like the cry of a child. Mostly, however, he behaves like a man on a mission, one freed from any obligation beyond removing himself from the earth, one who, with Sera, finds a ray of sunlight in which he can bask in the moment before it all goes dark. Sober, he shakes so hard he can't sign the check that will allow him to buy his next drink. Drunk, he's verbose and almost clever, the creativity that once powered his career still sending off sparks but never catching fire. His eyes and grin can still charm, but he looks unhealthy. (For the film, Cage lost his buff *Kiss of Death* physique via a crash diet of beef jerky and Twinkies.) Ben's good only at drinking, and he's starting to slip even in that task. He'd be hard to watch if Cage didn't make it impossible to turn away.

Critics quickly praised the film in reviews that focused heavily on Shue's and Cage's performances. Describing Ben as "Part buffoon, part poet, part lout, and part angel," the *Austin Chronicle*'s Marjorie Baumgarten wrote that "Cage plays the part with complete abandon, creating a searingly immortal character." Even those previously skeptical of him praised his work here. "A good actor who tends to overact spectacularly, [Cage] reins himself in to marvelous effect, delivering an impressive performance free of his usual tics and stunts," Rene Rodriguez observed in the *Miami Herald.* They also noticed the ways *Leaving Las Vegas* stood apart from films churned through the studio system. "The performances by Cage and Shue are deep-breathing of a sort that Hollywood almost never permits actors," Jay Carr wrote in his review for the *Boston Globe*.

The material's unrelenting bleakness didn't stand in the way of *Leaving Las Vegas* finding an audience. Picked up for North American release by United Artists, the film opened in just seven U.S. theaters on October 27, 1995, and only slowly fanned out across the country through the rest of the year before opening wide on February 9, 1996. By this point, it had picked up steam through word of mouth among those who'd seen it and created awards buzz, that intangible quality that attaches itself to films and performances as critics awards give way to the Golden Globes and, ultimately, the Academy Awards. By the time the film appeared nationwide on more than thirteen hundred screens, Cage had already won the Best Actor prize at the Golden Globes, beating out Richard Dreyfuss for *Mr. Holland's Opus*, Anthony Hopkins in *Nixon*, Ian McKellen in *Richard III*, and sometime friend Sean Penn in *Dead Man Walking*. This helped make Cage the front-runner when the Academy announced its nominees on February 13, a contest that would again pit him against Hopkins, Dreyfuss, and Penn, as well as Italian actor Massimo Troisi, the star of the art house hit *Il Postino*.

Troisi's unusual story—having postponed a heart transplant in order to play the role, he died mere hours after finishing filming—might have made him the favorite in another year. So might Dreyfuss's comeback role or Penn's intense work as an unrepentant death row inmate opposite Susan Sarandon, who would pick up a Best Actress trophy for her performance in the Tim Robbins–directed film. But this wasn't their year. In the run-up to the Oscars, prognosticators all pointed to Cage as the likely winner.

In an Oscars race, even the strongest performances benefit by being accompanied by a good narrative, and as awards night approached, the actor who once refused all interviews found himself doing a lot of talking. That he had a happy new story to tell, one in which he talked about putting his wild past behind him after reuniting with the love of his life, surely helped.

Cage's romance with Patricia Arquette was a new relationship with old roots. They'd met in 1987, at the LA land-mark Canters Deli when Arquette was eighteen. Cage vowed to marry her, leading Arquette to demand that he perform a series of Herculean tasks to win her hand, including retrieving a (nonexistent) black orchid and J. D. Salinger's autograph. He succeeded at both—if spray-painting a purple orchid counts—but the relationship sputtered during a trip to Cuba. A chance meeting—at Canters, no less—in 1995 renewed their chemistry. She proposed to him over the phone, and he said yes. Their strange, yearslong courtship allowed Cage to add another story of charming eccentricity to his repertoire, a story that became familiar through the retelling in the lead-up to the Sixty-Eighth Academy Awards ceremony on March 25, 1996.

Cage's likely win remained a constant during awards season, but debates flared up behind him. These included protests around the lack of diversity among the nominees—which seemed especially egregious in a year that included only one Black nominee and ignored strong 1995 performances from Denzel Washington, Laurence Fishburne, Angela Bassett, and others—and a curious disconnect between the films nominated for Best Picture and those nominated in acting categories. While *Leaving Las Vegas* (for which Shue had been nominated as Best Actress) and *Dead Man Walking* were shut out of a Best Picture race that would ultimately go to Mel Gibson's bloody historical drama *Braveheart*, seeming shoo-in performances like Tom Hanks's work in the Best Picture–nominated *Apollo 13* remained without recognition.

The crowd assembled that night seemed united in its admiration for Cage, however. His name inspired a response louder than the others when presenter Jessica Lange read out the list of nominees. When he won, a smiling Shue, who'd watched Sarandon win the Best Actress trophy minutes before, attempted to start a standing ovation. And though it didn't get much farther than her immediate neighbors, Cage still seemed moved by the moment. His acceptance speech put a special emphasis on Shue and Figgis, followed by O'Brien and Dingman, and concluded with warm words for Arquette and an "I love you" for son Weston. He gave the top of the speech, however, to some thoughts about what it meant to him to win for a tough-sell, low-budget film shot on 16 mm, thanking the Academy for, in his words, "helping me to blur the line between art and commerce with this award."

"I know it's not hip to say it," he continued, "but I just love acting, and I hope that there will be more encouragement for alternative movies where we can experiment and fast-forward into the future of acting."

In 1995, that unwritten future—for acting, for movies, and for Cage—seemed filled with possibility. Maybe this was the beginning of a new moment, one in which independent visions and challenging films fueled more by passion than dreams of box-office domination would redefine filmmaking as we knew it. Maybe 1995 would be remembered as a watershed year, like 1969, one that readjusted Hollywood's priorities. An artist like Cage could thrive in such a world. Maybe he could even help create it. In the days after his win, Cage and Arquette talked about costarring as the charming, boozy, crime-solving couple Nick and Nora Charles in a new take on *The Thin Man*. In interviews, Figgis didn't try to hide that he was writing his next film, *One Night Stand*, for Cage and that he wouldn't mind locking him down for the one after that, either. "When Scorsese found De Niro, that is how I feel," Figgis enthused to one interviewer. The two would never work together again. Cage's own future, whatever he imagined it might look like as he accepted the Oscar, would take him elsewhere, starting with an island prison in the San Francisco Bay.

8

Action Cage

By 1995, the old, reliable ways of making action films had started to feel too old and not reliable enough. It had been simpler in the '80s, when putting guns in the hands of musclemen bent on revenge could work at every budget level, whether in blockbusters headed by Arnold Schwarzenegger and Sylvester Stallone or low-budget efforts starring Chuck Norris and Charles Bronson. By the decade's end, the field had expanded a bit. Eddie Murphy's success in *48 Hours* and *Beverly Hills Cop* opened the gates for unlikely stars and comedic elements, setting the stage for Bruce Willis's Everyman hero in *Die Hard*, films like *Running Scared* (which made buddy cops of Gregory Hines and Billy Crystal), and the *Lethal Weapon* series, in which comic moments mingled with scenes of despair and graphic violence. Paul Verhoeven and James Cameron brought in science-fiction elements and an unusual degree of thematic complexity. Yet a meat-and-potatoes style dominated the genre, which was filled with films that strained to match the skill, intensity, and fleetness

Walter Hill brought to *48 Hours* (even Hill's own subsequent action movies).

The new decade found the genre in need of new ideas. While the directors Jan de Bont, John McTiernan, and Andrew Davis pushed the craftsman style forward with the films *Speed*, *Die Hard*, and *The Fugitive*, respectively, these films looked tradition-bound compared to trends emerging elsewhere. In France, Luc Besson's *La Femme Nikita* and Jean-Jacques Beineix's *Diva* helped create what became known as *cinéma du look*, which brought moody disaffection and striking visuals inspired by music videos and advertising to the action genre. The combination echoed and intensified the work of commercial- and video-inspired directors already working in Hollywood, like Tony Scott. Even more radical innovations would come from Hong Kong, where directors Tsui Hark, Ringo Lam, and John Woo set the elements of American action films to offbeat rhythms and made disturbing poetry out of bloodshed and stories of betrayal and twisted loyalties. Both approaches held a funhouse mirror up to the Hollywood action film. As the decade progressed, the Hollywood action film would itself start to resemble these innovative distortions.

It also needed new stars. Stallone became a hit-or-miss box-office draw, and Schwarzenegger started to branch out into comedy, scaling back on his action work apart from collaborations with Cameron and Verhoeven. Where martial artists Steven Seagal and Jean-Claude Van Damme once seemed poised to take their place, both found sustained success at the blockbuster level elusive.

Maybe the public didn't want musclemen anymore. Maybe they wanted more unlikely heroes. Maybe they wanted Cage.

❑ ❑ ❑

Over the course of a career in which he'd encounter rejection, distrust, and dislike, Michael Bay had learned to turn the chip on his shoulder into the source of his power. He'd gotten into movies early, taking a job as an intern at Lucasfilm at fifteen, helping out on a movie that he thought would be a disaster until he saw it cut together: *Raiders of the Lost Ark*. After studying English and film at Wesleyan University, Bay returned to his hometown of Los Angeles to further his education. Like *Raiders* director Steven Spielberg, he'd been turned down by the prestigious film program at USC and had to settle for his second choice, the respected but less sexy ArtCenter College of Design, in Pasadena. But to Bay, anything could be made sexy, even Donny Osmond. After graduating, Bay broke into the music video business directing Osmond's music video "Sacred Emotion," a 1989 attempt to reinvent the clean-scrubbed '70s fixture as a late-1980s pop star. The song sounded like a George Michael hand-me-down, but the video—a quick-cut barrage of largely monochromatic images of shirtless men and suggestively clad women building a barn in the desert—did what Bay was hired to do: push a familiar product by putting it in an irresistible new package.

Bay pressed on, scoring a job at Propaganda Films, a production house that became the first call for every artist wanting to make a cool video or attention-getting ad from the mid-1980s through much of the '90s. (The company also had a busy film wing, with productions that included *Wild at Heart* and *Red Rock West*.) It wasn't an easy fit. A core group of slightly older directors had founded the company, and though they asked Bay to join, that didn't necessarily make them fans of his work. This was especially true of David Fincher, Propaganda's most in-demand, and expensive, director, whom others at Propaganda recall having a fraught relationship with Bay. This didn't stop the two from being compared to each other, if not always flatteringly. Veteran record executive Jeff Ayeroff recalled Bay being pitched to him as "the little Fincher" and described as a director who's "not as artistic, but he's got drive, he's gonna chew through everything."

Bay could perform a sort of alchemy for uncool clients like Vanilla Ice or the band Winger. He could help push 1970s fixture Meat Loaf to an unlikely '90s comeback via a string of elaborate videos. He could create a buzzy ad for the least buzzy product imaginable: milk, as he did with a 1993 contribution to the Got Milk? campaign in which a history buff struggles to utter the name "Aaron Burr" to win a prize on a radio show thanks to a mouthful of peanut butter and an empty carton of milk. But every success meant Bay just had more to prove. He leapt to features in 1995 with *Bad Boys*, starring Will Smith and Martin Lawrence. But getting hired by producers Don Simpson and Jerry Bruckheimer—connoisseurs of flash who'd brought the MTV aesthetic to movies via films like *Flashdance*, *Beverly Hills Cop*, and *Top Gun*—seemed less like a triumph than an invitation to struggle: against those who didn't believe two Black stars could headline an action movie, against stars who didn't always understand his vision, and against a budget he felt was too low. (Bay even paid for one explosive shot out of his own pocket.) "I had to compete with the $120 million Arnold Schwarzenegger movie *True Lies*, which was coming out at the same time," Bay later recalled. "So I used everything I ever learned in videos and commercials on *Bad Boys*. I made fast cuts and shook the camera; anything to make it look different."

It looked, for the first time, like a Michael Bay movie, an American variation on the *cinéma du look* that seemed determined to make an impact on other senses as well. Soon, a *lot* of movies would resemble Bay movies, or try to. Bay's name would become shorthand for action films that privileged striking imagery and rapid cutting over classical editing styles and narrative coherence. The style would later come to be known as "Bayhem," a dismissive term that often lumped Bay in with his imitators, or ignored the style's connection to one of Bay's biggest influences: Hollywood musicals, particularly the films of Busby Berkeley, a spiritual godfather in his use of unexpected angles and kaleidoscopic compositions. It didn't always work, and Bay's later films would dip more frequently toward Bayhem, but *The Rock* largely finds Bay bringing a considered method to what could sometimes seem like a random assault of shots strung together in an attempt to overwhelm viewers' senses.

Where actors fit in wasn't always clear. Where an actor with strong artistic opinions and a habit of making eccentric choices fit in, even less so.

❑ ❑ ❑

The Rock's script had been floating around for a while and was largely considered a good idea in need of repair and reshaping. That idea: a group of soldiers takes over Alcatraz and threatens to unleash a deadly gas on the city of San Francisco if their demands for money to aid families of soldiers who died on unacknowledged covert missions aren't met. The finished script would bear the work of many, including several uncredited writers and leads Cage, Sean Connery, and Ed Harris. It would also feature a concussive soundtrack, brutal violence, more explosions than the average action film, and, because Bay thought the middle sagged a bit, an out-of-nowhere car chase through the streets of San Francisco. In the cinema of excess, the word *gratuitous* could have no meaning.

This didn't mean that the right actor couldn't provide some grace notes. To Cage, working in the action genre was like learning a new style of music. He'd been thinking about music a lot those days. Talking to Roger Ebert after *Leaving Las Vegas*'s premiere at the Toronto International Film Festival, he'd divided the film into three acts, comparing the first to blues, the second to jazz, and the third to opera. One of his contributions had been to have Ben sing a bit from Wagner's *Parsifal*—an opera Cage knew from growing up in a home where, thanks to August, music played constantly—as he entered the final stages of his descent. For an actor unafraid of big emotions, looking to opera for inspiration just made sense.

He needed other rhythms to make his characters work, however. On the set of *Vegas*, he'd used bongos to help work out the cadence of his delivery. Sometimes the characters emerged from the rhythms he created. "I'll start to use movements and vocal inflections, and it really becomes more or less musical for me," he explained in an audio commentary recorded for *The Rock*. "I feel quite comfortable with it on a musical level, where I can find rhythms and really hit the notes, which are the words, in ways I think will have a certain panache. Or sometimes I'll get into a mode where I don't want to think about it, and I'll allow myself two bars—I say two bars metaphorically—just like a couple of sentences where

I'm not going to think about it at all, and whatever happens accidentally will be interesting for me or not. And then I'll get back to what I've already choreographed or figured out beforehand." Elsewhere, he likened his work to "jazz riffs." He planned up to the point where he gave himself the freedom to throw out the plan.

Music wasn't a new influence. Where others heard Pokey the claymation horse in his *Peggy Sue Got Married* performance, Cage thought it akin to Lou Reed's work in the Velvet Underground, an out-of-tune delivery that took songs places they might otherwise not have gone. For *The Rock*, he looked to Miles Davis and the Beatles for inspiration. His contributions to his character, FBI Special Agent Dr. Stanley Goodspeed, included making Goodspeed into a self-described Beatlemaniac willing to spend six hundred dollars on an original vinyl LP because it sounds better.

Cage's contributions to the character didn't stop there. He helped reshape Goodspeed into a profanity-averse nerd more comfortable discussing the science of chemical weapons than wielding a gun. He's a wide-eyed, earnest good citizen surrounded by jaded pros. Already an odd fit for an action movie, Cage makes being an odd fit a part of the character. Musically speaking, he's the "off" beat that gives the film a curious, alluring rhythm that even rocket launchers can't drown out.

With some exceptions, critics generally approved of the film, sometimes because of Bay's style, sometimes in spite of it. In the *Austin Chronicle*, Marc Savlov called it "a ridiculously overblown summer testosterone blowout." Others balked at the style but found a redeeming factor in Cage. "There isn't a shot, scene or sequence in *The Rock* that doesn't move furiously, typically with colored lights flashing into our faces or onto those of the actors," Gene Siskel wrote in the *Chicago Tribune*. "The phrase 'all frosting and no cake' comes to mind," he continued, but Siskel found a bit of cake in Cage and Connery's chemistry. Closer to the film's fictional home, *San Francisco Examiner* critic Barbara Shulgasser felt that Cage's contributions helped temper Bay's excesses, calling him "one of the few actors working in movies today able to play a square, conservative science nerd with enough ingenuity and audacity to make him utterly winning. Goodspeed is a gentleman, a scholar, a romantic, a patriot and a decent person. Plus, he's funny. Although Cage has bulked up to play roughnecks convincingly, I think his gift is as a comedian. He has the touch. He's reedy and vulnerable, graceful and whippet-like. And he has great timing." Jazz-inspired timing, it could even be said.

The Rock became one of the biggest hits of a summer season that included *Independence Day*, *Twister*, and the Brian De Palma–directed *Mission: Impossible*. It also turned Nicolas Cage into an action star, a slot that had seemed impossible for him to return to after the disastrous *Fire Birds*. There's an unkind, and inaccurate, way to read this development, one of an actor cashing in on his artistic success via a blockbuster paycheck. But Cage had already lined up *The Rock* before winning the Oscar for *Leaving Las Vegas*, a film whose existence Bay learned about only after *The Rock* had entered production. Cage soon secured his next film, too, another Bruckheimer-produced action movie, called *Con Air*, Bruckheimer's first project without Simpson, who'd died of a drug overdose as *The Rock* filmed. In an interview with Siskel, Cage spoke of two ulterior motives for taking these roles: a desire to bring more "risk-taking" acting to the genre and the hope that success at this level would help green-light more artistically adventurous independent films, an echo of the desire expressed in his Best Actor acceptance speech.

The Rock itself doubles as an unkind reading of Cage's new direction. Where Goodspeed begins the film as a gun-shy lab rat prone to creative, profanity-skirting exclamations like "How in the name of Zeus's *butthole* did you get out of your cell?" he ends it as an F-word-spouting killing machine of the sort seen in countless action films. Did the action genre invariably sand away the rough edges that made an actor compelling? In the end, did that sort of music have any room for jazz riffs?

❑ ❑ ❑

Yet, as one action film begot another, Cage's work in the genre found him taking chance after chance, even when the movies didn't. *Con Air* paired him with another veteran Propaganda director, Simon West, who used the film as an opportunity to transition from videos and commercials to features. Like Bay, West brought the flash and frenetic energy of his past work to the action film. He didn't, however, bring Bay's command or consistency. *Con Air* is Bayhem without the vision—something that was already becoming the prevailing Hollywood action film aesthetic.

Then again, *Con Air* didn't necessarily require that much vision. Scripted by Scott Rosenberg, then best known for the witty, dialogue-heavy 1996 drama *Beautiful Girls*, the film starts with an unabashedly dopey premise and then sees how far it can run with it. Cage plays Cameron Poe, a discharged Army Ranger who, in the film's opening scenes, accidentally kills a creep harassing his pregnant wife and ends up sentenced to a lengthy prison stretch miles away from his Alabama home. Released early, he hitches a ride back home on a prison transport plane filled with the nation's nastiest criminals (played by John Malkovich, Steve Buscemi, Ving Rhames, and Danny Trejo, among other familiar indie movie faces). When his fellow prisoners hijack the plane, Poe is all that stands between them and mayhem.

The movie refuses to take itself seriously, which is both its most charming quality and its most wearying. It does, however, give Cage, sporting long hair and a sleeveless T-shirt for most of the film, an opportunity to bring a surprising amount of gravitas to lines like "Put the bunny back in the box!" yelled as he protects a stuffed animal he plans to give to the son he knows only from letters, and to a scene in which he savors his first breath of air as a free man (a wordless moment that would later become a favorite GIF). He's in tune with the film's absurdity yet never winks. But, unlike with *The Rock*, Cage doesn't feel essential to the film, or a key element of its creative fabric. For the first time in a while, he doesn't seem to be playing a character only he could have played. He's more actor than the part requires, which can be said of most of the cast, including John Cusack, here making his first foray into action films.

Having an overqualified cast didn't hurt the film, or its commercial prospects, however. *Con Air* debuted on June 6, 1997, to mixed reviews, with even champions like the *Washington Post*'s Rita Kempley half-apologizing for liking such a "[p]reposterous, predictable, but excessively entertaining" film. This didn't scare off moviegoers, however, who turned it into an early-summer hit. It was still hanging around a few weeks later when yet another Cage action film showed up, one that offered acting challenges beyond protecting a stuffed bunny.

❑ ❑ ❑

John Woo grew up, to use his term, in hell. Fearing persecution under Mao Zedong because of their Christian faith, the Woo family fled Guangzhou for Hong Kong when John was five, ending up living in a slum until a 1953 fire left them homeless. They landed in a neighborhood surrounded by crime and erupting in turf wars between local gangs. Woo's father's illness made the struggle to make ends meet even harder. The young Woo needed surgery on his spine, a procedure that made walking difficult for most of his boyhood. Only charity kept the family from falling through the cracks. And only two institutions kept Woo from falling into despair: his church and movie theaters, in his words, "The two places I found my heaven."

As a filmmaker, Woo kept trying to find ways to reconcile those two places of respite. He'd worked his way up through the Hong Kong film industry in the 1970s but had struggled to find his voice until making his 1986 breakthrough, *A Better Tomorrow*. An ultraviolent morality play set in Hong Kong's criminal underworld, it established Woo's stylistic and thematic trademarks: elaborately choreographed gun battles that would soon be dubbed "gun fu," characters whose aloof attitudes and cool outfits barely concealed their outsize emotions, carefully deployed freeze frames and unexpected moments of slow motion, broad symbolism, and a deep interest in depicting clashes between good and evil and the ways those two sides can mirror each other.

The film changed the direction not only of Woo's career, but of Hong Kong moviemaking. Other directors took their cues from its success, putting their own spin on the action genre. Like Woo, they seemed less interested in breaking with traditional filmmaking techniques than in pumping them full of adrenaline. Woo's follow-ups—a *Better Tomorrow* sequel, the brutal war film *Bullet in the Head*, the lighthearted *Once a Thief*, and his Western breakthroughs *The Killer* and *Hard Boiled*—looked less to music videos and commercials for inspiration than to the stylized violence of Sam Peckinpah, the moral conflicts of Martin Scorsese, and the existential isolation of Jean-Pierre Melville. Woo had found his voice making action films that doubled as blood-drenched explorations of his Christian faith.

But could it work in Hollywood? Journeying to America after the release of *Hard Boiled* in 1992, Woo found a system less accommodating to his distinctive voice, at least at first. He watched the studio recut *Hard Target* (a Jean-Claude Van Damme thriller Woo shot in New Orleans) in ways that deemphasized his style. Many of his trademark touches survived the process, however, and the film made money, as did his next Hollywood effort, 1996's *Broken Arrow*, in which John Travolta played a pilot with designs on stealing some nuclear missiles. With that success, Woo won the chance to make a proper John Woo film using all the resources a big-budget Hollywood production would allow.

He found a project tailor-made for him, however accidentally. Partners Mike Werb and Michael Colleary didn't know Woo's work when they wrote the script to *Face/Off*, a futuristic thriller in which a hero and a villain do battle after each assumes the other's identity, complete with an exchange of faces. (The title is designed to deliver on its promise, both literally and figuratively.) After seeing the trailer to Woo's *The Killer*, Werb and Colleary returned to the theater the next night to watch it again. When they saw the finished film—with its shifting loyalties and Manichaean clashes—they realized they'd written a Woo movie without knowing it.

Their script took a while to find its way to Woo, and to his eventual stars. As various filmmakers considered the film, pairings like Sylvester Stallone and Arnold Schwarzenegger, Michael Douglas and Harrison Ford, and Alec Baldwin and Bruce Willis, came and went. At one point, Johnny Depp emerged as a possibility to star opposite Cage. Eventually, after Woo asked the setting to be changed to the present day, the project found its stars: Cage would play the bad guy, the vivacious, amoral, flamboyant international terrorist Castor Troy, whom Cage took to calling "the Liberace of crime." Travolta would play the hero, Sean Archer, an FBI agent still grieving the death of his son at Castor's hands and hell-bent on bringing him to justice.

Sort of. The conceit of the film requires that its leads swap not only faces, but also identities, as Sean, wearing Castor's face, goes undercover at a prison to dig up information about an impending attack in Los Angeles and as the escaped Castor, having assumed Sean's identity, has to pass as the straight-and-narrow family man as he moves in with Sean's wife, Eve (Joan Allen), and rebellious teenage daughter, Jamie (Dominique Swain). Rather than demanding that its leads take on one character, *Face/Off* asked them to create two, with multiple variations: sometimes they play one character trying to pass himself off as the other, sometimes their character's original personality tries to surface from within his assumed identity, and sometimes their character loses himself in the personae he's assumed. Done right, it would be an acting clinic that doubled as a commentary on the craft of acting itself.

For Cage, it presented the chance to begin the film with the sort of big, flamboyant performance that had helped make him famous—another product of the *Vampire's Kiss* lab experiment he'd initiated years before—before shifting to become a brooding good guy doing his best to pass as the unrepentant baddie of the early scenes. After establishing Sean as a mournful man on a mission, Travolta had the opposite challenge, playing the lecherous, expressive Castor doing his best to hide behind the face of the upright (and uptight) hero—and taking wicked pleasure in the experience.

Their approaches offer a study in contrasts. Travolta echoes the Castor whom Cage sets up in the first act—a flashy, joyously malicious figure who revels in doing bad and pinches the backside of a choir girl while wearing the robes of a priest—but also draws on the tics of Cage's past work.

"I'd absorbed a lot of Nic watching him over the years," Travolta told *Entertainment Weekly*. "But it was all things I wanted permission to use." These included "that Nic Cage cadence . . . the way Nic slows down and enunciates and pronunciates [*sic*]. He's almost poetic in his talking." A skilled impressionist, Travolta would soon draw on that talent to great effect playing the Bill Clinton–inspired protagonist of *Primary Colors* (and decades later could still reprise his *Face/ Off* performance on demand to the delight of talk show hosts). Here, he offers an eerily precise take on Cage, playing Castor as a man awakening to new possibilities of wickedness from inside a cloak of goodness. The fun Travolta's having becomes disturbingly infectious, particularly when he administers swift, violent justice to Jamie's sexually aggressive date. It wouldn't be a Woo morality play without some sympathy for the devil.

Cage opts for less an impression than a reinterpretation of Sean—whom he plays as a man in agony after being separated, first, from his family and, then, from his identity. He's disturbed rather than delighted by the opportunities presented by the switch. In one of the film's most striking moments, Cage draws on the Expressionistic silent performances that made such a deep impression on him in childhood. Forced into a prison fight while posing as Castor, his Sean lets waves of emotion sweep across his face: first, horror at the violence he's forced to commit while other prisoners cheer him on; then an impression of the bug-eyed sadism Sean knows from having studied Castor for years; then a kind of dark joy at bending another man to his will; then the soul-deep regret of a righteous man compelled to perform dark deeds; then a flash of madness before he takes mercy on his prey. It's an entire Woo film compressed into a few wordless moments.

Cage found in *Face/Off* an action film that didn't require him to curb his artistic ambition and, in Woo, a collaborator attuned to his musical leanings, a passionate jazz fan who worked on an operatic scale. The film debuted to strong reviews, with even those skeptical of Woo's approach seeing it as the best possible expression of his art. Writing for *TV Guide*, Maitland McDonagh called it a "brutal, stunningly choreographed spectacle [that] weaves together lyrical beauty, blasphemy, sadistic cruelty and grotesque sentimentality with breathtakingly smooth assurance," a combination of seemingly incompatible elements that somehow worked anyway. Movie-goers responded positively as well, turning *Face/Off* into a hit that would ultimately outgross even *Con Air*. It was big and weird, and audiences loved it. It was everything Cage could want from an action movie, and it helped confirm his place as one of his generation's biggest stars, a dark horse who made an unexpected surge while others revealed they couldn't go the distance.

❑ ❑ ❑

In retrospect, it would look like a peak, both of Cage's venture into the action genre and of Woo's time in Hollywood. Where Woo was sometimes seen as the most "American" filmmaker in Hong Kong, with *Face/Off* he made the most Hong Kong action film imaginable within the Hollywood system, using all the resources a Hollywood budget would allow to craft a bullet-riddled exploration of virtue and sinfulness while tak-ing elements of the classic action film to their extremes. (Not content to end with a showdown in a church, Woo added a boat fight to make sure audiences went home satisfied.)

In the years that followed, however, it would be the Bay/Bruckheimer approach that prevailed, maximalism without the studied discipline of Woo and other Hong Kong direc-tors, whose upper ranks soon followed Woo to Hollywood but retreated before Woo made his own return. Making a film with Jean-Claude Van Damme became a kind of rite of passage for Hong Kong veterans like Ringo Lam and Tsui Hark, but nei-ther would stick around in the long run; nor would contempo-rary Ronny Yu, who brought some of the weird lyricism of his

Hong Kong work to the horror film *Bride of Chucky* before departing.

Action films found the Bay aesthetic easier to imitate, if not imitate well. Film scholar David Bordwell groups both Hong Kong– and Bay/Bruckheimer–influenced films under the umbrella of "intensified continuity," but in the latter, it's sometimes hard to find any continuity at all. In the decade that followed, what video essayist Matthias Stork would dub "chaos cinema" emerged as the default mode. In the years after Bay's rise, the multiplexes would fill with action films in which, in Stork's words, "every shot seems like the hysterical climax that an earlier movie might have spent several minutes building toward." Some used it well. While Bay struggled to marry this approach to more narrative-driven films like *Pearl Harbor*, he found a low-ambition, high-reward outlet in the *Transformers* series. Paul Greengrass's *Bourne* films used nausea-inducing handheld work to great effect. One of the pioneers of the form, Tony Scott, thrived and grew as audiences became even more receptive to his rapid-fire assault. Christopher Nolan wove pockets of seeming chaos into a more elegant, classical approach. These were the exceptions, however. Many others took the same shortcuts West took in *Con Air*, substituting movement for meaning and stimulation for thrills.

Face/Off also found its stars in a kind of imperial phase, both still wrapped in an aura of confidence and goodwill that comes with recent, unexpected, and undeniable triumph. In the years after *Pulp Fiction*, Travolta could seemingly do no wrong. The public embraced him. Older fans seemed to realize how much they missed having him as a star, but he also won over a new generation of admirers. The occasional disappointment aside, this affection helped make hits of most of the films that followed, a string of successes that stretched from *Get Shorty* to *A Civil Action* to the Simon West–directed *The General's Daughter*. But it wasn't just popularity and momentum on Travolta's side. He did the work, turning in remarkable performances in even lesser films. Whatever the X-factor was that made an actor into a bankable star, he had it.

Then he didn't. In 2000, Travolta produced and starred in *Battlefield Earth*. Not only a much-mocked flop, it contained one career-hindering speed bump after another, slathering Travolta in makeup to play a sneering alien villain and, as an adaptation of an L. Ron Hubbard novel, reminding moviegoers of Travolta's adherence to Scientology, a faith frequently likened to a cult and subject to allegations of human rights abuses. Travolta kept working, often in high-profile projects, but it was never quite the same.

But if it hadn't been that one tremendous misstep that soured Travolta's comeback, it might have been something else. Success, especially at a superstar scale, is tough to attain and tougher to maintain. One wrong move and it can slip away. Alternately, factors out of a star's control can wrest it away, whether changing tastes or studio politics. Cage's action films found him following one success after another as he found projects that synced up with what moviegoers wanted from blockbuster entertainment—and what they wanted of him. But that didn't mean they'd stay synced up forever.

For now, Cage's record could easily justify the swelling paychecks his services demanded, but he still had to figure out what to do next and how an actor who'd become a superstar by specializing in oddness could remain successful in a rarefied environment that seldom allowed the odd to thrive. Fifteen years after *Valley Girl*, Cage kept finding ways to make his misfit appeal work on an increasingly grand scale. Now all he had to do was keep making it work in movie after movie, year after year.

Born Nicolas Coppola, Nicolas Cage landed the role in *Valley Girl*, his first as a lead, after auditioning for director Martha Coolidge without revealing his family ties.

Cage's eccentric choices in the time-travel fantasy *Peggy Sue Got Married* didn't thrill everyone—including costar Kathleen Turner—but started a pattern of delivering bold, divisive performances.

Director Alan Parker, Cage, and Matthew Modine on the set of *Birdy*, a film that demanded emotionally raw work from its leads and inspired Cage to go to extremes to prepare for the role.

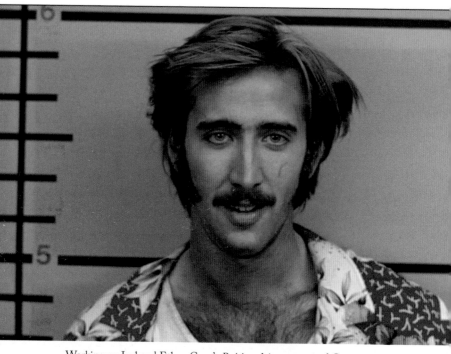

Working on Joel and Ethan Coen's *Raising Arizona* required Cage to summon a manic, cartoon-like energy for the story of a couple who decides to solve their fertility problems through kidnapping.

Cher insisted on Cage as her costar for *Moonstruck*, a warm romantic comedy that won Cher an Oscar and helped make Cage a household name.

Cage immediately followed *Moonstruck* with *Vampire's Kiss*. He'd later refer to the experience as a "laboratory" for acting ideas he could draw on in the future.

David Lynch's road movie fantasia *Wild at Heart*—costarring Cage and Laura Dern as lovers on the run—won the Palme d'Or at Cannes but split viewers and critics with its sex- and violence-filled vision of America.

Cage won the Best Actor Academy Award for his *Leaving Las Vegas* performance as an alcoholic writer finding love with a prostitute. Cage used his acceptance speech to say "I just love acting" and express a hope for more "alternative movies where we can experiment and fast-forward into the future of acting."

Producer Jerry Bruckheimer and Cage on the set of *Con Air*, one of a string of successful action films Cage made with Bruckheimer.

Cage, director John Woo, and John Travolta discuss a scene from *Face/Off*.

August Coppola, Cage, and Joy Coppola gather as Cage receives a star on the Hollywood Walk of Fame. Both deeply influential on Cage's life in different ways, the actor's parents divorced in 1976.

Francis Ford Coppola and Cage share a relaxed moment in 2003.

Martin Scorsese and Cage talk on the set of *Bringing Out the Dead*. The film, and Cage's intense performance, went largely overlooked amid a flood of great movies in 1999.

For director Spike Jonze's *Adaptation*, Cage played the dual roles of Charlie and Donald Kaufman, two temperamentally opposite brothers trying to make a living writing in Hollywood.

Reuniting with Bruckheimer, Cage enjoyed tremendous success as the star of *National Treasure* and its sequel.

Few saw Cage's performance in Neil LaBute's *The Wicker Man*, a remake of a horror classic, in the theaters, but an edited highlight reel became a much-mocked viral clip online.

Director Werner Herzog, Cage, and Eva Mendes film a scene for *Bad Lieutenant: Port of Call New Orleans*, in which Cage plays a New Orleans cop unhinged by addiction and struggling to do what's right.

Panos Cosmatos's phantasmagoric 2018 revenge thriller *Mandy* provided a reminder of how potent Cage could be given the right role at the end of an up-and-down decade defined by direct-to-VOD fare.

9

The Heights of Cage

Cage's movies got bigger. So did everything else: the money, the profile, the responsibility, the rewards of success, the risks of failure. Whether he liked it or not, his career wasn't just about acting anymore. It was about stardom. "Nic Cage has always been Nic Cage, and Nic Cage has always been a great actor," Michael Bay recalled while discussing the editing of *The Rock*. "But people were saying this is the movie that will make Nic Cage a movie star, [and] there's a difference between being a great actor and a movie star. A movie star is someone that has appeal around the world, that people want to see a movie because this actor is in it." The job of a star, a job that extends well beyond the time it takes to make a film, is to make sure audiences *keep* wanting to see movies because that star is in them.

It's not an easy job. The brutal saying "You're only as good as your last picture" has been around nearly as long as the movies themselves. Hollywood history is littered with exceptions, but such bits of received wisdom stick around for a reason. Cage's success opened up possibilities unimaginable just a few years before, making him a first call for the industry's biggest movies. But it also closed off other opportunities. As his quote went up, Cage's ability to step away to make the "alternative movies" he championed in his Oscars acceptance speech became more limited. To appear in anything but a blockbuster would mean taking a smaller paycheck—essentially leaving money behind. And some of Cage's new ambitions, such as forming his own production company, needed money to launch and sustain them. He also had a son to support and a lifestyle to maintain—one that involved buying a lot of stuff.

It was a habit he'd long enjoyed. Explaining his decision to return to studio filmmaking after *Wild at Heart* and *Zandalee* in a 1994 interview, Cage said, "I hadn't gone bankrupt—OK I was only three weeks away from it, maybe." While filming *Honeymoon in Vegas*, he spent time in the casinos, placing wagers big enough to trouble costar Sarah Jessica Parker. His bets, however unlikely, had paid off. Though, by his account, close to bankruptcy just a few years earlier, Cage had, by the time of his Oscar win, added a downtown penthouse to a collection that included a San Francisco mansion and a castle-like Hollywood home. "I think that having different environments is better, rather than having one huge, you know, space that you reside in all the time," Cage told *Entertainment Weekly*'s Steve Daly after mentioning he was also looking for a place in New York. He'd begun to count on the prospect of sustained success to support an increasingly lavish lifestyle, one that included multiple Lamborghinis and a growing collection of comic books, model trains, and other rare items. And why not? By the end of the '90s, the biggest stars in the world were making money on a scale never seen before.

❑ ❑ ❑

In the 1990s, movie stardom turned into an arms race. "Hollywood is caught in a salary-inflation cycle that's so out of control it would have Alan Greenspan weeping into his spreadsheets," *Entertainment Weekly* observed in 1996. A trend that would only intensify in the years that followed, it had escalated sharply in 1995 with the well-publicized news that Jim Carrey would take home a $20 million salary for appearing in *The Cable Guy*, a Columbia TriStar release the studio hoped would become the comedy blockbuster of the 1996 summer season. Carrey had the track record to back it up. In 1994 he'd followed *Ace Ventura: Pet Detective* with *The Mask* and then *Dumb and Dumber*. The following year, Carrey appeared in both *Batman Forever* and the sequel *Ace Ventura: When Nature Calls*, both tremendous hits. He'd earned the right to command an impressive payday, but $20 million seemed like the Hollywood equivalent of breaking the sound barrier.

It also arrived at a point when the model of throwing huge salaries at big stars to appear in super-size movies had already started to prove a bit creaky. In 1993, Arnold Schwarzenegger earned $13 million to appear in *The Last Action Hero*, a box-office disappointment whose profits didn't approach those of Schwarzenegger's previous film, *Terminator 2: Judgment Day*. Whatever soul-searching this might have prompted in 1993 proved short-lived, just as it did in 1996, when *The Cable Guy* similarly underperformed. A darker comedy than Carrey's fans expected, and one that attempted to comment on the corrosive effects of the same media-saturated culture that had helped make Carrey a star, it provided further evidence that films made on this scale, and for this much money, had better play it safe. With so much money going to stars, studios, rarely the most adventurous entities to begin with, would need to reduce risks elsewhere.

For *Face/Off*, Cage settled for a $6 million salary, which would have been considered a remarkable payday just a few years earlier. (As a point of comparison, Schwarzenegger reportedly earned $10 million for *Total Recall*, released in 1990, at the height of his fame.) *Face/Off*'s success, and that of the Cage-fronted action blockbusters that preceded it, made him more expensive. By the end of the decade, he'd also reach the $20 million level, by which point star salaries had become a regular part of the discourse around a movie, sometimes even overwhelming the discussion of the movie itself. In 1999, when a journalist at the Berlin Film Festival observed that whole festivals could be funded by the money Cage made from a single film, Cage replied simply, "Whatever the market rate is . . . is the market rate." He once likened his approach to punk. Now he had to face a familiar punk dilemma: How do you stay true to yourself after you've signed to a major label?

Some of the films Cage made during the period after his mid-'90s ascent to superstardom seemed to grapple with a similar issue, casting him as characters asked to choose between comfort and safety and a more authentic life, be it an angel drawn to earth by true love in *City of Angels*, a Wall Street titan who enters a fantasy world that shows him the life he might have had in *The Family Man*, or a screenwriter struggling to do something meaningful and true with an impossible assignment while others around him take the easy route to success in *Adaptation*. The period would have its successes but also more than a few dead ends, missed opportunities, and strong work that went underrecognized in its time. Becoming a star wasn't easy. Maintaining stardom presented challenges and frustrations of its own.

Among them: how to remind moviegoers that he wasn't *just* an unconventional action hero. Released in April 1998, *City of Angels* cast Cage as Seth, one of the divine beings charged with keeping unseen watch over Los Angeles, lending support to those in need and easing the dying into the next world. A loose remake of Wim Wenders's *Wings of Desire*, *City of Angels* deemphasized the original's metaphysical contemplation to focus on the romance between Seth and Dr. Maggie Rice (Meg Ryan), a devoted heart surgeon haunted by a recent failure—a romance with no future unless Seth gives up his angelic nature and takes on the life of a mortal man.

Directed by Brad Silberling from a screenplay by Dana Stevens, the film drew inspiration from Wenders while tapping into a decade-long interest in angels evident in everything from New Age best sellers to Tony Kushner's end-of-the-century meditation *Angels in America* to a string of angel-themed films that included a remake of *Angels in the Outfield* and Nora Ephron's John Travolta–starring *Michael*. For Cage, *City of Angels* offered a departure not just from action films, but from the expectations of past performances. His character speaks in hushed tones when he speaks at all, and Silberling's use of close-ups allows Cage to again draw on the influence of silent movie performances. Cage lets much of the performance rest on his big, expressive eyes, even refraining from blinking when playing Seth in his angelic form. He also develops a delicate chemistry with Ryan, an actress, like Cage, trying to break away from the sort of roles in which she was in danger of being typecast.

It worked, too, drawing largely polite reviews from critics, debuting at number one at the box office, and lingering in the top five for weeks. And though unmistakably a Hollywood gloss on the Wenders original, it features disarmingly beautiful imagery of the often-maligned Los Angeles and climaxes in an ending more bittersweet than that of its source material. It's a film designed for broad appeal but intent on maintaining its artistic integrity. If the road ahead was filled with similar projects, it would be a smooth one.

It wasn't. In August, *Snake Eyes* debuted to an audience of summer moviegoers hungry for another Cage action film. Instead, they got a twisty, recursively structured thriller directed by Brian De Palma featuring some jaw-dropping moments of cinematic showmanship—including a seemingly unbroken thirteen-minute opening shot that whisks viewers through the belly and onto the floor of an Atlantic City arena playing host to a heavyweight championship bout—and a climax that doesn't work.

Working again with a master filmmaker of the generation that emerged alongside Francis Ford Coppola, Cage offers a vivid performance—one filled with the sort of manic gestures and explosive line readings that would resurface in later work—as a gleefully corrupt cop who stumbles his way toward redemption after discovering that a childhood friend (Gary Sinise) has masterminded a conspiracy. Though *Snake*

Eyes had much to recommend it, particularly for longtime admirers of De Palma and Cage, collections of compelling elements that fail to gel into coherent movies rarely become hits. Hampered by middling reviews—in the *LA Weekly*, Manohla Dargis described it as "running on fumes" after its memorable opening—and bad word of mouth, it struggled at the box office.

At least no one found it repellent. Cage next returned to screens the following February, starring in *8mm*, a thriller penned by Andrew Kevin Walker, writer of *Seven*, which restored David Fincher's footing in Hollywood after the troubled *Alien 3*, and directed by Joel Schumacher, a resilient Hollywood veteran who'd enjoyed more success than respect with a list of hits that included *St. Elmo's Fire*, *The Lost Boys*, and a pair of John Grisham adaptations. Still smarting from the frosty reception that greeted the uninhibitedly campy *Batman and Robin*, his second Batman film, Schumacher had passed on directing a third Grisham movie and taken a break to recuperate in Mexico. But the rumor of a script others described as a "really a dangerous piece of material" helped lure him back.

That piece of material concerned Tom Welles (Cage), a middle-class Pennsylvania-based private investigator hired by a tycoon after she finds a disturbing item among her late husband's effects: a short film that appears to depict the murder of a teenage girl. As Welles's investigation proceeds, he's drawn deeper into the world of underground pornography, guided by Max California (Joaquin Phoenix), a sarcastic clerk at an adult book store. As it stretches on, the journey starts to chip away at his soul.

Schumacher initially conceived the film as a "handheld, gritty thriller" he could shoot on a relatively small budget—by the standards of Schumacher and Hollywood—starring Russell Crowe, an Australian actor whose work in *L.A. Confidential* had helped make him an in-demand, but still modestly priced, star. When Cage expressed interest, Schumacher offered Sony the choice: make the smaller-scale version with Crowe or the more expensive version with Cage. They opted for Cage, and why not? He was, in Schumacher's words, "hot as a pistol" at that time.

For Cage, *8mm* presented a chance to play a character who internalizes his mounting pain and disgust in a performance that simmers quietly until finally boiling over in the final act. (Schumacher later recalled the actor saying, "I want to do a role that's internalized. I don't want to do all my stuff. You know, my schtick.") It's one of the few subtle touches in a film that otherwise marinates in luridness. So, for that matter, was *Seven*, but Schumacher lacks Fincher's chilly command and gift for building suspense. The director's attempt to restructure the script prompted Walker's disgruntled departure, leaving Schumacher to rework it on his own. This included the addition of a hopeful ending, one Walker would later say "bleaches anything the script was meant to be about."

Though *8mm* had its admirers, it largely disgusted critics. After admitting that Schumacher and others must have had some reason to want to make such a film, the *Los Angeles Times*'s Kenneth Turan opined, "Even the most powerful microscope couldn't discover what's in this demeaning ordeal for anyone else." The film debuted at number one and then plummeted quickly. But, like *Showgirls* and other films dealing with behaviors moviegoers might feel timid watching in public, it found a lively second life on home video. "The DVD sales were through the roof," Schumacher noted years later. "I said to the studio, 'A lot of people can't go see it on a date night, they can't see it with their wives. But they're going to watch it. It'll be their secret little thing.'" Appearing in a "secret little thing" that men watched alone probably wasn't why Cage had signed on to the movie.

❑ ❑ ❑

These weren't the movies he was supposed to make, literally if not figuratively. In 1996, Cage met with Terrence Malick, the revered, mystery-shrouded director who had made two lyrical masterpieces, 1973's *Badlands* and 1978's *Days of Heaven*, and then stepped away from Hollywood with no apparent plans to return. This was set to change thanks to *The Thin Red Line*, an adaptation of James Jones's autobiographical novel that drew on the author's experience serving in the Pacific in World War II. Malick's return became a lure for talent. Cage and the director hit it off, but Cage had changed his number when Malick attempted to phone him months later. Taking offense, and apparently uninterested in making an additional phone call to track the actor down via his agent, Malick shut him out. When the film debuted in 1998, it featured an array of up-and-coming and established actors, including former Cage costars John Cusack, John Travolta, and Sean Penn, all of whom had shipped out to the Solomon Islands and remote stretches of Australia for the demanding shoot, leaving Cage behind.

Another missed opportunity looms even larger over this

period of Cage's career. In early 1997, word started to circulate that Cage had all but signed the contract to star in *Superman Reborn* (later retitled *Superman Lives*), a new take on the Man of Steel to be directed by Tim Burton. Burton had already enjoyed tremendous success with *Batman* in 1989 and with its 1992 sequel, *Batman Returns*, though the grim imagery and undisguised kinkiness of the latter would make the film divisive (and pave the way for Schumacher to take over the series with *Batman Forever*). Nonetheless, Warner Bros. brought Burton into the project, handing him a screenplay by Kevin Smith (a comic book fan and in-demand talent thanks to the indie breakthrough *Clerks*) based on a recent, much-publicized comic book story line centered on Superman's death (and subsequent rebirth, hence the title).

For Superman, the studio turned to the Burton-approved Nicolas Cage—to the concern of vocal fans, some of whom had balked at the casting of Michael Keaton as Batman just a few years earlier. One difference: this time they had the fast-emerging internet to amplify their concerns (and insults), most prominently via a site called "People Against Nicolas Cage/ Tim Burton for the Upcoming Superman Movie," whose content included everything from alternate casting suggestions to limericks. ("There was a young man named Cage / Whose hairline receded with age . . ." etc.) Superman became, for Cage, an unavoidable topic. On the set of *City of Angels*, costar Dennis Franz jokingly mocked Cage's anxiety about shooting a scene on the girders of an in-progress skyscraper, saying, "Come on *Superman!*" Of the ribbing, Cage said, "I have a good idea what my future holds."

The future had other plans. *Superman Lives* seemed ready

to go after Cage made his involvement official, signing a contract (for twenty million dollars) that guaranteed he'd be paid whether or not the film happened. Equipped with hair to match Superman's shaggy '90s comic book look, he even took part in a series of costume fittings, trying on various prototypes of the tights-and-cape ensemble he'd wear on-screen. This screen test would be as close as Cage came to playing Superman until making a vocal cameo years later in the animated feature *Teen Titans GO! To the Movies*. As progress slowed, hampered in part by difficulties in hammering out a revised script that worked within a reasonable budget, the proposed summer-of-1998 release date slipped away. Eventually, Burton left to pursue other work. Cage remained attached, but the lights eventually dimmed on *Superman Lives*.

Years later, on the set of *Superman Returns*, a self-conscious throwback to the Christopher Reeve–starring films of the 1970s and '80s, director Bryan Singer reportedly would use Cage's costume test photos to mock what might have been and to justify his own, more traditionalist instincts. It seems wrong to dismiss *Superman Lives* as an avoided folly, however. Jon Schnepp's 2015 documentary *The Death of "Superman Lives": What Happened?* includes some of the conversation around those costume fittings, talk that captures a director and star who sound deeply engaged with, even giddy about, a film that would treat Superman as the ultimate outsider, a misfit being with no innate connection to humanity in spite of his appearance, and a weirdo or, in Cage's words, a "beautiful freak."

Cage didn't join the project on a whim. "I have very specific ideas about Superman and reasons for wanting to be Superman," he told an interviewer in 1997. Calling it an example of "a character that other so-called important actors would probably say is beneath them," he explained that Superman "affects children around the world, and I want to say something to children around the world." Specifically, he saw his take on the character as striking a blow against teasing: "I would like to see that weird, different kid get a break because I was that kid." Memories of being bullied as a child, and of the alternate identity he constructed to stop that bullying, still didn't seem far away.

"I don't know if it'll work," he admitted later in the interview. And maybe it wouldn't have. It might have been a disaster. Or a triumph. Either way, it would have shifted the direction both of Cage's career and, undoubtedly, of superhero movies, which would soon become central to blockbuster filmmaking. At the time, Cage spoke of it as part of a fantasy trilogy to complement the "Sunshine" and action trilogies that preceded it, the centerpiece of a triptych that would include *City of Angels* and the Tim Burton–directed *The Defective Detective*, another ultimately unrealized project. Instead, he had to make other plans, discovering that reaching the upper echelons of stardom sometimes means surrendering, rather than seizing, control.

❑ ❑ ❑

If it wasn't always obvious at the time, it became increasingly clear in the years that followed that 1999 was a landmark year for movies. Moviegoers saw innovation at every level, from the beyond-low-budget found-footage horror film *The Blair Witch Project* to boundary-pushing studio projects like the Fincher-directed *Fight Club*, and from game-changing blockbusters like *The Matrix* to films that confirmed the emergence of bold new voices, like *Election*, *Being John Malkovich*, *Rushmore*, *Three Kings*, *Magnolia*, and *Boys Don't Cry*. To Cage, it might have felt as if the alternative movie revolution he wished for was happening without him. He'd turned down a role in *The Matrix*, and though *City of Angels*'s Brad Silberling had only one film to his credit when they made *City of Angels* (*Casper*, a live-action adaptation of *Casper the Friendly Ghost*), Cage had largely gravitated toward more experienced hands such as De Palma and Schumacher. For his final film of the 1990s, Cage would continue this trend by starring in *Bringing Out the Dead*, directed by Martin Scorsese and written by Paul Schrader.

Schrader and Scorsese had teamed up three times before, working together on *Taxi Driver*, *Raging Bull*, and *The Last Temptation of Christ*. An adaptation of Joe Connelly's auto-biographical novel of the same name, *Bringing Out the Dead* heavily echoes that first collaboration, focusing on a troubled man struggling to hold on to his soul as he cruises the streets of New York after dark. There's no mistaking Frank Pierce for *Taxi Driver*'s Travis Bickle, however. A sleepless paramedic who treats his job as a nightly chance to atone for his per-ceived mistakes, Pierce lives in a New York City filled not with dragons he needs to slay but with the ghosts of those he couldn't save. It's a draining existence, one that threatens to break him over the course of the three nights depicted in the film, during which he's paired with three starkly contrasting partners (played by John Goodman, Ving Rhames, and Tom Sizemore) and strikes up a tenuous relationship with Mary, the daughter of a heart attack victim barely clinging to life. As Mary, Scorsese cast Patricia Arquette. It would be the only film in which the couple appears together, and a not-entirely-expected pairing given that the two were leading largely separate lives by the end of the 1990s.

Cage delivers a tour-de-force performance of a sort he'd never offered before. Frank experiences a few familiar Cage moments of (usually chemically induced) manic energy, but weariness defines him. His eyes, limpid and searching in *City of Angels*, become clouded and then hooded, the eyes of a man who's seen too much too quickly yet who feels obligated not to look away from the horrors around him, be they drug casualties, self-destructive mental patients, abusive coworkers, or victims of bad luck. He serves as another contribution both to Schrader's gallery of God's Lonely Men and to Scorsese's collection of Christ figures. It seemed the sort of film destined to earn universal praise for all involved.

Yet while *Bringing Out the Dead* attracted some critical champions, more critics treated it as a worthwhile but flawed effort, and some regarded it as an outright disappointment. The familiar territory might not have helped. In *Salon*, Stephanie Zacharek wrote that it had "the feel of a hollow exercise: Nothing about it is particularly unexpected or surprising, despite the fact that it lunges at you every chance it gets." In the *Village Voice*, J. Hoberman similarly complained of "déjà vu." In some ways the movie itself invites frustration by depicting frustration. Mimicking Frank's mind-set (and his occupation), *Bringing Out the Dead* doesn't so much move forward as run in circles. There's no breakthrough here, just Frank's dawning revelation that he'll be able to climb out of hell only slowly, and with the help of others.

It now seems odd that a film so ambitious and filled with

remarkable moments could be taken for granted, but such was the spirit of '99. Scorsese had to compete for attention with a clutch of fresh names, and *Bringing Out the Dead* arrived in theaters already filled with awards season releases. The film opened wide on October 22, landing at a disappointing fourth place and then dropping precipitously in the weeks that followed. Any hope that Cage would earn a second Oscar nomination dropped with it. The Best Actor prize would eventually go to Kevin Spacey, whose *American Beauty* performance beat out the performances of Russell Crowe, Richard Farnsworth, Denzel Washington, and Sean Penn.

Penn had a habit of finding his way into Cage's story, whether Cage wanted him to or not. Profiled by Lynn Hirschberg for the *New York Times Magazine* in 1998, Penn expressed weariness with acting itself, and then volunteered, "Nic Cage is no longer an actor. He could be again, but now he's more like a . . . performer." Such a high-profile diss stung coming from Penn, who'd just visited Cage and Arquette on the set of *Bringing Out the Dead*. Cage and Penn's relationship had had its ups and downs, but Cage regarded Penn as a friend. It also meant he'd be asked about it for the foreseeable future. "The door to our friendship is now closed," Cage said while doing press for *8mm*. Profiled for a *Rolling Stone* cover story to coincide with the release of *Bringing Out the Dead*, he attempted to strike a more gracious note before defending his action films, saying a sellout "is only a sellout if you're being paid to do something you don't want to do. I want to make these movies. I like working with Bruckheimer. I like the work we've done together."

It wasn't the only topic he found himself obligated to talk about that he'd likely prefer to keep private. He now spoke openly of his mother's struggles, of his tumultuous relationship with his father, and, more obliquely, of his relationship with Arquette. *Bringing Out the Dead* brought them together professionally, but in February 2000, Cage would file for divorce. An attempt at reconciliation failed, and Arquette filed her own divorce papers in the fall.

There was no keeping it out of the press. It seemed at times that there was no keeping anything out of the press. After initially eschewing interviews, Cage started presenting himself as a charming eccentric, karate-kicking his way onto talk show sets and telling stories of fried grasshopper sandwiches and the Herculean labors he'd performed with Arquette. Now the public wanted more, be it about Cage's love life, his houses, or his collection of expensive cars.

An object of fascination for some, he became a target for others. Nick Nolte echoed Penn, saying, "Nic's gone.... [He] was this marvelous actor.... Then, bam!" Stephen Baldwin called him "ugly." Though few would ordinarily pay attention to anything Stephen Baldwin said, talking about Cage attracted attention. Still, the sense that Cage wasn't living up to his full potential spread elsewhere. *Orlando Sentinel* columnist Dean Johnson (writing under the name "Commander Coconut") put it bluntly: "What on earth is the matter with Nicolas Cage? He needs to back that career up. Of course, it's his life but because we pay good money for movie-ticket prices we get a bit of input." (Twisting the knife, Johnson also suggested Penn should have won the Oscar in 1996 instead of Cage.) Cage's imperial phase, the moment in which he could seemingly do no wrong, had passed.

❑ ❑ ❑

Johnson's column was inspired by the trailer for *Gone in 60 Seconds*, a reunion with producer Jerry Bruckheimer that returned Cage to the world of big-budget summer action films. Cage plays "Memphis" Raines, a gone-straight car thief who reluctantly returns to a life of crime to save his brother, Kip (Giovanni Ribisi), from a pitiless gangster (Christopher Eccleston). His task: steal fifty rare cars within seventy-two hours. Directed by Dominic Sena, a Propaganda Films founder who made his feature debut a few years earlier with the Brad Pitt–starring thriller *Kalifornia*, *Gone in 60 Seconds* loosely remakes a low-budget 1974 film of the same name that had become legendary for its outrageous, special effects–free car-chase sequences. With such a simple but compelling premise and a cast that included Angelina Jolie and Robert Duvall (both fellow Oscar winners), it seemed like a sure thing.

In a sense, it was. In the summer of 2000, audiences showed up, and the movie performed roughly on par with *Con Air*, Cage's preceding team-up with Bruckheimer. In doing so, audiences ignored the almost universally negative reviews at their own peril. (*The Dallas Observer*: "[B]arely a movie at all; more like a thousand car commercials spliced together in an hour.") Though not without some winning touches, including Duvall's performance as a genial gearhead and a scene of the thieves passing the time by identifying the makes and models of TV characters' cars, *Gone in 60 Seconds* has little to offer but noise and confusion. Cage drew on Steve McQueen for his low-key performance and trained with professional drivers in order to perform his own stunts, but his choices do little to liven up a character who's dead on the page, and the choppy editing ensured that little evidence of his newfound skills made it into the film.

It's the sort of movie that leaves even the least-demanding summer audiences feeling a bit ripped off. The films that followed did little to reverse the impression that Cage had strayed from what had seemed a carefully considered path. Gone was talk of trilogies. First, in their stead, came a holiday fantasy. Released just before Christmas in 2000, *The Family Man* casts Cage as Jack Campbell, a kind of benevolent Gordon Gekko who's seemingly perfectly happy, with a life of material success and romantic conquests. But performing a good deed for a supernatural messenger in disguise (Don Cheadle) sends him into an alternate reality in which he stays with his college sweetheart, Kate (Téa Leoni), in a middle-class existence filled with struggle but also with warmth and connection of the sort he's never known before.

Whatever the particular supernatural setup, *The Family Man* takes part in a tradition of Hollywood comedies in which errant men learn to focus on what really matters, a tradition that thrived in the 1990s via films such as *Mrs. Doubtfire*, *Groundhog Day*, *Hook*, and *Liar, Liar*. Maybe that's why its formula feels so, well, formulaic, despite some nice chemistry between Cage and Leoni. Or perhaps it's just that that film oozes insincerity, condescendingly depicting the middle-class New Jersey life that Jack slips into as vulgar while lionizing it as a somehow truer existence. *The Family Man* also arrived amid items about the lavish playboy lifestyle of Brett Ratner, its up-and-coming director, who'd recently enjoyed a huge hit with *Rush Hour*. Ratner had had to woo Cage back to the film after its original director, Curtis Hanson, departed. His approach included having Jack drive a Ferrari (a Cage favorite) and outfitting him in suits from Cage's favorite Italian designer. Movies are in the business of creating illusions, but sometimes those illusions feel a bit thin. The film performed decently, earning a few pat-on-the-head reviews (and more dismissals). But, oddly for a Christmas film, it's had little staying power, never picking up the long afterlife most holiday movies enjoy via December reruns (though the audio from a scene in which Jack searches for a piece of chocolate cake has enjoyed a second life on YouTube via an animated dance remix).

Cage's next film would make even less of an impact. For his follow-up to the Best Picture–winning *Shakespeare in Love*, director John Madden went big, taking on the adaptation of Louis de Bernières 1994 best seller, *Captain Corelli's Mandolin*, after its original director, Roger Mitchell, pulled out because of health problems. The story of a reluctant Italian soldier who falls in love with a doctor's daughter while occupying a Greek island in the waning days of World War II, it became a handsome, expensive production, sporting an international cast that included Penelope Cruz, John Hurt, Christian Bale, and David Morrissey—actors from Spain, Britain, and the United States speaking English dialogue in a hodgepodge of accents. This included Cage, who took on the role in part because of the challenge—and against the advice of his representatives. "They said to me: 'Look! You're an American star. People are comfortable with the way you talk and the way you look and now you're going to jolt them with something like this?'" Cage told the *Ottawa Citizen*'s Jamie Portman at the time, continuing, "And I said: 'I'm an actor first and as an actor I need to challenge myself and grow.'"

The instinct, however admirable, doesn't really pay off. Cage's natural speaking voice—the familiar precise, California-inflected pronunciation delivered in unexpected rhythms—slips through only once in a while, and he's convincingly upbeat as a soldier with no interest in fighting or in nationalist causes. But the film is at once shapeless and off-puttingly tasteful, the sort of bland, stately period drama favored by Miramax during the era, one released the year after the similar-in-spirit, but livelier-in-execution *Chocolat* earned the studio five Oscar nominations. Though a hit in Britain, *Captain Corelli's Mandolin* vanished quickly from North American theaters, and cultural memory, shortly after its August 2001 release.

"Should we worry about Nicolas Cage?" *Time*'s Richard Corliss asked in the opening of his *Captain Corelli's Mandolin* review, before further wondering, "a viewer has to wonder if Cage is tethered forever to the peculiar job description of Movie Star." And there was the double edge of stardom, and Bay's analysis of the difference between great actors and movie stars: not all movie star roles required, fostered, or even allowed for great acting. Cage had reached a point where challenges came not in the form of daring independent films, but in his veering slightly outside his usual range in the service of the blandly executed, risk-averse projects that could afford him. He'd apparently succeeded his way into a dead end. If there was a way out, it would be up to him to find it.

10

The Two Cages

On Tuesday, April 1, 2003, ABC aired a program originally scheduled for the previous Sunday. For years, a special installment of *The Barbara Walters Special* preceded the Oscars broadcast, featuring interviews with some of the nominees the veteran broadcaster considered most compelling. But the U.S. invasion of Iraq disrupted that tradition in 2003, prompting Walters to move the special to a later date, even though the Academy Awards proceeded as planned. When the special eventually aired, Walters tacked on an introduction, explaining that even though the "three huge and delightful stars" she talked to "didn't capture the Oscars, they did capture my heart—and I have a feeling they'll capture yours as well."

Walters's lineup included Julianne Moore, nominated as Best Actress for *Far from Heaven*; Renée Zellweger, up for the same prize for *Chicago*—both lost to Nicole Kidman's performance as Virginia Woolf in *The Hours*—and Nicolas Cage, who'd been nominated as Best Actor for the second time, thanks to his performance, or performances, in *Adaptation*. But Walters didn't want to talk about that. Walters wanted to talk about Elvis. Her intro described Cage as an "intense, kinetic, scenery-chewing inferno of talent—the least-predictable star of his generation," and her special's whirlwind recap of his career paused at the 1990 mark to describe his work in "the dark, sexually explicit thriller" *Wild at Heart* as "something that has dogged him ever since" thanks to his "peculiar acting choice of playing a variation on Elvis Presley."

The idea of Cage's *Wild at Heart* role haunting him was largely nonsense, and any evidence of an unhealthy obsession with Elvis mostly the stuff of tabloids, but Walters had other reasons to dwell on Presley. Cage's work in *Adaptation.* had earned great acclaim when it arrived the preceding winter, but his short-lived marriage to Presley's daughter, Lisa Marie, garnered even more attention in different corners of the press. The couple had met at Johnny Ramone's birthday party in 2001, broke up in early 2002, reunited later in the year, and married in August. Then, on November 25, two days after *Adaptation.*'s premiere—an event Cage and Presley attended together—Cage filed for divorce. In the time between, the couple had become the subject of wild stories, stories Cage was eager to put to rest.

"Again and again we read that you are obsessed with Elvis Presley," Walters says. Cage attempts to explain the *Wild at Heart* performance, as he had in the past, as an attempt to thumb his nose at the Stanislavski notion that a performance must never be an imitation. "I wanted to break that rule to see if you can do it," he replied. "So then I said, 'Who can I do this with?' And I thought, 'Elvis.' So I thought, 'Where can I try this new experiment?' And it was David Lynch directing *Wild at Heart*. And I went for it. He thought it was a great idea, and we tried this experiment to create a surrealistic interpretation of Elvis in the movie." That Cage later met and fell for Lisa Marie Presley was, by his explanation, just a coincidence, albeit one that had brought him into the orbit of gossip and outrageous stories that had surrounded Lisa Marie since birth. The rumor that he wanted to father Elvis's grandchild? Ridiculous. So were the other rumors. "There's no answering machine with my voice on it as Elvis. We weren't going to buy Graceland. We were never going to live in Graceland. I wasn't going to build Graceland for her on top of a ranch somewhere."

Lost in the conversation about Lisa Marie—which included Walters's seeming attempt to reunite the couple, who had yet to finalize their divorce—was any talk of *Adaptation.* or the rest of Cage's work. The setting might not have helped. Walters recorded the interview at Cage's LA mansion, which had previously been owned by Dean Martin and Tom Jones. It was one of four homes Cage owned at the time, and in the quick glimpses offered in the interview, it looks imposing, filled from floor to ceiling with art and collectibles, including a full-size replica of Robby the Robot from *Forbidden Planet*. After an intro making mention of his "love of exotic cars and motorcycles," the two chat, first by Cage's poolside pizza kitchen and then inside his home. He appears indulgent and gracious, despite clearly wanting to talk about anything else but his private life.

Yet giving up some privacy was part of the bargain, as Cage knew by now. If he had to talk about himself, he may as well talk about himself with Walters, an interviewer famed for her ability to put subjects at an often tear-inducing ease without probing too far beyond the surface of what had already become public knowledge. Cage's marriage to Lisa Marie had helped confirm his image as a colorful eccentric, even if he hadn't consciously played the role of a colorful eccentric for years. That didn't necessarily mean he didn't behave like a colorful eccentric. Nor did it necessarily mean that his interest in Elvis went no deeper than choosing him as a model for one role. (If nothing else, he'd channeled Elvis with eerie specificity, appearing as a pocket-size King in the "Tiny Elvis" sketch while hosting *Saturday Night Live* in 1992.) But the depths of any eccentricity, Elvis-related or otherwise, remained Cage's to keep to himself.

Being a public person means learning to compromise, however, to surrender protection of parts of yourself as a way to secure even more. Cage had become an in-demand movie star, but he'd also become a story, and it wasn't always easy being both at once. If talking to Walters offered the chance to balance the demand for access to his personal life while promoting his professional work, that might not be so bad. For now, he could draw a line at the spot of his choosing and keep behind it what he wanted to keep private. He understood how that sort of split worked.

❏ ❏ ❏

Cage had become unusually adept at playing men with divided identities and characters torn between different ways of life. The roles an actor takes on are rarely purely a matter of choice, and it's a mistake to confuse a filmography with an autobiography, but that doesn't make recurring patterns easy to ignore. He'd played a man divided in two in *Face/Off* and would have played another split personality in *Superman Lives*. He'd even considered splitting himself in two, at least in name. In 2000, Cage told the *Los Angeles Times*'s Amy Kaufman he wanted to adopt the name "Miles Lovecraft"—inspired by jazz trumpeter Miles Davis and horror writer H. P. Lovecraft—for edgier projects. "Whenever you saw Miles Lovecraft in a movie," he said, "you'd know it was going to be a dark subject matter, an independent film. It would be my own little internal protection device so people aren't going to *8mm* expecting to see *The Rock.* . . . Miles would work for scale . . . He'd have to build his way up the ladder. Nic Cage has been doing it for 20 years. Miles Lovecraft hasn't done anything. You've got to put in your dues." (Ultimately, Cage's representatives talked him out of the idea.) Sometimes the split was less literal, as in *City of Angels* and *The Family Man*, where he took on characters torn between comfort and safety and an authentic existence closer to their true selves.

Adaptation., among its other qualities, offered Cage a chance to explore those questions further, via a clever, deeply layered script by *Being John Malkovich* screenwriter Charlie Kaufman directed by *Malkovich* director Spike Jonze. Then married to Cage's cousin Sofia Coppola, Jonze had helped spearhead the wave of funny, self-reflexive, visually inventive videos that largely supplanted the glossy Propaganda style as the '90s progressed (though Propaganda produced Jonze's feature films).

The assignment didn't seem like an intuitive follow-up to its immediate predecessor, released over a year after the European debut of *Captain Corelli's Mandolin*. An occasionally shapeless but ultimately rewarding reunion with *Face/Off* director John

Woo, *Windtalkers* offers little of the action movie pleasures of their previous pairing. Instead, it tells the true story of the Navajo code talkers, a group of Native Americans whose language served as the basis for an unbreakable code during World War II. Cage plays Joe Enders, a war-weary sergeant charged with protecting Navajo private Ben Yahzee (Adam Beach) while fighting in the Pacific—or, failing that, killing him before letting him fall into enemy hands. Using graphic violence and situations demanding impossible choices to depict the horrors of war, the film bears a closer resemblance to Woo's brutal 1990 Vietnam War movie *Bullet in the Head* than to the action films that made him attractive to Hollywood.

Released in June 2002 opposite *Scooby Doo* and *The Bourne Identity*—the latter a less thorny sort of action film—the film attracted meager crowds, and most critics found little to celebrate, despite a past appreciation for Cage's and Woo's work. Even those who liked the film offered some warning signs about the direction of the star's career. Though writing that Cage was "perfectly cast" and "completely believable as a reluctant war hero who's more no-nonsense than jaded," *Salon*'s Stephanie Zacharek noted that "Cage has become so adept at playing the tortured, conflicted soul that many of us have become tired of seeing him do it." Maybe it was time for a change.

Adaptation. presented such an opportunity. More accurately, it presented two such opportunities. The doubling of Charlie Kaufman's script begins with the title, which refers to its screenwriter protagonist's attempt to turn Susan Orlean's wonderful but probably unfilmable nonfiction book *The Orchid Thief* into a screenplay. But it also refers to the process of botanical evolution described in the book, a process that mirrors the protagonist's need to change and grow beyond his crippling self-doubt and to move past his creative blocks. The protagonist's name: Charlie Kaufman. Beneath curly hair and sporting a sub-action star physique enhanced by a perpetual slouch, Cage plays Charlie as a nervous, self-lacerating creator with a hatred of artistic shortcuts and an allergy to the sort of formulaic screenplays created by script gurus like Robert McKee (a real-life story consultant played with forbidding authority by Brian Cox). Cage also plays Charlie's brother, Donald, a pleasant layabout with none of his brother's creative constrictions (or artistic standards), who steps on a fast track to Hollywood success when he uses McKee's formula to write a high-concept thriller called *The 3* (in which multiple personalities play a key role).

If Cage didn't seem like intuitive casting as the Kaufmans, he certainly understood how Hollywood could pull a creative person in two directions at once. The film industry drew talent into its orbit and then demanded that they direct their artistic impulses into increasingly narrow channels. He'd seen it, watching his uncle and others of his generation struggle to hold on to the freedom of the 1970s, and he'd lived it, trying to turn gargantuan action films into creatively fulfilling projects while exploring more adventurous work elsewhere. He'd wanted to split himself in two, but in the end there was no Miles Lovecraft, just as there was no Donald Kaufman. He had to reconcile what he wanted to do with what was expected of him and live with any contradictions, tension, or turmoil that this might create.

Cage took a pay cut to appear in the movie, as did Meryl Streep, who plays Orlean, first as witty woman of letters and then—as the film enters the third act and Charlie has spent a chunk of it struggling to write and has consequently filled it with Hollywood clichés inspired in part by his own encounter with McKee—as a depraved drug fiend in thrall to the unscrupulous orchid collector John Laroche (Chris Cooper). Like Cage, Cooper and Streep picked up well-deserved Oscar nominations for their work, with Cooper taking home the Best Supporting Actor prize. (The film also garnered a Best Original Screenplay nomination, for a script credited to "Charlie and Donald Kaufman.")

Though Cage had to watch as Adrien Brody accepted the Best Actor trophy (after commemorating the moment by giving an uninvited kiss to presenter Halle Berry), the film still served as a reminder of Cage's deft comic skills, in spite of his growing reputation as a specialist in playing serious, sorrowful men. He makes Charlie and Donald distinct, instantly recognizable characters and teases out the comedy in Charlie's neuroses without turning him into a punch line or losing a sense of poignancy, even when *Adaptation.* segues into manipulative, irony-encased late-film drama. Charlie's problems may be largely of his own creation, but that doesn't make the possibility that he could teeter into despair any less real.

It's not the sort of role that came around that often, and such roles now seemed to be coming around even less frequently than before. Nineteen ninety-nine had seen a flourishing of talent but not a fundamental reshaping of how Hollywood worked. Where *Easy Rider*'s unexpected success in 1969 carved room in the mainstream for distinctive directorial talents and offbeat visions, the Class of '99 still largely worked in the margins or for pseudo-indie mini-majors like Paramount Vantage, Warner Independent Pictures, Fox Search-light, USA Films, Miramax, and Sony Pictures Classics, many of which wouldn't survive the decade. Directors such as Jonze, Christopher Nolan, Paul Thomas Anderson, David Fincher, Wes Anderson, Sofia Coppola, and others wouldn't reinvent the business so much as claim their spot within it and hold on to that spot as best they could. Speaking to Brian Raftery for his book about the year, *Best. Movie. Year. Ever.*, producer Brad Simpson summed it up starkly: "I thought it was the beginning, but it was actually the end."

❑ ❑ ❑

To guard against Hollywood unpredictability, some stars formed their own production companies. By the end of the '90s, such so-called vanity shingles were practically de rigueur for actors who had reached Cage's level. Formed in 1997, the Cage-founded Saturn Films could have gone the way of Chris O'Donnell's George Street Pictures or Antonio Banderas and Melanie Griffith's Green Moon Productions, short-lived enti-ties that left behind little but flops, when they left anything at all. Cage had loftier ambitions for Saturn Films. Late 2000 saw the debut of *Shadow of the Vampire*, a clever horror film with an irresistible premise: What if Max Schreck, the actor who starred as Count Orlock in F. W. Murnau's silent clas-sic *Nosferatu*, were an actual vampire? Willem Dafoe played Schreck (picking up a Best Supporting Actor nomination for his work) opposite John Malkovich's Murnau. Though only a modest hit, it earned strong reviews and looked like a good first step for the company.

Saturn Films escalated its operations in 2001 with the

promotion of Norm Golightly to president in early 2001, a move that coincided with a mission statement from Cage, who told *Variety* he envisioned Saturn Films as "a safe haven for actors. . . . It's an actor-driven company, where performers can find material that's a little bit unusual, that studios might be wary of. It's a laboratory for actors, really." This included Cage, per Golightly, who added, "Having a company [allows] Nic to shepherd projects along instead of being reactive to what others in the marketplace are creating."

The pair also unveiled an impressive-sounding slate of upcoming films that included *The Life of David Gale*, a capital punishment thriller directed by Cage's *Birdy* director Alan Parker that eventually debuted to critical hostility and commercial indifference in early 2003. It arrived not long after another largely unnoticed Saturn Films production, *Sonny*, to date, Cage's only film as a director. Cage originally wanted to star in the story of a New Orleans gigolo trying to go straight after returning from a stint in the army when he encountered the script in the 1980s. Having aged out of the part, he cast emerging actor James Franco in the lead, surrounding him with a cast that included Brenda Blethyn, Mena Suvari, Harry Dean Stanton, and Seymour Cassel. (To help the film's commercial prospects, Cage reluctantly took the small role of "Acid Yellow," a gay pimp. For his costume, he chose an item from his personal collection: a jacket he'd acquired at Liberace's estate sale.) Apart from a screeching Blethyn performance, *Sonny* benefits from the generous room Cage gives his cast to develop their characters, but it suffers from a slack pace and a bland visual style. It played only a handful of theaters simultaneous to *Adaptation.*'s release.

Despite some initial disappointments, Cage would remain committed to Saturn Films, whose name and logo would appear on most of his films for the rest of the 2000s (and, less frequently, into the 2010s and 2020s). But the ability to shepherd projects would prove an imperfect bulwark against changes in the industry. In 2002, five of the six highest-grossing films were sequels. The sixth, *Spider-Man*, bore the name of a recognizable character and would launch sequels of its own. *Spider-Man's* success helped prove that *X-Men*, released two years before it, had not been a fluke and that superhero movies would continue to be a major part of the film landscape, which would increasingly be dominated by instantly recognizable properties. In 2003, the number of sequels and adaptations in the top ten would grow to seven, its ranks swelled by the debut of the Johnny Depp–starring *Pirates of the Caribbean* series, produced by Jerry Bruckheimer.

Within the span of Cage's career, blockbusters built around tent-pole films, designed to inspire sequels, merchandise, and theme park rides (when they weren't adapted *from* theme park rides), had gone from being one aspect of the industry to its driving force. For an actor, a successful franchise could offer safety, serving as an image-boosting sure thing and a hedge against risks taken elsewhere. *Superman Lives* could have been that, had *Superman Lives* not died. Cage had passed on both *The Matrix* and Peter Jackson's *Lord of the Rings* trilogy, for which he'd been offered the part of Aragorn. Instead, he'd have to look elsewhere for his franchise, a search that would meet with remarkable, if not long-lasting, success, via a history nerd man-of-action hero who could have been created just for him.

❑ ❑ ❑

But first, he'd watch as one of his best performances went largely unnoticed. After the rush of 2002, the following year saw the release of only one Cage movie, a difficult-to-categorize departure that featured a difficult, nuanced performance to rival his work in *Adaptation*. With *Gladiator*, *Hannibal*, and *Black Hawk Down*, director Ridley Scott had directed three massive films back to back (to back). Never one to slow down, Scott didn't want to stop working, but he opted for a smaller story as his next project—well, small by Scott's standards. The most successful of the school of directors to emerge from the British advertising world of the 1960s, Scott had developed into a peerless stylist with an extraordinary range, a director capable of mammoth, immersive but actor-friendly films like *Alien*, *Blade Runner*, and *Gladiator*. He could also zoom in on characters, as with the landmark *Thelma & Louise*, an intimate, complicated drama of two women, albeit one that plays out over the course of a cross-country crime spree. With Scott, small was relative, and human drama always unfolded within the confines of a technically accomplished piece of craftsmanship.

In his weaker efforts, the drama could get lost in the craftsmanship, but with *Matchstick Men*, Scott remained committed to keeping a tight focus on a pair of LA criminals and an interloper who seems to throw their well-oiled partnership out of balance. Cage plays Roy Waller, an experienced con man (or "con artist," as he prefers) who's found success in the field of his choice despite the obsessive-compulsive disorder he barely suppresses, most of the time, with medication. In some ways, his condition serves him well, aiding him in concocting schemes as meticulously ordered as his spotless house. His gregarious partner, Frank (Sam Rockwell), serves as a balance for his tendencies, setting up scores that Roy can then knock down. But when Angela (Alison Lohman), Roy's daughter from a long-ago love, shows up on his doorstep, Roy starts to rethink his priorities, and of ways to change his life after making one last score.

Roy's the sort of character who could easily be little more than a collection of tics and mannerisms. Instead, Cage makes the tics and mannerisms a barometer for Roy's emotional state. He's a man whose fragile psyche makes ordinary tasks into acts of Herculean will. But rather than his condition being the whole of the character, it provides the framework for the story of a man struggling to find stability and meaning after a life spent hiding behind false fronts. It's one of Cage's most delicate performances, apart from shocking bursts of rage and frustration, as when Roy, after impatiently cutting in line to fill a prescription, asks a fellow customer if he's ever "been dragged to the sidewalk and beaten until you *piss blood*?" Cage makes the last two words hit with the weight of a sledgehammer, but the loudness works only because of the quietness around it.

Matchstick Men earned mixed reviews but high praise from those who loved it, including Roger Ebert, who awarded the film four stars, writing, "Cage is accused of showboating, but I prefer to think he swings for the fences. . . . He has a kind of raging zeal that possesses his characters; what in another actor would be overacting is, with Cage, a kind of fearsome intensity. There's an Oscar nomination here for him." Ticket buyers didn't share this enthusiasm, however. The film debuted in second place when it opened in mid-September, well behind the chart-topping *Once Upon a Time in Mexico*. It fell steadily in the weeks that followed and was little remembered during awards season.

It might have been too tough a sell. Where *Once Upon a Time in Mexico* could announce itself as an action movie via posters and a trailer filled with guns and the familiar faces of Antonio Banderas, Salma Hayek, and Johnny Depp, *Matchstick Men* proved tougher to categorize. It's a mystery of sorts, but also a family drama, kind of, with a comedic element where the laughs come with a certain amount of discomfort. Of the three leads, only Cage had the fame to open a movie, but the posters featured him holding a briefcase, not a gun, establishing ahead of time that this wouldn't be a Nicolas Cage action movie. With more films coming out at any given moment than ever before, it could be tough to sound a clear signal through all the noise, particularly when sending that signal on a different frequency than audiences were used to hearing.

Marketing had always been a part of the moviemaking game, but it could now feel like the game itself. Studios thought in terms of the four quadrants: men under twenty-five, women under twenty-five, older men, and older women, and as Tad Friend noted in a 2009 *New Yorker* piece, a "studio rarely makes a film that it doesn't expect will succeed with at least two quadrants, and a film's budget is usually directly related to the number of quadrants it is anticipated to reach." Within each quadrant were perceived preferences for each audience: romance for older women, fashion and sensitive boys for younger women, and so on. The fewer easily recognizable, easily marketable elements a film possessed, the less a studio knew what to do with it. To whom do you push a film about an OCD con artist; a film with parental themes, left-field plot turns, and a tone that teeters between comedy and drama?

An adventure film based on American history, however, proved an easier sell, particularly one put together by Jerry Bruckheimer. Since Cage last worked with Bruckheimer, the producer had entered into a profitable partnership with Disney to make family-friendly films. This began with the inspirational sports drama *Remember the Titans*, released the same year as the R-rated Cage vehicle *Gone in 60 Seconds*, and then continued with *Pirates of the Caribbean: The Curse of the Black Pearl*, a mammoth (and four-quadrant success) directed by Gore Verbinski, who, like Cage, seemed interested in toggling between his commercial and artistic instincts. Reteaming with Bruckheimer meant switching into commercial mode, but it didn't necessarily mean losing all actorly ambition.

A long-gestating idea given shape by the husband-and-wife screenwriting team of Cormac and Marianne Wibberley, *National Treasure* uses American history as the backdrop for a treasure hunt story inspired in seemingly equal parts by the Indiana Jones movies and the cryptography-filled worlds of Dan Brown thrillers then dominating the best seller lists. Cage plays Benjamin Franklin Gates, a historian and treasure hunter with a family history that's deeply entwined with America's past. While on the trail of a massive stash of treasure brought to the States by the Knights Templar that he needs to prevent from falling into the wrong hands, Gates realizes he has no choice but to steal the item containing the next clue: the Declaration of Independence.

Like *Pirates of the Caribbean*, *National Treasure* worked

as a movie that kids and parents alike could enjoy, a kind of my-first-action-movie directed with sure-handed efficiency by Jon Turteltaub, an upper-echelon journeyman who'd been Cage's classmate at Beverly Hills High. (He'd even beaten out Cage when both were up for a part in the school's production of *Our Town*.) With Gates, Cage shaped a more wholesome variation on the nerd-as-action-hero he'd played in *The Rock*, a man driven by dutiful patriotism (even if that patriotism sometimes requires him to break the law). Though the plot takes silly turns, Cage's performance never suggests he feels above the material as Gates earnestly uses clues to make some of the wildest leaps in logic since Adam West played Batman.

It was a hit few saw coming, though they probably should have. *National Treasure* debuted at the top of the box-office charts on November 19, 2004, arriving in theaters already filled with kid-friendly fare like *The Incredibles*, *The Polar Express*, and a big-screen version of *SpongeBob SquarePants*. But rather than working against one another, the films seemed to bolster their competitors' performance, feeding the Thanksgiving season's seemingly bottomless appetite for films that could double as family outings. It held on to the top spot for three weeks and stayed strong deep into the Christmas season, fueled by good word of mouth that worked against decidedly mixed reviews that cited the movie's old-fashioned hokeyness as a detriment instead of a selling point.

❑ ❑ ❑

It was the sort of hit that could buy a star some creative freedom, up to a point. On the heels of *National Treasure*'s success, Cage lined up a pair of films even more difficult to sell than *Matchstick Men*. Such square-peg movies would become a recurring issue for Cage, who seemed aware of the problem when he talked to Ebert in the fall of 2005 about two new releases then playing simultaneously. "It's very risky for an actor who's a bankable star to make pictures like *The Weather Man* or *Lord of War*, because they inevitably promote them like big studio releases," Cage said. "And they're not big studio movies; they're more edgy, thought-provoking, independent-spirited films. What happens is, it goes into the computer and everyone says they can't open the movie because they thought it was X when it actually was Y. I want to make all kinds of movies. I do want to make big movies that are a lot of fun to go to, but I also want to make movies that are going to stimulate some thought and maybe raise some awareness."

Of the pair, *Lord of War* was the film designed to raise awareness. Writer and director Andrew Niccol had developed a specialty in high-concept dramas with science-fiction twists via his script for *The Truman Show* and his previous films as a writer and director, *Gattaca* and *S1m0ne*. But with *Lord of War*, Niccol turned his focus to a dangerous pocket of the real world. As arms dealer Yuri Orlov, Cage provides a steady anchor for a stylish, fact-filled film that often works better as an exposé than a drama.

If anything, *The Weather Man* proved tougher to classify. Written by Steve Conrad, whose script became the object of a bidding war, and directed by Gore Verbinski, the film casts Cage as Dave Spritz, a Chicago weatherman whose tremendous performance at a job that's, by his own description, not particularly hard hasn't made him feel any less of a loser. He's separated from his wife (Hope Davis) and senses disappointment radiating from his novelist father, Robert (Michael Caine). His children are growing up troubled and alienated, and though the public has elevated him profession-ally, his encounters with his viewers have taken a disturbing turn. Some even pelt him with milkshakes for no reason than a vague hatred of what he represents to them or who they believe him to be.

Ultimately a film about accepting defeat and personal limitations, driven by an introspective performance by Cage playing a character who doesn't always invite much sympathy, it would prove an even tougher sell than *Lord of War*, for both critics and audiences. *The Weather Man* picked up mixed reviews and failed to break into the top five during its first weekend of release. But, for Cage, it provided yet another chance to explore a character trying to sort out what's mean-ingful and what's superficial to place beside the protagonists of *The Family Man*, *City of Angels*, and *Adaptation*. Its plot also maps neatly onto the experience of being a star who could be built up and torn down by a fickle public.

Novelist Zadie Smith went even farther, writing a review for the *Daily Telegraph*, "The film's central concept is the aversion most people have to the actor Nicholas [*sic*] Cage, and he accepts this mantle so honourably and humbly that I think maybe now I quite like him. It's a deeply honest and comic performance and seems filled with all the genuine humiliations that one imagines Cage himself has suffered in the past 10 years."

While "suffering" might seem too strong a word, Cage must have felt at least a twinge of disappointment. He'd tried to play by the rules of stardom, smiling through interviews and taking on challenging parts, only to watch weariness creep into critics' assessments of his work and see ambitious films flop. No one was throwing milkshakes at him, but the protection of winning an Oscar and starring in action hits had started to wear off. He didn't mind giving audiences what they wanted, up to a point. With *National Treasure*, Cage had proven he could do hokey. In fact, he seemed to enjoy playing the wide-eyed, kid-friendly hero, particularly if he could balance out such parts with more complicated characters. And for much of the early 2000s, he tried to strike a balance between his more daring artistic instincts and commercial demands. The only problem: the dares weren't paying off. As satisfying as *Matchstick Men*, *Lord of War*, and *The Weather Man* might have been, they also looked like red marks on the ledger, not red enough to erase a hit like *National Treasure*, but suggesting that maybe Cage's name alone wasn't enough to open a film, that maybe it was necessary to give the market what it demanded a little more often. As the decade crept on, this would prove more difficult than ever.

The Unmaking of Cage

The 2000s wouldn't end well for Nicolas Cage. In fact, they would end disastrously, ensnaring Cage in a thicket of embarrassing public financial and legal problems that would come to light in 2009, problems tied to ruinous spending habits that had previously seemed like the whimsical indulgences of a superstar. The near-bankruptcy that the early '90s Cage had previously alluded to would look like a prelude once the bill came due on the cars, castles, and private islands he'd only thought he could afford. But these weren't the only troubles he would face in the back half of the 2000s. Box-office disappointments, including one outright disaster, outnumbered hits. Other actors found safe harbor in long-running franchises, and though *National Treasure* would spawn an even more successful sequel, it didn't offer the long-term job security its popularity might have suggested. Cage's second attempt to enter the world of comic book movies would be a measured success, one that arrived between the moment when superhero fatigue appeared to be setting in and the moment superhero movies became bigger than ever. Meanwhile, the public seemed to have grown weary of Cage himself. Even positive reviews started to sound more like defenses than celebrations. On the internet, the vague, free-floating distaste Zadie Smith sensed when writing about *The Weather Man* would mutate into not-always comforting, irony-tinged appreciations.

Cage was always in the public eye, even if there wasn't a Nicolas Cage movie in theaters—though he worked at such a pace that there often was. Yet he seemed more divided than ever. Rather than a dual identity, it could feel like there were multiple Nicolas Cages: the actor committed to seeking serious work; the name-above-the-title star of big-budget films; the oddball who turned up in tabloid stories and served as fodder for an entertainment press increasingly driven by click-generating, attention-grabbing headlines; the icon whose image could be repurposed as internet memes and clips selectively edited for comedic value; and, as the decade drew to a close, a cautionary tale whose time in the spotlight seemed on the verge of ending.

❑ ❑ ❑

It wasn't all bad news, however, at least not in 2004. Shortly after turning forty in January, Cage began dating Alice Kim, whom he met while Kim was working as a waitress at the LA sushi restaurant Kabuki. They married in July. In October 2005, they welcomed their son, Kal-El, named after Superman's true, Kryptonian name. "We wanted a name that was exotic, was American and stood for something good," Cage told journalist Anthony Breznican later that month. The actor called Kim an angel, spoke fondly of son Weston, while noting that his now fifteen-year-old, a black belt who stood at six foot six, could "easily kick my [butt]." Then, as before, he largely stopped talking about his marriage and his family.

Cage would, however, talk about movies and found himself having to do a lot of press the following year, for his high-profile role in Oliver Stone's *World Trade Center*, a film that arrived dogged by assumptions based on Stone's past work. After establishing himself as an in-demand screenwriter—his credits included Alan Parker's *Midnight Express*—Stone became synonymous with controversy thanks to politically charged films like *Platoon*, *Wall Street*, and *JFK*, the last a conspiracy theory–filled account of the Kennedy assassination that Stone described as a "counter-myth" to the official account of the event. Irresponsible conspiracy theories attached themselves to the 9/11 attacks from day one, reaching a high-water mark in the mid-2000s, in part thanks to widely circulated online videos.

Whatever Stone might have believed privately, however, he kept out of the film. "'The mantra is 'This is not a political film,'" he told the *New York Times*. To avoid politics, *World Trade Center* sticks to moment-by-moment events, recounting the destruction of the World Trade Center by focusing on the true story of two Port Authority police officers trapped in the rubble after the towers fell: John McLoughlin (Cage) and Will Jimeno (Michael Peña). The film pays scrupulous attention to the facts of the day, following McLoughlin and Jimeno as they respond to an emergency of a scale they can't comprehend. The two do their best to escort others to safety and then find themselves pinned and unable to convey their location to anyone who might be attempting to rescue them. Largely keeping politics in the background, the film begins as an intense, ground-level re-creation of the attacks before emerging as an affecting, if familiar, story of survival.

This didn't mean it wasn't risky. September 11 reshaped movies, prompting studios to delay the release of several films containing scenes of massive urban destruction of the sort that had become increasingly common in the years leading up to 9/11. Such images now found real-world echoes on the news, which replayed scenes of the attacks from every available angle. In its first issue back after the attacks, the satirical newspaper and website *The Onion* featured a headline reading "American Life Turns into Bad Jerry Bruckheimer Movie"; for a time, such images became scarce in action movies.

Films about 9/11 held the burden of depicting recent history that had killed thousands and left psychic scars that could still be felt in everyday life. Until *World Trade Center*, only one other studio project, the Paul Greengrass–directed *United 93*, had dealt directly with the events of that day, using the same middle-of-the-action approach that Greengrass had brought to the fact-based *Bloody Sunday* and the spy movie sequel *The Bourne Supremacy*. It earned acclaim and performed well enough to turn a profit on a relatively modest budget, but *World Trade Center*, a more expensive undertaking filled with stars and released in the summer movie season, presented a bigger risk.

The safe, respectful approach worked in the film's favor. However unnerving Stone's depiction of the attacks and the towers' subsequent collapse, it's the celebration of American resilience via a triumph-over-adversity story that ends up defining the film. Summoning the Everyman qualities of his early '90s comedies, but for a dramatic purpose, Cage's performance as the quiet, sturdy McLoughlin matches the tone of the film. He convincingly plays the part of a man summoning all his courage to push past fear and agony. (Cage's preparations included spending time in a sensory-deprivation tank.) Greeted by mostly positive reviews, the film opened at a strong third at the box office and performed well globally.

That Cage delivered memorable work in a prestigious film given wide release by a major studio and helmed by a name director didn't seem particularly notable in 2006. In fact, this had been the norm almost from the start. Even factoring out Francis Ford Coppola, few actors could claim a filmography that included filmmakers as notable as Martha Coolidge, Alan Parker, the Coen brothers, Norman Jewison, and David Lynch in just their first seven years. Since *Leaving Las Vegas*, Cage had added even more directors of note to that list. But in just a few years, *World Trade Center* would look like an exception, a point of departure from which he'd struggle to return.

❑ ❑ ❑

Much had changed since 1982. Studios largely lost interest in mid-budget movies and, correspondingly, scaled back on dramas, largely surrendering that territory to television, which had entered a dramatic golden age after the watershed arrival of *The Sopranos* in 1999. That shift also absorbed some of the writing and directing talent across several generations. Coolidge, for one, largely segued into directing television, and TV's reputation as a writers' medium made it aspirational for those who might have previously dreamed of working in movies.

Coolidge wasn't alone among Cage's old collaborators in moving elsewhere in the early years of the twenty-first century. Scorsese and Scott plugged away, but Francis Ford Coppola moved to the sidelines to make wine and smaller, more personal films. Lynch seemingly gave up on movies after releasing the three-hour experiment *Inland Empire* in 2006. Jewison directed his final film in 2003. Parker never made another feature after the Cage-produced *The Life of David Gale* that same year. Also in 2003, Figgis and Woo made their last stabs at working in Hollywood before retreating to London and Hong Kong, respectively. Andrew Bergman bowed out in 2000. De Palma worked less frequently, usually on smaller projects for overseas producers.

Cage's Saturn Films enjoyed some success, in part due to its attachment to projects like *National Treasure* and *World Trade Center*. But it never developed into the promised actors' lab, and its record of finding compelling projects for Cage to appear in proved increasingly spotty. So would its record of seeing projects through to the finish line. Saturn's initial slate included intriguing-sounding projects with Cage-friendly roles, films like *Tom Slick—Monster Hunter*, the true-life story of an eccentric oil magnate who searches for Bigfoot and other legendary creatures; a remake of *The Courtship of Eddie's Father* (whose TV incarnation, which Cage had name-checked in *Gone in 60 Seconds*, starred Cage favorite Bill Bixby); *Heartbreaker*, based on a story of Cage's own creation, about a man who takes jobs romancing and leaving women in order to send them back to ex-boyfriends; and *Press Your Luck* (inspired by the strange-but-true story of an unlikely game show champion). None were made. Nor were later films, like *Time Share*.

Announced in 2005, this film would have costarred Will Smith in Cage's first attempt at a straight-up comedy since *Trapped in Paradise* in 1994. After *Shadow of the Vampire* and *The Life of David Gale*, the company produced only two projects that didn't star Cage: the single-season Sci-Fi Channel series *The Dresden Files* and *A Thousand Words*, a fable-like Eddie Murphy comedy filmed in 2008 that sat unreleased until 2012.

Of the projects Saturn Films did produce, none would prove as regrettable as Cage's other 2006 release, a remake of the 1973 cult classic *The Wicker Man*. Written by playwright Anthony Shaffer and directed by Robin Hardy, the original film starred Edward Woodward as Sgt. Neil Howie, a devout policeman who travels to a remote Scottish island to investigate the disappearance of a young girl. There Howie finds a community dedicated to keeping alive the pagan ways of their ancestors and presided over by a smug patriarch, played by Christopher Lee. As Howie's investigation progresses, he accumulates evidence of an island-wide conspiracy before meeting a dark fate.

The job of writing and directing the remake fell to another creator with theatrical roots, Neil LaBute. LaBute made his filmmaking debut in 1997 with *In the Company of Men*, an adaptation of a play that created a stir when LaBute premiered it at Brigham Young University, his alma mater, a few years before. The story of two men who manipulate and torment a deaf woman, the film version proved equally controversial when it became an art house hit after a divisive Sundance premiere. LaBute filled subsequent efforts with similar depictions of cruelty, leading some to question whether he shared some of the views of his misanthropic, often misogynistic characters.

LaBute's vision for *The Wicker Man* did little to quiet those concerns. Moving the setting to an island off the coast of Washington State, he reimagined Summerisle as a matriarchal cult whose affinity with bees doesn't end with the honey that serves as its primary export. Cage plays the Woodward analogue, Edward Malus (pronounced MALE-us), a cop traumatized by witnessing a horrific car accident he couldn't prevent. Malus travels to the island after receiving a letter from his ex (Kate Beahan), pleading with him to find her missing daughter. Once there, Malus encounters strangely silent men and hostile women; the cult's queen bee, Sister Summersisle (Ellen Burstyn); and a classroom filled with spooky girls chanting the words "phallic symbol." The deeper Malus digs, and the more troubling evidence he finds that the missing girl is the target of an upcoming ritual sacrifice, the more unhinged he becomes. The film's frenetic climax finds him wearing a purloined bear suit and punching women.

LaBute's execution did his reconceptualization no favor. Malus spends much of the film wandering, occasionally biking, from place to place in the service of a shapeless mystery that never builds up the eerie atmosphere it needs. In the *New York Times*, A. O. Scott called it "comically inept as a horror movie," and ticket buyers stayed away when it premiered in September.

That could have been that. A few years earlier, a film like *The Wicker Man* might have disappeared, apart from the occasional revival by a cult of so-bad-it's-good movie enthusiasts. Instead, it became the first high-profile exhibit in Cage's complicated relationship with the internet.

Before year's end, audio clips of some of the film's more colorful moments surfaced on ytmnd.com, a site that allows users to upload repeating loops against text and tiled images. (The website's name is short for "You're the man now, dog," a line delivered, with gusto, by Sean Connery in the 2000 film *Finding Forrester* that served as the site's first and, for a time, only post.) While ytmnd.com was niche and lo-fi, the next home for *Wicker Man* appreciation would be a widely seen supercut constructed from out-of-context scenes from the film. On January 1, 2007, a YouTube user posted "Best Scenes from 'The Wicker Man,'" a video compiled from the film's DVD release. Cage spends much of the film brooding, but the "Best Scenes" video boils the film down to a florid two minutes of outbursts, including a moment featured only in the director's cut, in which Malus is subjected to torture by bees and screams, "Not the bees! My eyes!"

As of 2020, the video attracted more than 4.5 million views, and *The Wicker Man* had become synonymous with Cage shouting, "Not the bees!" Cage and LaBute have since said they intended *The Wicker Man* to play in part as a dark comedy and knew they were treading a line.

"I mean, were we aware that Nic Cage in a bear suit would be funny?" LaBute said in conversation with *The Believer* in 2013. "Yeah. But we knew that we were still going to kill him in the end. That balance of laughs and horror is always interesting, but sometimes we don't get it right." That same year, Cage also offered a defense of the film when speaking to IndieWire, saying it's "probably the best example of a movie where people are mystified because they think for some reason that we did not know it was humorous, even though I am dressed in a bear suit, doing these ridiculous things with the matriarchal society on the island—how can you *not* know that

Neil and I knew that this was absurdist humor? But okay, have at it. That was a misconception."

Misconception or not, *The Wicker Man* would prove tough to shake. Whether LaBute and Cage set out to create a send-up of misogyny or an edge-treading political provocation or just an effective horror film with a patina of sexual politics, there's a chasm between such intentions and the results, one only deepened by the general dullness of the film apart from those outbursts. A role that might have been forgotten in another era became one of Cage's best-known roles, a punch line even for those who would never see *The Wicker Man* in full.

Cage welcomed laughter when he inspired it on his own terms, however. A package of Robert Rodriguez and Quentin Tarantino short features that pays homage to the grimy exploitation films of the 1970s, the 2007 film *Grindhouse* also features a series of trailers to films that don't exist, directed by Eli Roth, Edgar Wright, and Rob Zombie. Zombie's *Werewolf Women of the S.S.* pays homage to a particularly sleazy strain of grindhouse, Nazi-themed shockers set in concentration camps, and it climaxes with the surprise appearance of golden age pulp villain Fu Manchu, played with maniacal glee by Cage. In *Ghost Rider*, Cage brings a similarly absurdist spirit to the role of stunt cyclist Johnny Blaze, the Marvel Comics hero who, thanks to a deal with the devil, turns into a flaming, motorcycle-riding skull to punish evildoers. Rather than play Blaze as a whiskey-swilling tough guy, Cage reinterprets him as a daredevil who spends his downtime eating jelly beans, listening to the Carpenters, and watching nature videos.

The film allowed Cage, at last, to play a comic book hero—and an odd one he seemed particularly well suited to play.

Introduced in 1972, Ghost Rider was born of a particular moment in pop culture history, inspired in equal parts by cyclist Evel Knievel's ascent to stardom and a loosening of restrictions by the comic book industry's self-censoring Comics Code Authority, which, since its implementation in 1954, had prohibited horror elements in mainstream comics. The character tapped into Cage's love of fast vehicles and the macabre and his attraction to outcasts. Ghost Rider was a misfit creation, a hero with satanic ties who sported chains and leather rather than tights and a cape. It wasn't Superman, but it had potential.

The film, however, does its best to smooth off the rough edges and make Ghost Rider fit into the mold of a standard movie superhero circa 2007, a year in which superhero movies seemed to be in decline. Where 2008 would bring *The Dark Knight* and *Iron Man*, the latter serving as the keystone for what would become the Marvel Cinematic Universe, the years leading up to it produced *Superman Returns*, a film whose tepid reception didn't bear out Bryan Singer's Cage-mocking instincts, and the widely disliked sequels *X-Men: The Last Stand* and *Fantastic Four: Rise of the Silver Surfer*. All the signs suggested that the genre didn't have much life left in it. *Ghost Rider* plays like an act of bet hedging, a dully directed film with not-quite-state-of-the-art special effects that follows a much-tinkered-with, formula-following script. It's as bland as a movie in which Peter Fonda plays the devil can be. It also doesn't benefit from hiding Cage's face behind fiery special effects during the action scenes.

Still, audiences turned out. Released in the usually sleepy month of February, *Ghost Rider* earned $45 million its opening weekend, the strongest debut for any Cage film. Even more showed up in December for *National Treasure: Book of Secrets*, in which Cage's Benjamin Gates has to clear the name of an ancestor unfairly linked to the Lincoln assassination by traveling the globe as he heads toward a climax within the bowels of Mount Rushmore. The film reunited the original's creative team, adding Helen Mirren, as Gates's mother, to a returning ensemble that already included Jon Voight, Harvey Keitel, Diane Kruger, and Justin Bartha. Despite earning largely so-so reviews, it became an even bigger hit than the first installment. It was the sort of success that usually led to sequels, offering a reliable sure thing for its star no matter what else might happen. But as the 2000s drew on, the changing business would redefine sure things.

For now, at least, it seemed that trouble lay elsewhere. Cage's other 2007 film release, *Next*, provided a signal that he and Saturn Films had begun to shift focus toward high-concept genre movies, a change in emphasis that would yield mixed results over the next few years. Loosely adapted from a Philip K. Dick story, *Next* casts Cage as Cris Johnson, a low-rent Vegas magician with an unwanted gift: he can see two minutes into the future. However clever the hook, the results proved pedestrian. Director Lee Tamahori never finds a compelling way to visualize Johnson's abilities until the finale, but any late-arriving goodwill is undone by a climax that feels like a cheat.

Unlike past missteps, it wasn't just a case of a strong Cage performance being stranded in an unworthy movie. Cage isn't bad in the film, but apart from his magic shtick, he does little to make Johnson into a distinctive character. Cage's ability to play tortured men ossifies here into a kind of all-purpose soulful glumness, one he could reprise, with slight variations, in films that demanded little more of him. Not much sets Cris Johnson apart from Joe, for instance, the gifted hit man Cage plays in 2008's *Bangkok Dangerous*. The Hollywood debut of the Pang Brothers, a Hong Kong filmmaking duo from the generation that followed John Woo, the movie captures little of the stylishness that distinguished their other work, apart from a few moments of florid violence. Nor is there much to distinguish either protagonist from John Koestler, the astrophysicist at the center of the vaguely religious science-fiction thriller *Knowing*, which premiered in March 2009 (and used 9/11-inspired scenes of chaos and destruction at several moments, a sure signal that the public's distaste for such images had melted away in the years since *World Trade Center*). Each character comes from different walks of life and faces threats as diverse as the Thai underworld and the end of existence itself. Each has also settled into a state of low-grade existential despair that make Cage's performances pretty much interchangeable.

One aspect did set *Knowing* apart from the others, however: it became a hit. Its 2009 success would prove to be an exception in what would otherwise be, for Cage, an annus horribilis.

❑ ❑ ❑

Nicolas Cage's troubles with money first became public in early 2008, but few noticed at the time. After all, was owing $800,000 after claiming limo rides and a Gulfstream as business expenses really *that* big a deal? Cage's more substantial troubles surfaced in early October of the following year, when the gossip website TMZ published notice of an IRS lien exceeding $6 million. This wasn't the end of the story. In the weeks that followed, Cage sued former business manager Samuel J. Levin for mismanagement. Levin, in turn, countersued, and then the details started to emerge—though, in Levin's telling, it was all pretty simple. Cage had bought stuff, so much stuff: $33 million in property, twenty-two cars, jewelry, art . . . and that was just in 2007. (Both suits would be dismissed in 2011.)

At the height of Cage's spending, he owned fifteen homes, including two castles (one in England and another in Germany), a private island in the Bahamas, and houses in Las Vegas, New Orleans, and on both coasts. He bought shrunken heads; rare comics; an octopus; dozens of cars, including several Rolls-Royces and a Lamborghini that had once belonged to the shah of Iran; two albino king cobras; and a dinosaur skull he had to give back to the government of Mongolia when it turned out to have been stolen. The list went on and would be repeated again and again, turning up in virtually every article written about Cage and providing fodder for websites looking for cheap hits with listicles. More trouble followed, including further claims of unpaid taxes and a lawsuit from ex-girlfriend Christina Fulton, mother of Cage's son Weston, alleging broken financial promises. (Cage and Fulton would come to an undisclosed agreement in 2011.)

Could anyone feel *that* much sympathy for a man who had frittered away a fortune, particularly while so many still struggled to recover from the financial collapse of 2008 and the long recession that followed? In turn, Cage became a joke, or at least a punch line.

"We felt really bad for Nicolas Cage when we heard he was flat broke and had to sell some properties—including two castles—and see others foreclosed upon, with his belongings auctioned off," *San Francisco Examiner* "entertainment writer and astrologer" Kitty Raymond stated at the beginning of a column that ended, "In the course of one year, the *Con Air* star is said to have bought three multimillion-dollar homes, 22 cars and 47 works of art. Yeah, so . . . we don't really feel all that sorry for Nic anymore."

The year got worse: Cage's father, August Coppola, died of a heart attack on October 29. His *Los Angeles Times* obituary included remembrances of him as a "flamboyant and eccentric" teacher. The headline mentioned that he was the "member of [a] noted film family."

Even creative satisfactions couldn't be counted on anymore. In 2008, Cage filmed *Bad Lieutenant: Port of Call New Orleans* with Werner Herzog, the venerable, singular German director. Herzog alternated between documentary and narrative films and had become known from his earliest days as a filmmaker for seemingly chaotic, but ultimately fruitful, shoots that included grueling trips into the Amazon rain forest and, for one film, hypnotizing his actors. One actor he couldn't hypnotize was Klaus Kinski, the wild-eyed, troubled leading man Herzog worked with frequently, and fractiously, until Kinski's death in 1991. *Bad Lieutenant: Port of Call New Orleans*—less a sequel or a remake than a companion piece to *Bad Lieutenant*, the intense, controversial, New York City–set Abel Ferrara drama released in 1992—might have seemed like an odd project for Herzog, but as usual he made it his own. Working from a script by William M. Finkelstein, Herzog created a darkly comic, occasionally absurd, but ultimately searing study of addiction and the difficulty of finding redemption.

Cage plays Terence McDonagh, a gleefully corrupt New Orleans police officer who, against the advice of his callous partner (Val Kilmer), rescues a prisoner from drowning as his cell fills with water from Hurricane Katrina. Commended and promoted for the rescue, but also injured while performing it, he patrols the streets to feed a drug habit when not making time with his girlfriend, Frankie (Eva Mendes, Cage's *Ghost Rider* costar), a high-end prostitute. McDonagh uses his authority to serve his own ends, often at the expense of others. But he's also haunted by a twinge of goodness that naggingly keeps manifesting as he investigates the murder of some Senegalese immigrants.

Herzog likes to work on a grand scale, and in Cage he found a game partner. "I wanted to be the California Klaus Kinski," Cage later told *GQ*. "I wanted to go out and even scare him at times to get to the core of that character." To get to the core, Cage reached back, way back, drawing on the silent film gestures of *Face/Off*, the Expressionistic experiments of *Vampire's Kiss*, and, ultimately, the vulnerability of *Birdy*. Wired on coke, McDonagh seems on the verge of madness, and Herzog matches the energy with hallucinatory shots of lizards and, in one memorable moment, a breakdancing ghost.

The film—from its extreme material to Cage's hold-nothing-back work—is, to put it mildly, a big swing. It also connects. Where Cage seemed penned in working in big-budget genre movies, here he seemed liberated working with a director and material that invited him to experiment. He also seemed to understand where he needed to draw the line. The film's excesses are calculated. Its wild touches magnify its power. In the end, Cage depicts McDonagh's urges and excesses as demons he might spend a lifetime trying to shake, but the effort itself might save his soul. The film's madness serves as a Trojan horse for an uncompromising morality tale.

It's the sort of movie that could remind those who saw it of what made Cage such an exciting talent. Its release, however, couldn't have arrived at a worse time, coinciding with Cage's much-mocked money problems and preceded by a trailer that spotlighted the film's oddest moments and became an article of viral fascination and mockery online. Critics largely went for it. In the *New York Times*, A. O. Scott praised its "maniacal unpredictability," noting that its originality served as a reminder of how the crime thriller, "once a repository of weirdness, wild emotion and sly cinematic invention, has recently devolved into a state of glum, routine sadism. The stories lurch toward phony and mechanical surprise endings, and the heroes tend to be glowering ciphers of righteous vengeance, exacting payback and muttering second-hand tough-guy catchphrases."

Those who saw the trailer seemed to outnumber those who sought out the film, however, which never played more than one hundred U.S. theaters during its release. It was never going to reach an audience as wide as a *National Treasure* entry, or even a *Bangkok Dangerous*, but that it would be so little seen, so widely misunderstood, and so entangled with tabloid stories of prodigal spending seemed like an unnecessary twist of the knife.

It's as if the public now wanted the stories of weirdness—in Cage's life and glimpsed in trailers and highlight reels—more than the work that made all that weirdness possible. Whatever control Cage once exerted over his public image had slipped away. His work had gotten overshadowed by bear suits and dinosaur skulls. The steps he took to steer his career had instead led him to an impasse. Now he had to find his way out of it working in a filmmaking environment increasingly averse to the risks he liked to take and to the films in which he liked to take them. It wouldn't be easy.

It might not even be possible.

12

Endless Cage

On August 2, 2010, Nicolas Cage walked away. Though due to start filming his latest movie, *Trespass*, in just two weeks, he'd left for parts unknown. Seemingly, no one knew how to reach him. Rumors suggested he'd gone to the Bahamas, where he still owned a private island, but who knew for sure? Who knew anything for sure about Cage anymore? In June he'd signed on to play the part of Kyle Miller, an over-leveraged Louisiana diamond dealer who becomes the victim of a home invasion. Nicole Kidman had agreed to costar as his wife, and the film would reunite him with his *8mm* director, Joel Schumacher. Then Cage had a change of heart, deciding he'd rather play one of the bad guys instead. The production accommodated him and began looking around for another actor to play his original part. Finally, Cage decided he'd rather not make the movie at all. Hero. Villain. Did it really matter what part he played anymore?

❑ ❑ ❑

It had been a rough stretch for Cage as the 2000s drew to a close and the 2010s began, one in which disappointment and financial strife played out in full view of a public that didn't know what to make of him anymore. Not that they'd forgotten him. Cage was still everywhere, in one form or another, his movies in constant rotation on cable and his face all over the internet, including in a bizarre meme that replaced his hair with a large bird and in an odd eBay auction that, for a million dollars, offered a photo of "Cage" from 1870. (The listing read "Nicolas Cage is a Vampire." The sale did not succeed.) He'd become a recurring character on *Saturday Night Live*, thanks to Andy Samberg's impression, which began primarily as a send-up of Cage's *National Treasure* character but had evolved into a more cutting parody of Cage's acting tics and personal woes. Two thousand ten also saw the appearance of another breakout YouTube clip, a kind of sequel to the *Wicker Man* compilation, entitled "Nicolas Cage Losing His Shit." That it was drawn almost entirely from the most extreme moments in a handful of movies—primarily *Vampire's Kiss*, *Zandalee*, and *Deadfall*—didn't seem to matter. This was Nicolas Cage now.

A big hit might have changed that, but hits of any size were becoming vanishingly rare for Cage. He'd found success in a colorful supporting role in early 2010, with *Kick-Ass*, an irreverent take on superheroes in which he played Big Daddy, a heavily armed vigilante/warm and supportive father in the process of turning his daughter into a killing machine. The film allows him to send up both *Batman* and the idealized vision of fatherhood he'd grown up watching on television, offering just the sort of offbeat role in which he excelled. As Big Daddy, he could mix big gestures, unexpected choices, and genuine emotion, and the film's success ensured that it was widely seen, even if he wasn't the name-above-the-title star this time.

Being the name-above-the-title star, however, wasn't working out as well as it used to. *The Sorcerer's Apprentice* reteamed Cage with producer Jerry Bruckheimer and *National Treasure* director Jon Turteltaub for another Disney summer blockbuster, this one loosely inspired by the *Fantasia* short of the same name and Cage's own interest in the mythology of King Arthur. The busy but joyless film found Cage playing a disciple of Merlin who, unlike *National Treasure*'s Benjamin Franklin Gates, seems more annoyed than enthused as he whisks a wizard-in-training (Jay Baruchel) around New York's most enchanted corners (in part via a one-of-a-kind antique Rolls-Royce from Cage's personal collection). Though it had all the elements required of a new franchise—a strong tie to Disney-owned intellectual property not least among them—its disappointing box office killed any sequel dreams.

Made before Cage's financial issues became widely known in October 2009, *The Sorcerer's Apprentice* seemed to confirm Cage's downward trajectory in the summer of 2010. Released in the dumping-ground month of January in the following year, so did *Season of the Witch*. A dreary, modestly budgeted medieval horror thriller filmed in 2008 and directed by *Gone in 60 Seconds*'s Dominic Sena, it was met with hostile reviews and audience indifference. The following month saw the release of *Drive Angry*, a supernatural action film in which Cage plays a man so bent on revenge that he escapes from hell to foil a satanic cult that's kidnapped his daughter. Filmed in 3-D and filled with a ratings-pushing amount of sex and violence—to say nothing of fast cars and not-quite-state-of-the-art CGI effects—it did little to lure moviegoers to theaters, debuting in ninth place.

These films might seem like the efforts of a star trying anything to see if it might work, but such were the times. Released at the end of 2009, James Cameron's *Avatar* would go on to gross nearly $2.8 billion, a staggering figure that seemingly justified, and undoubtedly intensified, a steroidal increase in scale for Hollywood filmmaking. Of the ten top-grossing films of 2010, only Christopher Nolan's *Inception* and the Disney animated film *Tangled* were not part of a larger franchise, neither serving as a sequel to another film nor designed to produce sequels of its own. In 2011, that number shrank to zero. The year's top ten reads like a roll call of twenty-first-century pop culture institutions (and some new takes on twentieth-century fixtures): the final *Harry Potter* film, the fourth *Fast and the Furious* sequel, a revival of *Planet of the Apes*, the first of three and counting *Thor* movies, and so on. A few outliers find slots a little farther down the list—*The Help*, *Bridesmaids*, *Super 8*—but the top twenty is otherwise dominated by X-Men, kung fu pandas, and Smurfs. Lower on the list lies the wreckage of the would-be franchise starters *Green Lantern* and *Green Hornet*. (Cage almost played the bad guy in the latter, even working on the Bahamian accent he thought would complete the character before ultimately leaving the film.) Franchises, already the name of the game, threatened to become the game in total.

Moviegoers wanted superheroes and superspies. Moviegoers wanted sparkly vampires and giant robots inspired by toy lines from the 1980s. Moviegoers wanted Avengers and charismatic car thieves. Studios wanted the same, particularly when those projects could compete internationally in an environment where what played in Chongqing now mattered as much as, or more than, what played in Peoria. Comedies and dramas didn't translate nearly as well as X-Men and Captain Jack Sparrow.

Movie stars (by the Michael Bay definition of the term) unattached to such projects could feel like players in a game of musical chairs still left standing when the music had stopped. Even then, sometimes those chairs could get yanked away. There would be no second *Sorcerer's Apprentice* film. More surprisingly, there would be no third *National Treasure* film. Though *National Treasure: Book of Secrets* outperformed the original, Disney saw no future in the franchise. In 2020, producer Jason Reed told the website Collider that Disney "was never able to capitalize on it as a franchise. It was more of a movie with a sequel and *National Treasure 3* would have been another sequel. . . . They never figured out a way to integrate it into the parks." To maintain the company's interest, a movie couldn't just be a movie anymore. It couldn't even be a big hit movie with sequel potential. It had to be a merchandisable, theme park–friendly element of a synergistic corporate strategy to be worth continued effort. It had to be a universe.

The world of superhero films, which would only expand in the coming years, also offered no refuge for Cage. He'd brought a Marvel Comics character to life for Lionsgate the year before *Iron Man* inaugurated what would become the Marvel Cinematic Universe, a sprawling series of connected films. The MCU would have no room for characters like Ghost Rider, which Marvel had previously licensed to other studios. Cage had named himself and one of his sons after superheroes—he'd nearly been Superman—only to find everyone else getting a shot at playing them when superheroes got *really* big.

With these options off the table, a star would have to pick from what was left, selections that grew even more limited for those on the far side of forty-five whose name no longer guaranteed crowds of paying customers and who'd recently experienced high-profile public humiliation, in the process becoming a talk show, sketch comedy, and internet punch line. It was enough to make anyone sit and wonder whether he'd be better off playing the hero or the villain of a movie. Or if it mattered. Or if it was worth doing at all.

❑ ❑ ❑

The *Trespass* crisis ended nearly as quickly as it began. By August 4, Cage was back on board, agreeing to play Kyle Miller as originally planned. But though his return saved the film from possible cancellation, it did little to guarantee its success. The sort of thriller that shoots for claustrophobic but settles for having its characters shout at each other for ninety minutes, Schumacher's film debuted at the Toronto International Film Festival in September 2011 on its way to theaters the following month. Some theaters. What little attention *Trespass* generated came from a release strategy that saw it debuting on video-on-demand services simultaneous to an extremely limited theatrical release in a handful of major markets. In retrospect, it would mark a major turning point in how films would be seen in the years ahead. This had been attempted before, but rarely with a film filled with name stars like Cage and Kidman, whose pairing, a few years earlier, would have counted as an event in itself.

The development brought Cage little joy. "I like movies to be seen the way the director wanted them to be seen, which is on the big-screen, with an audience with their popcorn," he told the Associated Press. "I want movies to be an event. I want people to get excited about it and go out for the night with their wife or their date, whatever it may be, and have it be an event. I don't want it to get smaller and smaller and wind up on a cell phone."

Cage couldn't have known it in 2011, but his words would prove prophetic, both for his career and for the industry in general. Over the course of the 2010s, theaters increasingly focused on event films—as the definition of what qualified as an event narrowed. A night out at the movies, more often than not, meant action and state-of-the-art effects (or sometimes animated animals). Most other movies could wait for home viewing and, increasingly, became accessible at home not long after playing theaters, if they played theaters at all. An alternate Hollywood of leaner budgets, smaller salaries, upstart production companies, frugal distributors, and directors of wildly varying abilities awaited those who lost their footing in the blockbuster world.

Though he might not have known it at the time, *Trespass* became a Rubicon for Cage. His next film, *Seeking Justice*, played in just 231 theaters and, though a step up from *Trespass* thanks in part to a villainous turn by Guy Pearce, earned poor reviews. When Cage did return to theaters in 2012, it was via *Ghost Rider: Spirit of Vengeance*, a sequel made on an appreciably smaller scale than the original. The film paired him with the innovative directing team of Mark Neveldine and Brian Taylor but featured little of the punkish spark of previous Neveldine/Taylor projects like *Crank*. Its cool reception would bring Cage's stint as a superhero to an end and send him back toward projects such as *Stolen*, a reunion with *Con Air* director Simon West in which he played a New Orleans ex-con scrambling to rescue his estranged daughter from a former partner.

Cage's films started to take on a kind of Mad Libs quality in the early years of the 2010s, sending one protagonist or another on a rescue and/or revenge mission in a southern city that offered generous incentives to film productions trying to save money. That Cage delivered some of his least creative performances during this stretch is almost certainly no coincidence. Though he doesn't visibly disengage like some actors given material they believe beneath them—see almost any film made by Bruce Willis in recent years—Cage's work in this era offers little evidence of the thought or creativity found even in subpar films like *Next*. Still, it was work, and work at a time when he had bills to pay. It's tough to discern to what extent financial expediency factored into his professional choices. Cage had almost always been prolific, but for the moment he didn't seem to take much pleasure in the work.

His behavior surrounding *Trespass* suggested a shift as well. Cage's days of acting out on the set of *The Cotton Club* and demanding that yogurt be poured on his toes while shooting *Vampire's Kiss* were now decades in the past. Directors tended to use words like *professionalism* to describe working with him. He wasn't, in other words, the sort of actor who walked out on a movie. Other events suggest he'd entered a troubled period. In April 2011, Cage was arrested following a loud, drunken argument with wife Alice Kim on the streets of New Orleans about the location of the apartment they were renting. That *Dog the Bounty Hunter* star Duane Chapman posted Cage's $11,000 bond did little to lower the profile of the embarrassing event.

Cage once owned a mansion in the city. Now he owned only a tomb. The previous year, he'd purchased a spot in New Orleans's historic St. Louis Cemetery No. 1. A mossy necropolis that serves as the final resting place of voodoo practitioner Marie Laveau and other city notables dating back to the late eighteenth century, the cemetery now housed a gleaming nine-foot-tall pyramid bearing the Latin words *Omnia ab uno* ("Everything from One"), a phrase associated with alchemists and Rosicrucians. But even if he knew where his ultimate destination would be, for now, Cage seemed a little lost.

❑ ❑ ❑

He needed a comeback, the sort of comeback that would vault him back to the top tier of stardom, the role that would put all questions to rest and push him toward the next phase of his career. He had strong prospects, too. The atmospheric feature debut of writer/director Scott Walker, *The Frozen Ground* paired him with John Cusack in a fact-inspired project that allowed both actors to play against type, with Cage taking the role of a nice-guy family man Alaska state trooper and Cusack as the Anchorage serial killer who eludes him. It, too, played only a few theaters before heading to VOD in 2013.

Maybe it would be a good idea to take some time to reflect and plan. Though a release schedule that saw *Ghost Rider: Spirit of Vengeance* followed at a regular clip by *Stolen*, the DreamWorks animated film *The Croods*, and *The Frozen Ground* doesn't reflect it, Cage essentially took a year off after shooting *The Frozen Ground* in 2011, apparently freed from the financial urgency of the preceding years. In the fall of 2012, he began shooting *Joe* in Texas for director David Gordon Green. The resulting film would feature one of the best performances of his career.

Based on a 1991 novel by Larry Brown, a Mississippi writer acclaimed for his knowing, unsparing depictions of the modern American South, *Joe* found Cage assuming the title role of Joe Ransom, a Texan who leads a crew that illegally poisons trees to provide cover for companies interested in clearing land for development. He's a man with a violent history, but his reputation has evened out over the years. He treats his workers fairly and does his best to stay out of trouble, most of the time. Years and accumulated wisdom have softened his edges, but they haven't erased them. When Joe takes Gary (Tye Sheridan), a teenage drifter with an abusive, alcoholic father (Gary Poulter), under his wing, he finds himself drawn into a cycle of violence of the sort he thought he'd found a way to escape.

The film dated back to director David Gordon Green's college days, when he helped out on a documentary about Brown. In the years since, Green had made a name for himself as a filmmaker of remarkable, but unpredictable, natural talent. His 2000 debut, *George Washington*, initiated a string of lyrical films filled with indelible images that drew inspiration from the work of Terrence Malick. With *Pineapple Express*, he'd pivoted into mainstream comedies before returning to the indie world with *Prince Avalanche* in 2013. Like Cage, he seemed averse to being pigeonholed.

Born in 1975, Green was also young enough to have grown up watching Nicolas Cage films as a movie-obsessed kid in the 1980s. Where Cage had previously worked largely with older directors and contemporaries, here was someone with a different perspective on what the actor could do, someone who showed little interest in hiring Cage to repeat himself. Instead, Green cast him in a part that could have been designed to erase his action star image. He made what he wanted clear via shorthand. "I want Robert Mitchum for this role," Green wrote in a letter he sent to Cage with the script, "but he died, so will you please help me out?'"

There's not much of Mitchum in the final performance, but the spirit of countless terse, haunted tough guys trying to stay out of trouble hangs over Cage's work in *Joe*. Green used Westerns as a model, particularly *Shane*. Cage drew on samurai films. The film is so rich in details of a particular time and place—small-town Texas hollowed out by the changes of the twenty-first century—and Cage's performance so particular to one man living in that place, however, that those influences seem secondary.

At times, *Joe* plays like a response to the "Nicolas Cage Loses His Shit" video. Cage delivers a carefully controlled performance as a man who comes to realize that his life, and the lives of others, might depend on him controlling his rage, that he has to put behind him the days of being wild that other characters mention in passing if he wants to have any days ahead of him. When he does lose his cool, when the seething anger finally boils over, it's terrifying. Cage had played characters in the grip of vengeance-fueled fury in the past, and he would soon play them again, but his work in *Joe* drains any dark pleasure from acts of violence. However righteous he might be, and however driven by his best instincts in his attempts to defend Gary, he knows he's still destroying the best part of himself.

Acting behind a bushy beard and limiting his voice to its lower register, Cage is at times unrecognizable as Joe. It's the sort of lived-in, naturalistic performance he hadn't attempted since *Birdy*, one that fits in nicely alongside a cast that mixes professional actors with newcomers and outsiders. (Gary Poulter, who does remarkable work, was a homeless Austin street performer who didn't survive to see the film's release. Green cast his next-door neighbor as a policeman.) In interviews promoting *Joe*, Cage would describe it as conscious departure. To explain his approach in the past, he'd coined terms like *nouveau shamanic* and *Western kabuki*. This, however, was different. "I had done some other kinds of movies," he told *Good Morning America* while promoting the film in 2014:

> experimented with different styles of film performance I call [it] "Western kabuki," a little more larger-than-life, more baroque. I'd taken a year off and I wanted to be very selective and try to find a character that I could invest all the wisdom from some of the mistakes I'd made in the past. Not have to act so much. Be more emotionally naked. Not put things on top of performance but take things off.

What remains is an unvarnished depiction of a middle-aged man at a crossroads with no guarantee he'll choose the right path—or if he'll get a chance to choose at all.

Joe picked up one glowing notice after another as it made

the festival rounds. The film "stands as a reminder of what a terrific actor Cage can be when he is able to harness and channel his wilder impulses. Here he comes padding bear-like across the yard with his tattooed biceps and his bushy grey beard, a cigarette burning between his knuckles. He looks at home, in his natural habitat," the *Guardian's* Xan Brooks noted in a review filed from the Venice Film Festival, where the film premiered in the fall of 2013. More acclaim greeted *Joe*, and Cage, in Toronto, and ahead of the film's April release, *Time's* glowing review arrived headlined "*Joe* Reminds Us that Nicolas Cage Is a National Treasure."

The acclaim felt like a confirmation of Cage's instincts. He could do small and naturalistic. He could go big. It was all part of the plan, all within the range of his abilities. In a *CBS Sunday Morning* profile shot to coincide with the film's release, Cage seemed relaxed and down-to-earth, even when, inevitably, asked to talk about eating a cockroach for *Vampire's Kiss*. And while *Joe* signaled a change of pace, Cage didn't consider it a retreat. "I don't believe in the term 'over the top,'" he says to interviewer Lee Cowan. "I believe in the term 'outside of the box.' Let's take chances, let's keep trying new things, and that's how you reinvent yourself. And that's how you stay fresh."

The problem: not many saw the movie. *Joe* opened in a mere forty-eight theaters, premiering simultaneously on VOD. It's hard to determine definitively whether this expanded its audi-ence as hoped—VOD numbers remain nebulous and tough to access—and either way, *Joe* was never going to do the block-buster numbers of, say, the film that topped the box office the weekend it opened, *Captain America: The First Avenger*. An indie movie wasn't expected to reach such heights. But it also wasn't expected to serve as an example of how good movies could fall through the cracks or of the increasing rarity of art house hits. Any hopes that the film or Cage would be talked about at year's end, when the conversation turned to awards, had faded by the fall.

❏ ❏ ❏

There would be no comeback, not of that sort, anyway. But there would be work, and with work came opportunity. Some opportunities would be better than others. In some respects, 2014 would serve as a microcosm for the years that followed, years filled with ambitious misfires and low-ambition genre films. Cage began 2014 with the release of *Rage*, another forgettable Mad Libs–style revenge thriller (former gangster; murdered daughter; Mobile, Alabama). *Left Behind* followed in October, a second adaptation of a wildly popular book series about life during and after the Rapture that had found a fervent following among Evangelical readers. Despite Hollywood's declining interest in niche markets, the early years of the 2010s found producers and distributors large and small rushing to exploit a demand for faith-based entertainment. It would become Cage's most widely seen film in years.

Twenty fourteen ended with what ought to have been a highlight and another opportunity to stretch as an actor. *Dying of the Light* reunited Cage with *Bringing Out the Dead* writer Paul Schrader, this time with Schrader serving as both writer and director for a film in which Cage plays a CIA agent suffering from a rare form of dementia who attempts to assassinate a terrorist before his condition worsens. The film was taken out of Schrader's hands, leading the director, Cage, and costar Anton Yelchin to protest its treatment. Cage and Yelchin's on-screen rapport remains evident in the final product, but the movie still plays like a creatively hobbled effort.

The work continued, resuming a feverish pace. Cage could be seen in virtually every sort of minimally released, modestly budgeted film that appeared in the mid-2000s, from international coproductions (*Outcast*), to earnest dramas (*The Runner*), and horror movies (*Pay the Ghost*). He'd find an occasional gem like *The Trust*, a nasty, stylish, darkly comic heist thriller that paired him with Elijah Wood and, for one scene, childhood hero Jerry Lewis. But even devoted fans could be forgiven for getting lost in the flood of Cage content.

The Trust also found Cage working on what was now his home turf. Though he'd lost his Las Vegas mansion as part of his financial troubles, he'd settled elsewhere in the city that had served as the backdrop for some of his most notable films. His life changed in other ways as well. Now grown, Weston had become an actor and musician whose songs had started to turn up on the soundtracks to Cage films and who played the younger version of his father's character in *Rage*. In 2014, Weston's wife, Danielle, gave birth to Cage's first grandchild, Lucian Augustus Coppola Cage, his middle name inspired by August. Weston and Danielle would divorce in 2016. So would Cage, who ended his marriage of twelve years to Alice Kim the same year.

But there was always work. And even if he no longer needed it to pay off debts, he needed it for other reasons. "If I don't have somewhere to go in the morning and a job to do, it can be very self-destructive," he told the *Guardian*'s Hadley Freeman in 2018. "Then I'm just going to sit and order two bottles of red wine and dissolve, and I don't want to be that person, so I have to work." And work came in many forms: a small role in Oliver Stone's *Snowden*; a costarring role opposite Willem Dafoe in another Schrader film, the brutal crime comedy *Dog Eat Dog*; a lead part as a scapegoated World War II captain in *USS Indianapolis: Men of Courage*; and a broad comic performance in Larry Charles's fact-inspired *Army of One*.

The latter three all appeared on VOD in a two-week span in the fall of 2016, serving as a sampler both of what Cage had been up to and of the increasing variety of films to premiere on VOD (sometimes accompanied by a token theatrical run, often not). Here was Cage playing noble captain in *USS Indianapolis*, going mean and scuzzy for *Dog Eat Dog*, and offering a strange, Jerry Lewis–inspired turn in *Army of One* (another film taken out of the hands of its director, though one too odd to reshape into a conventional film). At the *Daily Beast*, Jen Yamato took notice, writing:

> The three films beg the question: If Cage kept his current A-list king of direct-to-VOD crown, well, would that be such a bad thing? VOD is the new direct-to-video, but it's not exactly the new direct-to-video. The term used to be shorthand for low-budget movies not good enough to warrant a theatrical release, or at least not good enough to convince distribution execs to spend the marketing cash it would take to get butts in seats. But in the age of streaming, Netflix, Netflix and Chill, Amazon, Hulu, and video on demand, non-theatrical releases only widen opportunities for eyeballs for smaller independent films to be seen at a fraction of the cost—and great indie films have benefited for it.

With lowered stakes came new chances to take risks, and this new, lower-profile world might double as a new laboratory. "I like to break forms, try different things, and I don't think studios are comfortable with that. But in an independently spirited film, I can do that," Cage told Freeman. Some of the time, anyway. Working in VOD could mean doing time in uninspired efforts like *Vengeance: A Love Story* and *Inconceivable*. But it also presented the chance to act alongside his brother Christopher and revive *Deadfall*'s Eddie King, awful wig, makeup, and all, for the crime thriller *Arsenal*. Because . . . why not? Who working on that film would tell him it was a bad idea?

Occasionally the films were weird or moodily compelling or both, such as *Looking Glass* and *Between Worlds*, a pair of David Lynch–inspired thrillers. The latter featured a sex scene in which Cage's long-haul trucker reads from an erotic book bearing the title *Memories* and credited to the author "Nicolas Cage." Because, again, why not? If heist movies like *211* and dystopian science-fiction thrillers with ideas their budgets could realize, like *The Humanity Bureau*, allowed less room to play, he could still bring some striking body language or odd inflection to keep it interesting. He was an actor with a job to do. That meant something.

Sometimes it even meant getting a great part. Thirty-two years after his teary scene with Kathleen Turner, Cage found himself in another basement having another heated conversation between husband and wife about disappointment and regret for the film *Mom and Dad*. Though the setting remains small-town America, just about everything else has changed from the days of *Peggy Sue Got Married*, from the budget to the genre to his character's age. Cage plays Brent Ryan, a suburban dad who'll spend much of the movie trying to murder his two children thanks to some unexplained phenomenon—maybe a disease, maybe mass hysteria—that's prompting all parents in their area to attempt to kill their offspring. Written and directed by Brian Taylor (half of the *Ghost Rider: Spirit of Vengeance* team), it's a violent, low-budget, high-concept black comedy powered by outrageous set pieces. It's also a sincere exploration of middle age and the waves of reflection and regret that come with it.

The heart of the movie arrives about halfway through, via a flashback. As punk music blares, Brent lovingly assembles a pool table in his basement while wearing a Misfits T-shirt, smoothing out the felt, meticulously making sure the table is level, reveling in his work and forgetting his troubles until his wife, Kendall (Selma Blair), interrupts. She objects to the pool table—they can't afford it, and besides, he doesn't even like pool—triggering an explosion of dissatisfaction that culminates in his smashing the table with a sledgehammer while singing "The Hokey Pokey" before saying, "You're right, honey. I hate pool."

It's a big moment, the sort beloved by meme makers and creators of YouTube clips with titles like "Nicolas Cage Freakout Power Hour." Yet, in context, the moment has meaning. Brent's fit of anger gives way to a disarmingly moving disgorgement of his disappointments and fears, a monologue about obsolescence, waning virility, and encroaching mortality that follows the sledgehammering, almost as if he had to exhaust himself to arrive at a moment of honesty with Kendall. He hates his job selling machine parts because it's "not exactly what I had in mind as a young dude," and he can't understand how time has passed so quickly. He yells not to yell but to be heard, because it's been a long time since anyone's heard him. "I remember," he says, "that kid I used to be like it was four fucking minutes ago." But that time has more than passed.

It's also hard not to think of Cage, once one of the highest-paid actors in the world, when Brent tells his wife, "My salary went from making a hundred and forty-five thousand dollars to forty-five thousand dollars," words that echo a Cage email Paul Schrader once shared with IndieWire in which the actor described himself as "an A-list actor doing A-list work who is being forced into B-list presentations because I had some hits in action films a million years ago." Cage delivers the line in the middle of a smart, compelling film made by a simpatico director. But even factoring out a pair of roles in animated films, *Mom and Dad* is just one of six Cage films released that year, all shot for a fraction of the budget of the films Cage had made a few years earlier, not all of them with a collaborator as talented as Taylor.

Some, however, were even better. A major studio would never make a film like *Mandy*, in which director Panos Cosmatos creates a melancholy fever dream of a movie from the stuff of old heavy metal album covers and bottom-shelf horror movies from the VHS era set in the forbidding forests of the Pacific Northwest in 1983. Cage stars as Red Miller, a logger who shares a home in the woods with his wife, Mandy (Andrea Riseborough), a shy artist who works at a rural gas station. When Mandy falls prey to Jeremiah Sand (Linus Roache), Red dedicates himself to taking him down.

In bare description, it's familiar stuff, the sort of revenge fantasy Cage had played many times. In execution, it's at once heartbreaking and unsettling, a film rich in atmosphere and shot through with a sense of loss, thanks to Cosmatos's command of imagery and the work of Riseborough and Cage, who begins the film with some of the tenderest work of his career and ends it in a blood-drenched frenzy. Cosmatos and a production team that included Cage's *The Trust* costar Elijah Wood wanted him for the part of Sand. Cage was interested only in playing Red, however, and the film bears out his thinking. In its most striking scene, the underwear-clad hero, moments after his wife's murder, pants and screams in despair and pain while downing most of a bottle of vodka, a dark moment of the soul that plays out in one long, unbroken shot in a harshly lighted bathroom. It's at once sad, funny, and more than a little terrifying, a raw moment of a man slipping over the edge. It wasn't written for Cage, but only he could have played it.

He was an actor with a job to do, but wasn't he something more as well? Hadn't he gone the distance? Eric Stoltz had made fun of him on the set of *Fast Times*, but who, nearly forty years later, gave much thought to Eric Stoltz? Had anyone put on a film marathon dedicated solely to the work of Eric Stoltz? And if they did, would Stoltz himself crash it, as Cage did the Alamo Drafthouse "Caged" Marathon in Austin in 2017? Would he favor them with a dramatic reading of Edgar Allan Poe's "The Tell-Tale Heart," as Cage did? Would he put it all out there for them?

Was the appreciation sometimes ironic? Did it matter? In a memorable 2014 episode of the sitcom *Community*, one character, Abed Nadir, approaches the brink of madness by forcing himself to consider a seemingly simple question: "Nicolas Cage: good or bad?" Abed's professor tells the class, "I promise you, the question has no answer." By episode's end, Abed reluctantly has to agree. As one of his classmates puts it while watching an unseen film consisting largely of Cage grunting in distress, how can the words *good* or *bad* apply to a performance in which Cage "seems scared to smell [a] flower but happy to get shot?"

But, in reality, the question did have an answer, at least in the mind of *Community* creator Dan Harmon, who said of the episode, "unless you're a total cynical dick, you have to embrace the fact that Nicolas Cage is a pretty good actor. He's done a lot of weird, dumb movies, but that was supposed to be the point of the episode—that Nicolas Cage is a metaphor for God, or for society, or for the self, or something. It's like—what is Nicolas Cage? What is he? Is he an idiot? Or a genius? Can you write him off, or is he inexplicably bound to your soul?"

Sometimes irony has a way of looping back around to sincerity. And sometimes an actor becomes more than the sum of his roles, a magnet for interest simply by being himself. In 2019, Cage embarked on a four-day marriage that ended with his filing for divorce, claiming he was too intoxicated to realize what he was doing. In the midst of it all, he showed up at an LA karaoke bar to deliver a fevered rendition of Prince's "Purple Rain." The cameras were watching. He had to know they would be, that this would become yet another weird Nicolas Cage story. But maybe it didn't matter. "It was more like primal-scream therapy," Cage told a reporter for the *New York Times* when asked about the moment, an answer that only raises more questions.

All the while, the movies kept rolling out, one after the other: *A Score to Settle*, *Running with the Devil*, *Kill Chain*, *Primal*, *Grand Isle*, *Jiu Jitsu*, *Color Out of Space*, and so on. Of the bunch, only the last, a bizarre, stylish H. P. Lovecraft adaptation, was especially good, but they all had *something* to recommend them. And they all offered Cage a chance to act.

In 2018, Cage told an interviewer he'd like to retire from acting in three or four years, but he showed no signs of slowing down. The roles kept coming in. He kept accepting them. A-list work, B-list presentations—it was all work, and it seemed to be working for him. Over the course of Cage's career, Hollywood had changed, undergoing shifts as profound in their own way as the advent of sound is for *Sunset Boulevard*'s Norma Desmond. But he wasn't in retreat, holed up in a mansion living among memories of past glories. He still got close-ups all the time, and he was always ready for them.

In 2019, Cage received a screenplay then making the rounds by the comedy writing team of Tom Gormican and Kevin Etten. A sample script the writers thought no one would ever make, it was written as a way to demonstrate that they could change gears. In it, Cage, its central character, is an actor struggling with his B-list status, hungry for a comeback and in frequent communication with his younger self, a cocky young actor disappointed with what Cage has made of himself. After his latest professional disappointment, Cage takes a gig attending the birthday party of a wealthy fan who lives in a house filled with movie memorabilia, including some key pieces from Cage's own career, intensifying his reflection as he comes to realize that not all is what it seems and that he might have stumbled into a scenario out of one of his own movies.

The script is a meditation on stardom and Hollywood self-absorption, changing tastes, shifting fortunes, and Cage's eccentric public image, one that depicts him as burdened by his past triumphs and a bit battered by his reversed fortunes but still capable of greatness, still a star like nobody else. Gormican and Etten called it *The Unbearable Weight of Massive Talent*. The title was a joke, but not really, not in the ways that counted.

Cage agreed to play the part they'd written for him.

Afterword: Cage to the Future

On July 13, 1981, Nicolas Cage (then Nicolas Coppola) made his national debut via the *The Best of Times*. Two thousand twenty-one will mark his fortieth year as a professional actor. That nice, round number provided some of the inspiration for this book. The announcement of *The Unbearable Weight of Massive Talent*, with its meta-Cage hall-of-mirrors premise as I was writing the book confirmed the instinct that now was the right time to dig into Cage's career. The confirmations kept coming throughout 2021, a personally tumultuous year for Cage in which lost his mother and married for the fifth time. January saw the Sundance premiere of *Prisoners of the Ghostland*, a memorably strange film by cult-favorite Japanese director Sion Sono in which Cage wears a costume inspired by the leather jumpsuit worn by Elvis in his *'68 Comeback Special* and pushes his delivery of the word *testicles* to amusing extremes. February brought *Willy's Wonderland*, a horror comedy in search of a cult following that pits Cage against possessed robot animals in an off-brand Chuck E. Cheese. At the dawn of the 2020s, Cage seemed less averse to plunging into weirdness than ever.

It's easy to detect a creeping sense of winking self-awareness in some of these projects, but maybe it's just a newfound self-confidence, an understanding that Cage's name brings with it certain expectations and that he's better off acknowledging and maybe subverting those expectations than running away from them. In a short documentary about the making of *Spider-Man: Into the Spider-Verse*—for which Cage provides the voice of the hardboiled Spider-Man Noir—Paul Watling, the project's head of story, recounts director Rodney Rothman offering notes on Cage's performance. Cage's reply: "Oh. You want me to go full Cage." An understanding of who you are and what you do may be the best shield against irony. Or maybe it's sometimes best to drop all shields. July 2021 saw the release of *Pig*, which from a distance doesn't look *that* different from other Cage projects. A first feature directed by Michael Sarnoski, who cowrote the script with producer Vanessa Block, *Pig* stars Cage as Robin Feld, a woods-dwelling hermit who makes his living selling rare truffles he finds with the help of his pig. When his pig is stolen, however, tracking her down becomes his sole reason for living.

That may sound like a film designed to mimic *John Wick* or *Taken*, a blood-soaked tale of revenge with a staggering body count. It's not. Instead, it's an eccentric exploration of grief and forgiveness, the struggles between fathers and sons, and the way art often conflicts with commercial success anchored by a deeply moving Cage performance in which scenes of terseness and silence give way to remarkable monologues. It's a performance of rare vulnerability, one in which elements of absurd comedy live beside moments of crushing emotion. If this book were *only* an attempt to provide a definitive answer to the question, "Nicolas Cage: good or bad?," *Pig* would have made it irrelevant. The answer's right there.

This book may be finished, but I'll keep watching Cage's movies. I've been watching Nicolas Cage's work for almost as long as there's been a Nicolas Cage, inspired as an eighth-grader to check out a weird-looking movie called *Raising Arizona*, thanks to a glowing review from Gene Siskel and Roger Ebert. After that, I kept an eye out for Cage (and for the Coens and Holly Hunter and others involved with the film). I'm sure I'm not the only moviegoer for whom Cage's work has helped open up new horizons, whether through his collaborations with David Lynch, the Coens, and Spike Jonze or by his providing an intriguing element of oddness in an otherwise conventional film.

From the start, I hoped this book would serve two purposes. I wanted to provide a sincere, if clear-eyed and not-uncritical, appreciation of Cage as a unique talent. And I wanted to use his life and work as a lens through which to consider the ways filmmaking has changed over the course of his career. I've seen the movies change radically, both by increments and in grand shifts, over the course of a career spent writing about them (and, prior to that, simply watching them). Even when Cage hasn't been a part of those changes—and he often has—he's been affected by them. And in retrospect, he's often been ahead of the curve, most recently by appearing in movies meant to be seen at home before streaming services normalized watching movies at home and before COVID-19 made it compulsory. Simply by persevering, he's seen it all, and his movies capture the face of a changing industry.

The first question most people asked me when I said I was writing this book was whether I'd be talking to Cage. I always said I didn't expect to. Early in the project, I reached out to his representation to gauge interest but never got a response—which didn't surprise me. Cage's days of refusing to talk to press might be well behind him, but talking about himself is clearly not an activity he relishes. That's fine by me. I conceived this as a book about Cage's movies and Cage as a public figure whose distance, unusual performances, and occasionally enigmatic interviews have allowed others to interpret him as they like and whose career intersected with a lot of shifts in the foundation of Hollywood. (I made a point of never trying to find out anything about Cage's private life beyond what's already in the public record, both out of politeness and because it fell outside the scope of the book.) Talking to Cage would have made this a book about his perspective on his life and career, and while that's a book I'd love to read, it's not the one I set out to write.

I *did* talk to Cage once, however. During a Chicago press tour for *Adaptation.* in 2002, I interviewed him, Spike Jonze, and Charlie Kaufman at the same time. The strategy of putting together three people who did not particularly like doing interviews was seemingly designed to disarm them, in the hope that the discussion would be less awkward for all involved. It worked. We had a pleasant, if not particularly revealing, conversation about the film that lasted about twenty minutes, after which the next interviewer showed up and likely asked variations on the same questions and yielded variations on the same answers. Such is the business of interviewing famous people (except on the rare occasion when you encounter someone who relishes telling stories or who has stopped caring what anyone thinks of them or whom they piss off).

You do, however, occasionally get to meet celebrities face-to-face, which is usually an unnerving experience. Some are shorter than you'd imagined or more ordinary looking or, occasionally, even more glamorous up close than on the big screen. Cage looked like, well, Nicolas Cage: intense, sincere, a little unreadable. But when the conversation turned to how he allowed himself to be depicted on posters, he made a ridiculous face and . . . ah, there was the kid who grew up watching silent movie actors, who filed away ideas and then refined and built on those ideas while falling in and out of fashion with the changing times. There, for a moment, was the full Cage.

The Complete Cageography:
A Capsule Guide to the Films of Nicolas Cage

(Presented in release order and rated on a scale of * to
****. These ratings refer to the film as a whole, not just
Cage's performance. All opinions are the author's. Any
disagreements are welcome.)

Best of Times (1981 TV Pilot) **

Even as top-name actors have turned to television during prestige TV's
boom years, Cage has remained steadfastly committed to movies. Nonetheless, the seventeen-year-old actor then known as Nicolas Coppola made his
debut in this pilot for a never-to-be series starring his friend Crispin Glover
as a normal (!) '80s teen trying to figure out girls, grown-ups, and other
pressing matters. A series of vignettes—some comic, some dramatic, some
musical—the project feels like the work of a middle-aged creator trying to
figure out what's up with the kids these days. Often shirtless, Cage plays a
vaguely Stallone-ish beach-loving slab of muscle who gives Glover advice
on the opposite sex and delivers a heartfelt monologue about fearing the
draft and being sent to fight in El Salvador.

Fast Times at Ridgemont High (1982) ****

Cage makes only a blink-and-you'll-miss-him appearance as "Brad's Bud"
in this classic teen comedy, the cast of which doubles as a list of up-and-
coming stars.

Valley Girl (1983) ***1/2

For his breakthrough role, Cage dropped his family name and won the part
of a Hollywood kid caught in a *Romeo and Juliet*–inspired romance with a
girl from the San Fernando Valley (Deborah Foreman). Packaged like a
sex romp in the *Porky's* mold, the film works beautifully as both a sweet (if

not particularly deep) love story and a historical document of a particular moment in California teen history. Martha Coolidge brings a light touch, and Cage arrives as an intense, smoldering presence, his movie star magnetism already in evidence (even with chest hair puzzlingly shaved into the shape of a triangle). Bonus points for having one of the best soundtracks of its era (or maybe of any era).

Rumble Fish (1983) ***1/2
Filmed before *Valley Girl* but released after, this S. E. Hinton adaptation directed by Francis Ford Coppola gave Cage his first notable role. Here he plays Smokey, sidekick to a sensitive teen rebel played by Matt Dillon and standing out even in a cast that includes Mickey Rourke, Dennis Hopper, and Diane Lane and in the midst of a film defined by Coppola's striking use of black-and-white photography. The shoot wasn't easy, however, and the mockery of others helped inspire Cage to change his surname.

Racing with the Moon (1984) **1/2
Actor turned director Richard Benjamin followed his well-loved directorial debut, *My Favorite Year*, with this sweet-natured, sensitive (if a little pokey) Steve Kloves–penned coming-of-age story starring Sean Penn as Henry, a young man who spends his final days before shipping off to fight in World War II romancing a pretty girl (Elizabeth McGovern) whom he mistakenly believes to be a well-to-do "Gatsby." Cage plays Nicky, Henry's wild, wrong-side-of-the-tracks pal who drinks too much and asks Penn to help him earn money to pay for his girlfriend's abortion. Cage works as a pinsetter alongside Penn, plays a drunk scene in which he tries to get a tattoo, and gets the chance to deliver an impassioned rendition of the song "Tangerine" while cleaning up in a bowling alley.

The Cotton Club (1984) ***
A famously troubled production, *The Cotton Club* reunited Francis Ford Coppola with his *Godfather* collaborators Mario Puzo and Robert Evans. It didn't go as well this time, though the film is filled with electric moments (most of them musical). Richard Gere stars as "Dixie" Dwyer, a musician who reluctantly gets swept up in the business of New York gangster "Dutch" Schultz (James Remar) as the Roaring Twenties turn into the less-roaring Thirties. Cage plays Dixie's brother, Vincent, who's far more enthusiastic about gangster life. It's easy to see the appeal here. Later dubbed "Mad Dog," Vincent is a supporting but key player in the film. If this were *The Godfather*, he'd have the Sonny role. But it's not, and while Cage brings a lot

of wiry energy to the movie and gets some memorable moments, he mostly sinks into the ensemble. Frustrated at all the parts he had to decline during the film's long production, he made this the final time he appeared as an ensemble player in any movie.

Birdy (1984) ****

Probably the best use of the Alan Parker aesthetic, this stylish but disturbing adaptation of William Wharton's 1978 novel casts Cage as Al, a suave kid growing up in 1960s Philadelphia who befriends his oddball classmate and next-door neighbor, nicknamed "Birdy" (Matthew Modine) because of his fondness for birds. The film flashes back and forth from their time growing up to a period after their return from Vietnam, when Al's been badly wounded and Birdy has withdrawn into a semi-catatonic state that finds him frequently adopting the mannerisms of birds. Cage famously had some past-their-prime baby teeth pulled and stayed in bandages for weeks to help get into character, but for all the Method-inspired prep work, it's one of his most naturalistic performances. It's also one of his best, particularly his raw, wounded postwar scenes in which he desperately tries to save Birdy from being permanently committed. We see him as a teenage ladies' man and as a broken veteran who can only weep when a sympathetic nurse offers herself up to him.

The Boy in Blue (1986) *1/2

In this by-the-numbers underdog sports biopic about a legendary Canadian sculler, Cage plays Ned Hanlan as a backwoods rascal whose raw talent rescues him from a life of moonshine running. He seems puzzled about how to make the character, or the material, interesting in any way, though his intense physical preparation shows in his bulked-up physique.

Peggy Sue Got Married (1986) ***1/2

This time-traveling fantasy directed by uncle Francis Ford Coppola contains one of the key Cage performances, one in which he plays a high school dreamboat as a pompadoured kid with weird fake teeth and a voice borrowed from Gumby's horse sidekick, Pokey. Costar Kathleen Turner hated the performance, and Cage would almost certainly have lost his job if not for Coppola's intervention. Yet the movie bears out the wisdom of Cage's choices, giving the lie to the nostalgic fantasies of the man her estranged husband used to be that have filled Turner's character with regret. It turns out he was just a goofy, vulnerable boy with his own unfulfilled dreams all along.

Raising Arizona (1987) ****

Cage reportedly didn't always see eye to eye with Joel and Ethan Coen, but he fits perfectly into their live-action cartoon world as a trying-to-go-straight criminal who kidnaps one of five babies born to a wealthy family in an attempt to create the family denied him and his wife (Holly Hunter) by infertility. Cage rises to the physically demanding challenges of the role but also serves as its soulful emotional anchor as a man who'll do anything to keep the love of his life happy. Like the Coens, he's wild and constantly moving but also, especially in the film's final moments, incredibly touching, tapping into the deep yearning at the heart of the story.

Moonstruck (1987) ****

In Cage's most romantic performance, he plays an opera-loving, one-handed baker who falls for his brother's fiancée (Cher). Despite his often-deserved reputation for going to extremes, he's convincing as a man who finds his excesses unexpectedly tamed by the love of a good woman. Cher fought for Cage to play the part, which didn't stop him from clashing with director Norman Jewison or suggesting that he found the movie too tame during the acting-as-punk-rock phase of his career, but the sweet, lyrical film benefits from his misfit presence.

Vampire's Kiss (1989) ****

The font from which all future Cage weirdness sprang, this low-budget horror movie casts him as a literary agent who may or may not be a vampire after being bitten by a strange woman (who may or may not exist). Cage would later refer to this film as his "laboratory," and he clearly revels in the creative freedom to try out any idea that pops into his head, whether eating a live cockroach or delivering an increasingly crazed recitation of the alphabet. It's sometimes hard to shake the sense, especially in later moments of untamed exuberance, that he would have been perfectly happy making variations on this movie for the rest of his career.

Time to Kill (1989) **

For this true obscurity, which barely even made it to American video stores, Cage traveled to Africa to play an Italian soldier in Ethiopia for director Giuliano Montaldo. He's good. The movie, essentially an overextended metaphor for Italian colonialism, isn't.

Fire Birds (1990) **

Cage's first attempt at action stardom asks him to play a cocky, all-American military hero. It's outside his skill set, but the movie around him—rightly dubbed "*Top Gun* with helicopters" and filled with war-on-drugs-era right-wing bravado—doesn't do him any favors.

Wild at Heart (1990) ***1/2

In David Lynch's dark fantasia of an America obsessed with sex and violence, Cage plays a parolee deeply in love with the girl he left behind when he went to prison (Laura Dern). Cage channels Elvis Presley for a smoky, lustful performance in which both he and Dern hold on to their characters' essential innocence as the world goes to hell around them. It never quite gels into a masterpiece like some of Lynch's other films, but it's a pleasure to watch Cage and Dern match the energy of Lynch's let's-try-anything spirit.

Zandalee (1991) **

An erotic (or "erotic") drama filled with rich New Orleans atmosphere, graphic sex, and unintentional laughs, *Zandalee* imagines a love triangle with the eponymous Zandalee (Erika Anderson) at one point and Cage and Judge Reinhold at the other two. The male leads fight a battle for the silliest facial hair to a draw, but Cage otherwise blows everyone else off the screen with his explosive performance as a frustrated artist who at one point covers himself in black paint (symbolism!).

Honeymoon in Vegas (1992) ***

Cage wandered back into the mainstream with this romantic comedy about a sweet private eye with commitment issues whose too-good-for-him girlfriend (Sarah Jessica Parker) agrees to spend the weekend with a gambler (James Caan) to pay off his debt. Romantic chaos ensues, climaxing in a bunch of Elvis impersonators skydiving into Las Vegas with Cage's character in tow. Director Andrew Bergman excels at making crowd-pleasing comedies with heart and a little bit of edge, and Cage's performance as an increasingly frantic straight man fits nicely into Bergman's comic vision.

Amos & Andrew (1993) *1/2

The best that can be said about this tone-deaf race relations comedy in which Cage plays a criminal set up to take the fall when a racist police force racially profiles a celebrity academic (Samuel L. Jackson) is that all involved probably meant well.

Deadfall (1993) **1/2

A favorite of those who seek out Cage's most unhinged moments, *Dead-fall* finds him sporting a Halloween costume–quality wig, mustache, and fake teeth and speaking in a ridiculous voice to play violent criminal Eddie King in a film directed by brother Christopher Coppola. Cage is fun, and the bizarre film also features a parade of stars that includes James Coburn, Charlie Sheen, Peter Fonda, Talia Shire, and Mickey Dolenz (!). Eddie King would return years later in the loose 2017 sequel and/or prequel, *Arsenal*.

Red Rock West (1993) ***1/2

In John Dahl's sun-baked film noir that became an unexpected art house hit, Cage plays a wounded veteran looking for work in the American South-west only to stumble into a murder-for-hire plot. Like Dahl, Cage has fun playing against noir expectations, in this case as a down-on-his-luck man of innate decency trying his best not to be corrupted by a vice-filled world.

Guarding Tess (1994) ***

Sitcom great Hugh Wilson's comedy about a terse Secret Service agent (Cage) unhappily assigned to protect a temperamental former First Lady (Shirley MacLaine) falls apart in its too-serious finale, but it's a joy to watch the two stars play against one another until then. Cage's early career often found him playing against equally memorable female costars, whether as a romantic interest or a sparring partner, a dynamic that would occur less frequently after he became an A-list star.

It Could Happen to You (1994) ***1/2

In another Andrew Bergman comedy, and another pairing with remarkable chemistry, Cage plays a New York cop who promises a waitress (Bridget Fonda) half of any winnings on a lottery ticket when he finds himself without cash to leave a tip. The twist: he hits it big, a development that invites trouble into his marriage but opens up new romantic possibilities. Cage and Fonda radiate virtue as they fall for each other against the backdrop of a fairy-tale New York City—albeit one filled with New Yorkers who some-times aren't as selfless as the central lovebirds. After *Honeymoon* and *Tess*, the film closed out what Cage would later call his "Sunshine Trilogy" of upbeat comedies.

Trapped in Paradise (1994) **

A fun idea—criminals rob a small-town bank at Christmas and then find themselves stranded amid a bunch of friendly locals—gets turned into a dismal comedy in which Cage plays a brother to thieving doofuses played by Dana Carvey and Jon Lovitz. After a run of comedies, Cage seems a bit trapped himself. Maybe that's part of why he took to the decidedly non-comic script sent to him while he was filming the movie, the story of an alcoholic who moves to Las Vegas to die.

Kiss of Death (1995) ***

This remake of a noir classic was supposed to make David Caruso a movie star. Caruso's fine as the glowering ex-con hero, but it's Cage who steals the film as the musclebound, asthmatic gangster with the doubly diminutive name of "Little Junior Brown." He's magnetic as a bad guy who's essentially a slab of coiled menace (or, as Junior might put it, a "BAD" guy, made up of little but "balls, attitude, and direction").

Leaving Las Vegas (1995) ****

Even if Cage had never won the Best Actor Oscar for his depiction of a self-destructive screenwriter living out his last days in Sin City—if the film had never been widely seen, as Cage once suspected would be the case—this is the sort of performance that would have lived on, talked about with reverence by those who found it. Cage brings all his skills to bear here, playing the doomed Ben Sanderson with a mix of bravado, dark humor, and frightening vulnerability. Winning helped elevate him to another level of stardom, one that made it hard for him to return to small projects that demanded this kind of high-wire work.

The Rock (1996) ***

Nicolas Cage: action star. Just a few years earlier, this seemed like a fairly ridiculous idea, and part of the appeal of this first foray into the world of 1990s action blockbusters comes from the way Cage plays the wonderfully named Dr. Stanley Goodspeed as a nerd with little interest in kicking ass and blowing away bad guys. By film's end, however, he's every inch the action movie hero. So was Cage.

Con Air (1997) **1/2

Beneath flowing locks, Cage plays a good-hearted tough guy on his way home from prison who ends up aboard a plane filled with the most hardcore criminals in America. (The trip hits some turbulence.) *Con Air* benefits from a lack of seriousness—a trait embodied by Cage's knowingly big performance—but by the time it comes down for a climax on the Las Vegas Strip, it's also become pretty exhausting.

Face/Off (1997) ****

An exploration of the thin line between good and evil, a meta-meditation on acting and movie stardom, the purest distillation of director John Woo's

Hong Kong–born sensibility, and the best action film in which Cage would ever appear, *Face/Off* casts Cage as a flamboyant terrorist-for-hire who changes identities with the FBI agent hunting him (John Travolta). Travolta does a killer Cage impression. Cage takes the opportunity to play the role of a man tormented by being forced to become what he hates. It's a masterpiece that allows him the room he needs to explore every possibility suggested by the film's bizarre premise.

City of Angels (1998) ***
Cage plays an angel drawn to earth by his attraction to a troubled surgeon (Meg Ryan) in a remake of Wim Wenders's *Wings of Desire*. The film affords both leads a chance to break out of the boxes their stardom helped create for them, giving Ryan a character that's anything but the sort of cutesy rom-com role that made her famous and letting Cage play a being who's almost too sensitive to live in the world of men. Director Brad Silberling makes great use of LA landscapes and both stars' big, expressive eyes.

Snake Eyes (1998) ***
Sold as another Cage action film, this twisty Brian De Palma thriller confused moviegoers expecting more blood and bullets. That the film, even on its own terms, has problems didn't help, but Cage has fun playing a cop who loves being on the take and who enjoys everything corruption brings him—until he has to face a moral reckoning.

8mm (1999) **
A nasty, exploitative work about underground pornography and snuff films, this Joel Schumacher film is almost redeemed by its performances, particularly Joaquin Phoenix as a porn store clerk who thinks himself above the world he's come to know too well. Cage is good, too, dialing back his instincts to play a man trying to keep his cool and hold on to his soul despite the nastiness around him.

Bringing Out the Dead (1999) ****
A dream team-up that put Cage in the hands of screenwriter Paul Schrader and director Martin Scorsese, *Bringing Out the Dead* didn't find the audience it deserved in 1999. That means moviegoers missed the creative team behind *Taxi Driver* making a return trip to New York City's underside, this time through the weary eyes of Frank Pierce, an ambulance driver who has seen too much and can't imagine a time when his calling might allow him to

look away. Some manic flashes aside, Cage leans into the exhaustion, playing it as a state that produces a kind of madness all its own.

Gone in 60 Seconds (2000) **

Cage went to the action movie well one too many times with this headache-inducing tale of LA car thieves. The star's love of exotic cars and Steve McQueen shines through, but it doesn't prove infectious.

The Family Man (2000) **1/2

Can a New York business tycoon find happiness in an alternate time line in which he marries his college sweetheart and has to live in—gasp!—New Jersey? A sense of insincerity (and condescension) colors the Capraesque aspirations of this holiday fantasy, though Cage and costar Téa Leoni have some nice chemistry.

Captain Corelli's Mandolin (2001) **1/2

This splashy adaptation of a best-selling novel with a cast of international stars features Cage playing a bon vivant Italian soldier (with an accent to match) but feels like a product of the prestige picture assembly line.

Windtalkers (2002) ***

War is hell in this second team-up with John Woo, in which Cage plays a soldier charged with protecting (or, failing that, killing) a World War II Navajo code talker. It's not the action movie audiences might have expected, but it *is* a fine, uncompromising war film.

Adaptation. (2002) ****

In a movie about screenwriting mechanics and the difficulties of maintaining artistic integrity in a film business driven by profits and imitation, Cage deftly plays both Charlie and Donald Kaufman, twins with decidedly different approaches to Hollywood. It's both the sort of performance(s) only Cage could deliver and like nothing he'd ever done before. And as an actor with a professed fondness for both distinctive visions and blockbuster entertainment, he's especially well suited to play a man torn between the demands of each.

Sonny (2002) **

Cage's sole film as a director benefits from New Orleans locations and a fine cast led by James Franco, but it's a bit too shapeless and indistinct to be memorable.

Matchstick Men (2003) ****

Like *Bringing Out the Dead*, another overlooked pairing with a top-tier director, this Ridley Scott film features Cage playing a con man struggling with obsessive-compulsive tendencies who's forced to reexamine his life when his daughter resurfaces. What could have been an invitation for a gimmicky performance instead allows Cage to craft a three-dimensional portrait of a man whose tics serve as symptoms of a deeper crisis.

National Treasure (2004) ***

Cage returned to the world of blockbuster action films by way of this goofy, kid-friendly delight in which he plays a fortune hunter who's a patriotic history nerd at heart.

Lord of War (2005) ***

As much long-form magazine piece as thriller, this Andrew Niccol film explores the dark world of arms sales. Cage plays an unrepentant master of the game for whom any moral concerns sound as faint echoes at best.

The Weather Man (2005) ***

Playing another man at a crossroads, Cage stars as a Chicago weatherman with a dying father, marital problems, and troubled children who's forced to confront his own limitations. Essentially an indie drama with the budget of a much bigger film, this darkly comic look at celebrity and looming middle age bombed at the box office but deserves a second look.

The Ant Bully (2006) **

An all-star cast that includes Julia Roberts and Meryl Streep supplies the voices for this annoying, frenetic, if well-intentioned story of a bullied kid who learns some lessons about compassion and self-reliance when he's shrunk down to ant size. Cage mostly plays it straight as Zoc, the ant wizard who does the shrinking.

World Trade Center (2006) ***

Oliver Stone turns an extraordinary tragedy into a defiantly human-scaled tale of survival that allows Cage to play an ordinary Joe whose selfless sense of duty leaves him injured and stuck in the rubble of the 9/11 attacks.

The Wicker Man (2006) *

Both Cage and director Neil LaBute have defended this remake of a classic horror film, and Cage's meltdown-filled performance, as stabs at dark comedy. On paper, that works. As a viewing experience, however, the plodding story goes nowhere and any comedy seems purely unintentional.

Ghost Rider (2007) **

A lifelong comic book fan, Cage finally got to play a superhero in this big-screen adaptation of a cult-favorite Marvel character. All the eccentric touches he brings to the role can't make the film feel any less soulless and tame, however.

Next (2007) **

Some of the same problems evident in *Ghost Rider* would plague this loose Philip K. Dick adaptation in which Cage plays a magician who can see into the future—but not very far. Neat gimmick. Dull movie.

National Treasure: Book of Secrets (2007) ***

More of the same as in the first *National Treasure*, but the same worked last time, so why not? This fun sequel doesn't take any chances, but it works anyway.

Bangkok Dangerous (2008) *1/2

Hong Kong's Pang Brothers broke into action movie filmmaking in 1999 with a film about a deaf-mute master assassin. This remake with the same title throws out the central conceit, leaving Cage to play a master assassin with no real defining characteristics. The movie around him is similarly indistinct. In thrillers, Cage sometimes struggles to animate underwritten protagonists beyond giving them a glower and an air of deep concern, a habit that can be traced back to this period and that would recur in the years to come.

Knowing (2009) **1/2

Animating an underwritten character is not a problem here, in a film in which Cage brings a sense of loss and worry to the role of an MIT professor who comes to believe an elementary school classroom might predict the end of the world. The movie, however, seems to exist mostly to showcase scenes of mass extinction before building to a ridiculous ending.

G-Force (2009) **1/2

In an animated film produced by Jerry Bruckheimer, Cage plays a mole named Speckles, part of a band of intelligent rodents recruited to work as spies. It's about as good as that premise suggests, though Cage does a memorably silly voice.

Astro Boy (2009) **

The classic anime hero gets an unimpressive Westernized remake via a cheap-looking animated feature. Cage plays it straight as Dr. Tenma, Astro's dad/creator.

Bad Lieutenant: Port of Call New Orleans (2009) ****

A perfect match of material, director, and star, this spiritual sequel to *Bad Lieutenant* finds Cage's corrupt addict policeman running amok in the Crescent City even as he's drawn into the case of some murdered immigrants. Cage uses his gift for big, Expressionist performances to depict his character as a man struggling to hold on to his soul before it slips away from him for good. The viral trailer promised excesses, but the film as a whole beautifully matches grand gestures with nuanced touches and a deep concern for its characters' struggles.

Kick-Ass (2010) **1/2

Cage plays a square, loving father who's also a bloodthirsty vigilante hell-bent on revenge and willing to turn his daughter into a murderer in this irreverent superhero send-up. The film has more attitude than insights (or heart), but Cage is fun as a kind of sitcom dad by day, off-brand Batman by night.

The Sorcerer's Apprentice (2010) **

Another attempt at a kid-friendly, Disney-produced blockbuster, this tale of Arthurian sorcery in the twenty-first century lacks the charm of the *National Treasure* films. (That Cage plays a far less likable protagonist doesn't help.) What could have started a new franchise became a dead end, and a farewell to big-budget studio movies built around his star power.

Season of the Witch (2011) **

Cage battles demons alongside Ron Perlman in a medieval Europe ravaged by the Black Death. That sounds like the setup for a fun horror movie, but it's mostly a slog.

Drive Angry (2011) **

A supernatural action film designed to take advantage of the short-lived 3-D craze, *Drive Angry* casts Cage as "John Milton," a restless spirit who returns to earth to drive fast cars, exact revenge, and save his granddaughter from Satan worshippers. Think an R-rated, tongue-half-in-cheek *Ghost Rider*, but not as much fun as that might sound (though William Fichtner has some nice moments as the demonic "Accountant" sent to drag Milton back to hell). It set the table for the many revenge stories in which Cage would star in the decade that followed.

Trespass (2011) *1/2
Vivid work from Cage and costars Nicole Kidman and Ben Mendelsohn can't paper over the shortcomings of a lurid, loud, but overly familiar hostage drama. The film played a handful of theaters but essentially debuted on video-on-demand services, the first time since *Deadfall* that a Cage movie essentially skipped theaters.

Seeking Justice (2011) **1/2
Cage stars as a New Orleans schoolteacher who, after the rape of his wife (January Jones), gets drawn into a secret society that dispenses punishment to those who evade the law. With lots of location photography and a menacing supporting performance from Guy Pearce, it's far from the worst of its type.

Ghost Rider: Spirit of Vengeance (2012) **1/2
Cage's second outing as Johnny Blaze is an appreciably lower-budget adventure with the *Crank* team of Neveldine and Taylor offering only a few flashes of their over-the-top style. The image of Ghost Rider peeing fire earns it half a star.

Stolen (2012) **
Cage reunites with *Con Air* director Simon West for a heist film/hostage drama set in New Orleans. Cage plays a criminal trying to go straight while Josh Lucas gets the most florid moments as a friend turned evil lunatic. It's a watchable time-waster.

The Croods (2013) ***
In a pleasant DreamWorks comedy, Cage provides the voice of "Grug," a risk-averse caveman forced to explore the world when he'd rather remain safe at home.

The Frozen Ground (2013) ***
A fact-based story about an Anchorage detective (Cage) on the trail of a serial killer, this moody procedural suffers at times from too many familiar-seeming elements (particularly Cage's character's had-it-up-to-here wife), but it also smartly lets its two leads chillingly underplay their roles. Both

Cage and Cusack bring a slow burn that works nicely against their snowy surroundings.

Joe (2013) ***1/2

For this low-key but violent drama directed by David Gordon Green, Cage returns to the naturalistic approach of *Birdy* to play a well-meaning but demon-plagued man who befriends a teenage boy (Tye Sheridan) with an abusive father. The style suits him just as well in middle age. Disappearing behind a bushy beard and speaking in a low grumble, he turns in a performance that suggests an actor who's discovered a new gear.

Rage (2014) *

Joe would ultimately prove an outlier in the 2010s, however, a decade that mostly found Cage pursuing work in low-budget, VOD-friendly fare like this revenge story in which he plays a Mobile, Alabama–based gangster who falls back into a life of crime to avenge the death of his daughter. Cage's sullen performance matches the dreary execution, but the movie offers virtually nothing to recommend it. It's the worst movie he ever made.

Left Behind (2014) *1/2

The 2010s saw the mainstreaming of faith-based entertainment, including this second adaptation of a popular series of novels set during and after the events of the Book of Revelation. Cage stars as an airline pilot whose copilot and others disappear mid-flight thanks to the Rapture. Though kind of fascinating as a cultural artifact, it's a lousy film.

Dying of the Light (2014) **1/2

The streak of bad luck continued with this Paul Schrader–directed thriller in which Cage plays a CIA agent suffering from a rare form of dementia who tries to capture a terrorist before his condition worsens. The film was taken out of Schrader's hands, but Cage and costar Anton Yelchin are quite good, and you can see the more intriguing version of the film beneath the surface. Schrader would later release to torrent sites an approximation of his original cut (under the title *Dark*) that bears this notion out and includes a hallucinatory, abstract ending reminiscent of *2001: A Space Odyssey*.

Outcast (2014) **1/2

The Chinese market became increasingly important in the 2010s, leading to occasional coproductions that mixed Western and Eastern talent and settings. Cage lets loose to play the "White Ghost," a disillusioned Knight Templar who walks away from the Crusades to start a new life in China. He's more supporting character than star—that role belongs to Hayden Christensen—but he brings considerable flavor to a mostly by-the-book period action film.

The Runner (2015) ***

Cage plays a lauded-then-disgraced New Orleans politician attempting a comeback in a solid, no-frills political drama that serves as a reminder of how good he could be in a straightforward role.

Pay the Ghost (2015) **1/2

What do you do when you lose your son on Halloween night and suspect otherworldly forces might have taken him? If you're Mike Lawford (Cage), you keep looking, no matter how strange the search gets. A supernatural drama in the M. Night Shyamalan mold, *Pay the Ghost* ultimately doesn't go anywhere, but Cage brings some emotional heft to the lead role.

The Trust (2016) ***

By the mid-2010s, Cage was making movies at such a rapid pace that it became a challenge for even the most dedicated fans to keep up (and releasing enough duds to discourage all but completists from trying). This meant that gems like this nasty, stylish, darkly comic heist thriller sometimes got lost in the mix. Cage plays a Las Vegas cop who ropes his coworker (Elijah Wood) into robbing some bad guys of their ill-gotten fortune.

Snowden (2016) ***

This Oliver Stone film dramatizes Edward Snowden's (Joseph Gordon-Levitt) decision to leak classified information about privacy-threatening overreach in the intelligence community. Playing a veteran instructor/cautionary tale, Cage shows up in only a couple of scenes, but they provide some key moments.

USS Indianapolis: Men of Courage (2016) **

A sprawling, budget-impaired attempt to tell the horrific story of the U.S. cruiser sunk in the Pacific Theater after delivering the atom bomb, leaving hundreds of sailors to attempt to fend off sharks, this film comes to life only in a final act, in which Capt. Charles McVay III (Cage) gets railroaded into serving as a scapegoat for the incident.

Dog Eat Dog (2016) **

Another team-up with Paul Schrader, and a reunion with *Wild at Heart* costar Willem Dafoe (star of the Cage-produced *Shadow of the Vampire*),

Dog Eat Dog is notable mostly for its unpleasant integrity. Cage plays a just-paroled con who immediately gets drawn back into crime via a kidnapping job that promises a big payout.

Army of One (2016) **1/2

In his first unabashedly comedic performance in years, Cage stars as Gary Faulkner, a real-life weirdo who travels to the Middle East to kill Osama bin Laden at the direction of God (Russell Brand). Directed by Larry Charles, no stranger to bizarre comedic premises, the movie gives Cage room to fully commit to Faulkner's oddness. (Though, when the real Faulkner shows up in the closing credits, Cage's performance starts to look like a deeply studied attempt to channel the real man.) That's *almost* enough to make up for the sense that the movie is mostly running in place (though producer Bob Weinstein reportedly heavily recut the version that ultimately saw release). It also doubles as a *Birdy* reunion: Matthew Modine shows up for a few scenes as Faulkner's doctor.

Arsenal (2017) **

Arsenal might have been standard VOD fare were it not for a few touches: (1) director Steven C. Miller has a fondness for strange, slow-motion sequences; (2) the movie seems to have been filmed on a four-block radius of an ordinary Biloxi neighborhood; (3) Cage costars alongside his brother Christopher Coppola, director of *Deadfall*; and (4) Cage revives his *Deadfall* character/caricature Eddie King.

Inconceivable (2017) *

Cage largely recedes into the background of an our-new-friend-is-crazy thriller that plays like the 1990s never ended.

Vengeance: A Love Story (2017) **

The source material, Joyce Carol Oates's novel *Rape: A Love Story*, suggests aspirations that this standard revenge thriller, in which Cage plays a cop who takes the law into his own hands, never realizes. Cage almost directed the film.

Mom and Dad (2017) ***1/2

Not for the faint-of-stomach, this darkly comic horror movie stars Cage and Selma Blair as parents infected with an uncontrollable compulsion to kill their children. Get past the giddily staged violence, however, and you'll find a rueful consideration of midlife regret.

Looking Glass (2018) ***
Veteran director Tim Hunter (*Over the Edge*, *River's Edge*) helms a solid thriller in which a married couple (Cage and Robin Tunney) tries to escape it all by buying a roadside motel, not realizing the previous owner's secrets included a room with a one-way mirror.

The Humanity Bureau (2018) *1/2
In the not-so-distant future, America sends its "inefficient" citizens to the paradise of New Eden—or so it claims. Cage plays a government agent who gets woke. It's not a bad idea for a movie, but that doesn't make the results any less of a trudge.

211 (2018) **
Cage plays a grieving cop in a by-the-book heist movie.

Teen Titans Go! To the Movies (2018) ***
Cage gets to voice Superman, at long last, in this fun adaptation of the clever kids' show. He shows up only for a cameo, however.

Mandy (2018) ****
A darkly poetic tale of vengeance and loss that turns the stuff of B-movies, heavy metal music, and lurid horror posters into high art. Cage fits right into a meticulously crafted film that almost justifies the many less-imaginative revenge movies he made in the years leading up to it.

Spider-Man: Into the Spider-Verse (2018) ****
In this endlessly inventive animated take on Marvel's web crawler, Cage provides the husky voice of Spider-Man Noir, a visitor from a black-and-white universe in which no one can be trusted.

Between Worlds (2018) **1/2
A struggling trucker (Cage) romances a woman who can communicate with the dead when she's being strangled (Franka Potente). It just gets weirder from there in a heavily improvised oddity inspired by David Lynch.

A Score to Settle (2019) *1/2
When Frank (Cage) is released from prison after serving nineteen years, will he use the opportunity to reconcile with his son or exact revenge? Why not both?

Love, Antosha (2019) ***1/2

One of the most promising actors of his generation, Anton Yelchin died in a freak accident at the age of twenty-seven. This revealing, compassionate documentary details his brief life and previously undisclosed battle with cystic fibrosis. Cage, cast at the request of Yelchin's parents, gives sensitive voice to his *Dying of the Light* costar's letters and diary entries.

Running with the Devil (2019) **

First-time director Jason Cabell brings some flair to a *Traffic*-inspired drug-smuggling drama with a low-key Cage performance as a high-level operative with a day job as restaurant chef.

Kill Chain (2019) **

Cage at least gets some colorful dialogue in a confusing noir-inspired film in which he plays a hotel owner with underworld connections.

Color Out of Space (2019) ***1/2

Cult favorite director Richard Stanley made his return after a seventeen-year absence with a spirited adaptation of an H. P. Lovecraft story. Cage plays an academic trying to keep his family together by moving to his late father's farm. A crashing meteorite has other plans in a film that's part gooey throwback to 1980s horror films, part family drama that lets Cage play a character pushed to the brink of madness.

Primal (2019) **1/2

Chaos ensues when a grizzled poacher of exotic animals (Cage) gets trapped on a ship with a government-trained assassin gone rogue. Though not *quite* as fun as its premise, the film does feature a running gag in which Cage's character gets angry at a parrot.

Grand Isle (2019) **

Cage and costar Kelsey Grammar go big in a lurid, but ultimately pretty unmemorable, thriller with Tennessee Williams pretensions.

Jiu Jitsu (2020) **1/2

As a half-crazed martial arts expert helping a select group of elite fighters make a last stand against an alien, Cage has only a few scenes, but wearing an outfit inspired by Dennis Hopper in *Apocalypse Now* and talking about his love of making paper boats, he makes them count.

The Croods: A New Age (2020) ***

Grug returns for more amiable prehistoric adventures, this time involving a conflict with the bougie Bettermans, who look down on the Croods' primitive ways.

History of Swear Words (TV series, 2021) ***

A dapperly clad Cage hosts a comedic/informative Netflix series about the origins of various four-letter words. It's breezy fun, and Cage appears to enjoy playing with his image.

Willy's Wonderland (2021) **1/2

Cage plays a muscle car–driving drifter who agrees to spend a night cleaning what turns out to be a cursed pizzeria filled with murderous animatronic characters. Though not quite as fun as a movie with that log line should be, Cage's wordless performance keeps it compelling.

Prisoners of the Ghostland (2021) ***

Sion Sono's postapocalyptic action film is set in a world inspired in equal parts by *Mad Max*, classic Westerns, and samurai films. Cage plays a criminal charged with rescuing a young woman from the wasteland while wearing a leather suit that will kill him if he doesn't perform the task by a deadline set by a ruthless warlord. It's more weird than enjoyable, but you won't see anything else like it.

Pig (2021) ****

Cage delivers one of the most affecting performances of his career in this assured, deeply moving, hard-to-categorize first feature from Michael Sarnoski. Cage stars as a truffle hunter living in the depths of the Pacific Northwest who's forced to return to civilization, and a past he'd prefer to forget, when thieves abduct his beloved pig. That might sound like the setup for a bare-knuckled revenge thriller, but the film dodges expectations at every turn as it spins a story of loss, fine dining, and the meaning of integrity.

Works Cited

Interviews with the Author
Coolidge, Martha. Interview with author, February 8, 2020.
Dahl, John. Interview with the author, October 18, 2020.
Hatfield, Carol. Email correspondence with the author, January 21, 2020.
Muller, Eddie. Email correspondence with the author, June 30, 2020
Pillsbury, Sam. Interview with the author, March 16, 2020.

CHAPTER 1
Coppola, August. *The Intimacy*. New York: Grove Press, 1978.
Coppola, Francis Ford. "Audio Commentary." *Rumble Fish (The Criterion Collection)*. Directed by Francis Ford Coppola. New York: Criterion Collection, 2017. Blu-ray Disc.
Cowie, Peter. *Coppola: A Biography*. New York: DaCapo, 1994.
Gardella, Kay. "'Young Lives' Is Old Hat & Cardboard, at That." *New York Daily News*, July 13, 1981.
Gross, Terry. "Nicolas Cage." Interview by Terry Gross. *Fresh Air*, NPR, February 13, 2002. Audio, 49:32. https://freshairarchive.org/segments /actor-nicolas-cage.
Huber, Dean. "A Teenage World in Wild Caricature." *Sacramento Bee*, July 9, 1981.
Noland, Claire. "August Coppola Dies at 75; Professor Was Father of Nicolas Cage and Brother of Francis Ford Coppola." *Los Angeles Times*,

October 30, 2009. https://www.latimes.com/local/obituaries/la-me
-august-coppola30–2009oct30-story.html.

Pall, Ellen. "Nicolas Cage, The Sunshine Man." *New York Times*, July 24, 1994. https://www.nytimes.com/1994/07/24/movies/film-nicholas -cage-the-sunshine-man.html.

Schruers, Fred. "Nicolas Cage Is a Hollywood Samurai." *Rolling Stone*, November 16, 1995.

Schumacher, Michael. *A Filmmaker's Life*. New York: Crown Publishers, 1999.

Sheff, David. "Playboy Interview: Nicolas Cage." *Playboy*, September 1996.

"Vogelsang, Louise Adrianne (obituary)." *Los Angeles Times*, December 28, 2010.

Wilmington, Michael. "Nicolas Cage—Wild and Full of Heart." *Los Angeles Times*, August 12, 1990.

CHAPTER 2

Arar, Yardena. "Nicolas Cage's Strange Taste in Film Roles." *Los Angeles Daily News*, August 31, 1990.

Attanasio, Paul. "The Road to Hollywood." *Washington Post*, August 7, 1985.

Blowen, Michael. "They Could Call It 'Rocky Goes Rowing.'" *Boston Globe*, January 18, 1986.

Carson, Greg. "In Conversation: Martha Coolidge and Nicolas Cage." *Valley Girl: Special Edition*. Directed by Martha Coolidge. Los Angeles: Shout! Factory, 2018. Blu-ray Disc.

———. "Valley Girl in Conversation." *Valley Girl: Special Edition*. Directed by Martha Coolidge. Los Angeles: Shout! Factory, 2018. Blu-ray Disc.

Caulfield, Deborah. "Summer's Hot Faces (Part Five): Nicolas Cage: 'Valley Girl.'" *Los Angeles Times*, September 3, 1983.

Ebert, Roger. "Birdy." *Chicago Sun-Times*, January 1, 1984.

Fristoe, Roger. "Show Talk with Nicolas Cage." *Louisville Courier-Journal*, September 16, 1990.

Handelman, David. "Joel & Ethan Coen: The Brothers from Another Planet." *Rolling Stone*, May 21, 1987.

Mann, Roderick. "Nicolas Cage Opens Up." *Los Angeles Times*, October 19, 1986.

Marchese, David. "Nicolas Cage on His Legacy, His Philosophy of Acting, and His Metaphorical—and Literal—Search for the Holy Grail." *New York Times Magazine*, August 7, 2019.

Marsh, Betsa. "'Valley Girl' Gentle Display of Teen Woes." *Cincinnati Enquirer*, May 31, 1983.

McKenna, Kristine. "A 'Moonstruck' Nicolas Cage Opens Up." *Los Angeles Times*, February 21, 1988.

Norman, Barry. "Birdy: Film 85." *Film 85*. BBC, 1985. https://www.youtube.com/watch?v=FehHQ2skj_U.

Parker, Alan. "Audio Commentary." *Birdy (Indicator Series)*. Directed by Alan Parker. London: Powerhouse Films, 2019. Blu-ray Disc.

Rea, Steven. "Teen Sex—You Know—And Kind of Grody." *Philadelphia Inquirer*, June 10, 1983.

Rosenberg, Jane. "The 'Valley Girl'—Era or Fad—Lives on in Merchandising." *Los Angeles Times*, May 8, 1983.

Schruers, Fred. "The Passion of Nicolas Cage." *Rolling Stone*, November 11, 1999.

CHAPTER 3

Bergen, Ronald. *The Coen Brothers*. 2nd ed. New York: Arcade Publishing, 2016.

Canby, Vincent. "'Peggy Sue Got Married,' Time Travel by Francis Ford Coppola." *New York Times*, October 5, 1986.

Corliss, Richard. "Just a Dream, Just a Dream: 'Peggy Sue Got Married.'" *Time*, October 13, 1986.

GQ. "Nicolas Cage Revisits His Most Iconic Characters." Video interview, September 18, 2018. https://www.gq.com/video/watch/nicolas-cage-revisits-his-most-iconic-characters.

Kael, Pauline. "Peggy Sue Got Married." *New Yorker*, October 20, 1986.

Mann, Roderick. "Nicolas Cage Opens Up." *Los Angeles Times*, October 19, 1986.

Marchese, David. "In Conversation, Kathleen Turner." *Vulture*, August 7, 2018. https://www.vulture.com/2018/08/kathleen-turner-in-conversation.html.

McCreadie, Marsha. "Raising Arizona: Movie Does State No Favors." *Arizona Republic*, March 29, 1987.

Nayman, Adam. *The Coen Brothers: This Book Really Ties the Films Together*. New York: Abrams, 2018.

Rambeau, Catharine. "Lack of Logic Cramps Style of 'Peggy Sue.'" *Detroit Free Press*, October 10, 1986.

Schruers, Fred. "The Passion of Nicolas Cage." *Rolling Stone*, November 11, 1999.

Travers, Peter. "Picks & Pans Review: 'Peggy Sue Got Married.'" *People*, September 29, 1986.

Turner, Kathleen. *Send Yourself Roses: Thoughts on My Life, Love, and Leading Roles*. New York: Grand Central Publishing, 2008

CHAPTER 4

BBC. "Why Cher Was So Upset When Everyone Laughed at Her First Role." *The Graham Norton Show*. Excerpted on YouTube, June 22, 2018. https://www.youtube.com/watch?v=1ANCcQKaG9Q&feature=emb _logo.

Bierman, Robert, and Nicolas Cage. "Audio Commentary." *Vampire's Kiss*. Directed by Robert Bierman. Los Angeles: Shout! Factory, 2015. Blu-ray Disc.

Bull, Debby. "Modine & Cage Are at Head of Class." *Rolling Stone*. Reprinted *Boston Globe*, April 4, 1985.

Cain, Scott. "Nicolas Cage: One Shy Guy." *Atlanta Journal-Constitution*, April 4, 1987.

Chase, Chris. "Mama Mia! Now This Is One Full 'Moon'!" *New York Daily News*, December 16, 1987.

Cher, Norman Jewison, and John Patrick Shanley. "Audio Commentary." *Moonstruck*. Directed by Norman Jewison. Los Angeles: MGM, 2011. Blu-ray Disc.

Davis, L. J. "Hollywood's Most Secret Agent." *New York Times Magazine*, July 9, 1989.

Fristoe, Roger. "Show Talk with Nicolas Cage." *Louisville Courier-Journal*, September 16, 1990.

Geller, Lynn. "Moving Images." *Spin*, March 1989.

Gelmis, Joseph. "Actor Nicolas Cage Allows Peek Under His Veil of Privacy." *Newsday*. Reprinted *Hartford-Courant*, October 12, 1986.

Maslin, Janet. "'Moonstruck,' with Italians in Love." *New York Times*, December 16, 1987.

McKenna, Kristine. "A 'Moonstruck' Nicolas Cage Opens Up." *Los Angeles Times*, February 21, 1988.

Rickey, Carrie. "'Vampire's Kiss': Nicolas Cage Goes Batty." *Philadelphia Inquirer*, June 3, 1989.

Schonfeld, Zach. "Truly Batshit: The Secret History of 'Vampire's Kiss,' the Craziest Nicolas Cage Movie of All Time." *The Ringer*, June 13, 2019. https://www.theringer.com/movies/2019/6/13/18663380/nicolas-cage -vampires-kiss-breakout-performance-30-years.

Taggart, Patrick. "'Vampire's Kiss' Has the Bite of Originality amid Bland Fare." *Austin American-Statesman*, August 4, 1989.

Weaver, Caity. "Cher Everlasting." *New York Times Magazine*, December 27, 2020.

Wuntch, Philip. "Nicolas Cage Likes to Leave Them Laughing." *Dallas Morning News*, September 2, 1992.

———. "Try to Relax and Enjoy Weird 'Vampire's Kiss.'" *Dallas Morning News*, June 2, 1989.

CHAPTER 5

Arar, Yardena. "Nicolas Cage's Strange Taste in Film Roles." *Los Angeles Daily News*. Reprinted *Chicago Tribune*, August 31, 1990.

Ebert, Roger. "David Lynch Gives Filmgoers All They Can Handle." *Chicago Sun-Times*, May 27, 1990.

———. "Wild at Heart." *Chicago Sun-Times*, August 17, 1990.

Green, David. "Audio Commentary." *Fire Birds*. Directed by David Green. New York: KL Studio Classics, 2018. Blu-ray Disc.

Hamilton, Erik. "'Wild at Heart' Tweaks 'Peaks' Freaks." *Los Angeles Times*, August 25, 1990.

Maychick, Diana. "Under the Tawdry Dress There's a Heart of Gold." *The Record*, May 5, 1991.

Rodriguez, René. "Nicolas Cage Still Doing Things His Way." McClatchy Newspapers. *Akron Beacon Journal*, February 16, 2012.

Soto, Alfred. "Defining the Poppy Bush Interzone." *Humanizing the Vacuum*, March 10, 2020. https://humanizingthevacuum.wordpress.com/2020/03/10/defining-the-poppy-bush-interzone/.

Strailey, Jonathan. *Love, Death, Elvis & Oz: The Making of 'Wild at Heart.'* Produced by Jonathan Strailey. Los Angeles: Shout! Factory, 2004.

Wilmington, Michael. "Nicolas Cage—Wild and Full of Heart." *Los Angeles Times*, August 12, 1990.

CHAPTER 6

Birnbach, Lisa. "If Only I Were a Cleveland Indian." *Parade*, November 8, 1987.

Christian, Terry. "Nicolas Cage Interview on 'The Word.'" Channel 4, September 7, 1990. https://www.youtube.com/watch?v=SpB7E7fPg8A&t=166s.

Ebert, Roger. "Amos & Andrew." *Chicago Sun-Times*, March 5, 1993.

Faillace, Adrienne. "Hugh Wilson Interview." Television Academy Foundation, November, 16, 2015.

Hornaday, Ann. "Film Noir, 'Tweener' or Flub?" *New York Times*, April 3, 1994.

Kelly, John F. "It Could Happen to You." *Washington Post*, July 29, 1994. https://www.washingtonpost.com/wp-srv/style/longterm/movies/videos/itcouldhappentoyoupgkelly_a09dfb.htm.

Pall, Ellen. "Nicolas Cage, the Sunshine Man." *New York Times*, July 24,

1994. https://www.nytimes.com/1994/07/24/movies/film-nicholas-cage -the-sunshine-man.html.

Pooley, Eric. "The Unknown King of Comedy." *New York Magazine*, May 27, 1985.

Ryan, Mike. "Nicolas Cage on 'Ghost Rider: Spirit of Vengeance,' Almost Starring in 'Dumb and Dumber' and Why He Is Led Zeppelin." *Huffington Post*, February 14, 2012.

Sheff, David. "Playboy Interview: Nicolas Cage." *Playboy*, September, 1996.

CHAPTER 7

Baumgarten, Marjorie. "Leaving Las Vegas." *Austin Chronicle*, November 22, 1995.

Beck, Marilyn. "Hollywood: Banderas Still the Busiest Actor Around These Days." *Press Democrat*, April 10, 1995.

Beck, Marilyn, and Stacy Jenel Smith. "Caruso Still in the Film Game." *Santa Maria Times*, November 8, 1995.

Bochco, Steven. *Truth Is a Total Defense: My Fifty Years in Television*. Scotts Valley, CA: CreateSpace, 2016.

Carr, Jay. "'Vegas': A Nocturne in Neon." *Boston Globe*, November 10, 1995.

Cerone, Daniel Howard. "Det. Kelly's Public Hell." *Los Angeles Times*, March 12, 1995.

Daley, Steve. "Caged Heat: Bugged-Out to Moonstruck: A Quirky Actor Dissects His Roles." *Entertainment Weekly*, March 15, 1996.

———. "High Spirits." *Entertainment Weekly*, March 15, 1996.

———. "Nicolas Cage: He's Staggeringly Brilliant as a 'Vegas' Drunk." *Entertainment Weekly*, February 28, 1996.

Ebert, Roger. "Cage Relishes Operatic Role in Tragic 'Leaving Las Vegas.'" *Chicago Sun-Times*, November 5, 1995.

Gleiberman, Owen. "Leaving Las Vegas," *Entertainment Weekly*, October 27, 1995. https://ew.com/article/1995/10/27/leaving-las-vegas-3/.

Hinson, Hal. "'Kiss of Death': Nicolas Cage Uncaged Leaves David Caruso, Well . . . Rather Flat." *Washington Post*, May 3, 1995.

Hunter, Stephen. "The Hunt for Oscar Predictions." *Baltimore Sun*, March 24, 1996. https://www.baltimoresun.com/news/bs-xpm-1996-03-24 -1996084102-story.html.

Imbesi, Peter. "Viva, 'Las Vegas!'—Interviewing Director Mike Figgis." AMC, 1996. https://www.amc.com/viva-las-vegas.

Kagan, Jeremy. "Visual History with Mike Figgis." Directors Guild of America, May 27, 2014. https://www.dga.org/Craft/VisualHistory /Interviews/Mike-Figgis.aspx.

Nashawaty, Chris. "John O'Brien's Bittersweet Departure." *Entertainment Weekly*, November 10, 1996.

Rea, Steven. "Success of 'Las Vegas' Has Mike Figgis on a Roll." Knight-Ridder. Published in *Hartford Courant*, March 21, 1996.

Rodriguez, René. "'Vegas' Tells a Story of Self-destruction." *Miami Herald*, November 22, 1995.

Schruers, Fred. "Nicolas Cage Is a Hollywood Samurai." *Rolling Stone*, November 16, 1995.

Simon, Jeff. "How Nicolas Cage Gambled on 'Vegas'—And Came Up Big." *Buffalo News*, February 18, 1996. https://buffalonews.com/news /how-nicolas-cage-gambled-on-vegas—-and-came-up-big/article _9fe58490-cc2d-5203-b630-a4e4bd70963b.html.

Stone, Jay. "A Good Girl Turns Bad." *Ottawa Citizen*, January 9, 1996.

Strauss, Bob. "Caruso Thinks 'Media Frenzy' Is Waning." *Baltimore Sun*, May 1, 1995.

Turan, Kenneth. "Mike Figgis Likes Looking at Life on the Dark Side." *New York Times*, January 21, 1990. https://www.nytimes.com/1990/01/21 /movies/film-mike-figgis-likes-looking-at-life-on-the-dark-side.html.

———. "A Potent 'Kiss of Death.'" *Los Angeles Times*, April 21, 1995.

UPI Staff. "Nicolas Cage Wins Best Actor Oscar." UPI, March 26, 1996. https://www.upi.com/Archives/1996/03/26/Nicolas-Cage-wins-best -actor-Oscar/5989827816400/.

Wyatt, Gene. "Cage Quenches Thirst for Tragic Role." *Tennessean*, February 9, 1996.

CHAPTER 8

Bay, Michael, Jerry Bruckheimer, Nicolas Cage, and Ed Harris. "Audio Commentary." *The Rock*. Los Angeles: Buena Vista, 2008. Blu-ray Disc.

Bordwell, David. *Planet Hong Kong*. Cambridge, MA: Harvard University Press, 2008.

Colleary, Michael, John Woo, and Mike Werb. "Audio Commentary." *Face/ Off: Special Collector's Edition*. Los Angeles: Paramount Pictures, 2007. Blu-ray Disc.

Daly, Steve. "Face to Face." *Entertainment Weekly*, June 20, 1997.

Ebert, Roger. "Cage Relishes Operatic Role in Tragic 'Leaving Las Vegas.'" *Chicago Sun-Times*, November 5, 1995. https://www.rogerebert.com /interviews/cage-relishes-operatic-role-in-tragic-leaving-las-vegas.

Kempley, Rita. "'Con Air': Extreme Turbulence at Cruising Altitude." *Washington Post*, June 6, 1997. https://www.washingtonpost.com/wp-srv /style/longterm/movies/review97/conairkemp.htm.

Koltnow, Barry. "'Rock' Director Found Fame in Commercials." *Orange County Register*, June 7, 1996.

Macaulay, Scott. "'What Is Bayhem?' The Secret of Michael Bay's Shots." *Filmmaker*, July 3, 2014. https://filmmakermagazine.com/86534-what-is-bayhem-the-secret-of-michael-bays-shots/#.YCWZQY9Kj0o.

Marks, Craig, and Rob Tannenbaum. *I Want My MTV: The Uncensored Story of the Music Video Revolution*. New York: Dutton Penguin, 2011.

McDonagh, Maitland. "Face/Off." *TV Guide*, June 1997.

Savlov, Marc. "The Rock." *Austin Chronicle*, June 7, 1996.

Shulgasser, Barbara. "The Rock." *San Francisco Examiner*, June 7, 1996.

Siskel, Gene. "Wisecracking Nicolas Cage Saves Hyperactive Thriller 'The Rock.'" *Chicago Tribune*, June 7, 1996.

Stork, Matthias. "Chaos Cinema Part 1." Video essay published to Vimeo, 2012.

———. "Chaos Cinema Part 2." Video essay published to Vimeo, 2012.

CHAPTER 9

Abramowitz, Rachel. "Welcome to the Jungle." *Premiere*, January 1999.

Associated Press. "First an Angel, then Superman . . . Nicolas Cage Just Loves to Fly." *Daily Advertiser*, May 1, 1998.

Bay, Michael, Jerry Bruckheimer, Nicolas Cage, and Ed Harris. "Audio Commentary." *The Rock*. Los Angeles: Buena Vista, 2008. Blu-ray Disc.

Corliss, Richard, "The Saga of Nic the Nice." *Time*, August 27, 2001. http://content.time.com/time/subscriber/article/0,33009,1000646,00.html.

Dargis, Manohla. "T.K.O.: De Palma—All Camera, No Content." *LA Weekly*, August 13, 1998.

Entertainment Weekly Staff. "This Week in Hollywood." ew.com, March 26, 1999. https://ew.com/article/1999/03/26/this-week-hollywood-7/.

Frankel, Daniel. "Cage Writes Off Penn." *E! Online*, March 17, 1999. https://www.eonline.com/news/37884/cage-writes-off-penn.

Goldstein, Patrick. "He's Better than Good in a Room." *Los Angeles Times*, December 26, 2000.

Hirschberg, Lynn. "Restless." *New York Times Magazine*, December 27, 1998. https://www.nytimes.com/1998/12/27/magazine/restless.html.

Hoberman, J. "Metaphysical Therapy." *Village Voice*, October 26, 1999. https://www.villagevoice.com/1999/10/26/metaphysical-therapy/.

Johnson, Dean (writing as "Commander Coconut"). "Second City Blooms in 2 New Films." *Orlando Sentinel*, April 14, 1999.

Macnab, Geoffrey. "Nicolas Cage: From Hollywood A-lister to King of the B-Movies." *Independent*, September 3, 2020. https://www.independent

.co.uk/independentpremium/culture/nicolas-cage-primal-leaving-las-vegas-oscar-con-air-rock-wild-heart-a9700371.html.

Pall, Ellen. "Nicolas Cage, the Sunshine Man." *New York Times*, July 24, 1994. https://www.nytimes.com/1994/07/24/movies/film-nicholas-cage-the-sunshine-man.html.

Partridge, Harry. "Nicolas Cage Wants Cake." Directed by Harry Partridge. YouTube, June 15, 2010.

Persall, Steve. "Nicolas Cage Would Cast Superman in His Own Image." *Tampa Bay Times*, June 3, 1997.

Portman, Jamie. "Cage Pursues Image as Versatile Actor." *Ottawa Citizen*, August 11, 2001.

Roach, Mary. "The Unlikeliest Action Hero." *USA Weekend*, June 1, 1997.

Salisbury, Mark. "Butcher My Script and I'm Outta Here." *Guardian*, April 9, 1999. https://www.theguardian.com/film/1999/apr/09/features.

Samuelson, Edwin. "8mm in 35mm with Joel Schumacher." *8mm*. Los Angeles: Shout! Factory, 2019. Blu-ray Disc.

Schnepp, Jon. *The Death of 'Superman Lives': What Happened?* Directed by Jon Schnepp. Los Angeles: Showtime Networks, 2015.

Schruers, Fred. "The Passion of Nicolas Cage." *Rolling Stone*, November 11, 1999.

Schumacher, Joel. "Audio Commentary." *8mm*. Los Angeles: Shout! Factory, 2019. Blu-ray Disc.

Svetkey, Benjamin. "Are the Stars Worth Their Salaries?" April 12, 1996. https://ew.com/article/1996/04/12/are-stars-worth-their-salaries/.

Turan, Kenneth. "'8mm' Is Descent into Hell." *Los Angeles Times*, February 26, 1999.

Wilonsky, Robert. "Going, 'Gone.'" *Dallas Observer*, June 8, 2000. https://www.dallasobserver.com/film/going-gone-6395081.

Zacharek, Stephanie. "Bringing Out the Dead." *Salon*, October 22, 1999. https://www.salon.com/1999/10/22/dead_2/.

CHAPTER 10

Barbara Walters Special. Directed by Bill Geddie. ABC, 2003.

Cohen, David. "Saturn Sets into Orbit with Spirited Film Slate." *Variety*, March 7, 2001.

Ebert, Roger. "Matchstick Men." *Chicago Sun-Times*, September 12, 2003. https://www.rogerebert.com/reviews/matchstick-men-2003.

———. "Talkin' About the Weather with Cage." *Chicago Sun-Times*, October 30, 2005. https://www.rogerebert.com/interviews/talkin-about-the-weather-with-cage.

Friend, Tad. "The Cobra." *New Yorker*, January 12, 2009. https://www.newyorker.com/magazine/2009/01/19/the-cobra.

GQ. "Nicolas Cage Revisits His Most Iconic Characters." Video interview, September 18, 2018. https://www.gq.com/video/watch/nicolas-cage-revisits-his-most-iconic-characters.

Kaufman, Amy. "It's in His Eyes." *Los Angeles Times*, November 12, 2000.

Raftery, Brian. *Best. Movie. Year. Ever: How 1999 Blew Up the Big Screen*. New York: Simon and Schuster, 2019.

Smith, Zadie. "An American Revolution." *Daily Telegraph*, March 5, 2006. https://www.telegraph.co.uk/culture/3650748/An-American-revolution.html.

Zacharek, Stephanie. "Windtalkers." *Salon*, June 15, 2002. https://www.salon.com/2002/06/14/windtalkers/.

CHAPTER 11

BBC Staff. "Nicolas Cage Returns Stolen Dinosaur Skull to Mongolia." BBC News, December 22, 2015. https://www.bbc.com/news/entertainment-arts-35159082.

Breznican, Anthony. "Nicolas Cage's Outlook: Mostly Sunny." Gannett News Service. *Binghamton Press and Sun Bulletin*, October 30, 2005.

Chernikoff, Leah. "Nicolas Cage Sued by Ex Christina Fulton for $14 Million for Fraud and Breach of Contract." *New York Daily News*, December 9, 2009. https://www.nydailynews.com/entertainment/gossip/nicolas-cage-sued-christina-fulton-13-million-fraud-breach-contract-article-1.434396.

Cohen, David. "Saturn Sets into Orbit with Spirited Film Slate." *Variety*, March 7, 2001.

Duke, Alan. "Nicolas Cage Settles Lawsuit with His Son's Mother." CNN, June 15, 2011. http://edition.cnn.com/2011/SHOWBIZ/celebrity.news.gossip/06/14/nicolas.cage.lawsuit/index.html.

Enoonsti (YouTube username). "The Best Scenes from 'The Wicker Man.'" YouTube, January 1, 2007. https://www.youtube.com/watch?v=e6i2WRreARo.

GQ. "Nicolas Cage Revisits His Most Iconic Characters." Video interview, September 18, 2018. https://www.gq.com/video/watch/nicolas-cage-revisits-his-most-iconic-characters.

Halbfinger, David M. "Oliver Stone's 'World Trade Center' Seeks Truth in the Rubble." *New York Times*, July 2, 2006. https://www.nytimes.com/2006/07/02/movies/oliver-stones-world-trade-center-seeks-truth-in-the-rubble.html.

Jordan, Julie. "Nicolas Cage Will Pay IRS $14 Million." *People*, January 15, 2010. https://people.com/celebrity/nicolas-cage-will-pay-irs-14 -million/.

Kiang, Jessica. "Berlin Interview: Nicolas Cage Explains Why 'Wicker Man' Is Misunderstood, His Career Choices, & More." IndieWire, February 20, 2013. https://www.indiewire.com/2013/02/berlin-interview -nicolas-cage-explains-why-wicker-man-is-misunderstood-his-career -choices-more-101425/.

Mr. Bumhole #1 Fan of Osaka (Know Your Meme username). "Know Your Meme: Nicolas Cage." knowyourmeme.com, 2012. https://knowyour meme.com/memes/people/nicolas-cage.

Noland, Claire. "August Coppola, 1934–2009." *Los Angeles Times*, October 30, 2009.

The Onion. New York: Onion Inc., September 27, 2001.

People Staff. "Nicolas Cage Losing His Treasures." *People*, December 7, 2009. https://people.com/archive/nicolas-cage-losing-his-treasures-vol-72 -no-23/.

Raymond, Kitty. "Scoop: Nicolas Cage Said to Have Squandered Fortune." *San Francisco Examiner*, November 19, 2009. https://www.sfexaminer.com /entertainment/scoop-nicolas-cage-said-to-have-squandered-fortune/.

Reuters Staff. "Nicolas Cage Sues Ex-Manager for 'Financial Ruin.'" Reuters, October 17, 2009. https://www.reuters.com/article/entertainmentNews /idUSTRE59F4RM20091017.

Scott, A. O. "Learning All About the Girls and the Bees," *New York Times*, September 2, 2006.

———. "A New Orleans Mystery: A Cop So Bad He's Good." *New York Times*, November 19, 2009. https://www.nytimes.com/2009/11/20 /movies/20badlieutenant.html.

Strong, Rider. "An Interview with Neil LaBute." *The Believer*, September 1, 2014. https://believermag.com/an-interview-neil-labute/.

TMZ Staff. "Nic Cage—Debt Man Walkin'." TMZ, October 9, 2009. https://www.tmz.com/2009/10/09/nic-cage-debt-man-walkin/.

CHAPTER 12

Brooks, Xan. "'Joe'—Venice 2013: First Look Review." *Guardian*, August 31, 2013. https://www.theguardian.com/film/2013/aug/31/joe-venice -review-nicolas-cage.

Corliss, Richard. "Joe Reminds Us that Nicolas Cage Is a National Treasure." *Time*, April 9, 2014. https://time.com/55304/joe-movie-review -nicolas-cage/.

Cowan, Lee. "The Fearless Nicolas Cage." CBS News, April 6, 2014. https://www.cbsnews.com/video/the-fearless-nicolas-cage/.

Dolak, Kevin. "Dog the Bounty Hunter Bails Out Nicolas Cage." ABC News, April 17, 2011. https://abcnews.go.com/Entertainment/dog-bounty-hunter-bails-nicolas-cage/story?id=13394003.

Fitzpatrick, Kevin. "'Community' Season Five Is Finally Doing Dan Harmon's Nicolas Cage Episode." *ScreenCrush*, December 10, 2013. https://screencrush.com/community-season-5-nicolas-cage-introduction-to-teaching/.

Fleming, Mike. "HE'S BACK: Nicolas Cage Changes Mind, Returns to Millennium's 'Trespass.'" *Deadline*, August 3, 2010. https://deadline.com/2010/08/nicolas-cages-abrupt-departure-leaves-millennium-drama-trespass-in-lurch-59076/

Freeman, Hadley. "Nicolas Cage: 'If I Don't Have a Job to Do, I Can Be Very Self-destructive.'" *Guardian*, October 1, 2018. https://www.theguardian.com/film/2018/oct/01/nicolas-cage-if-i-dont-have-a-job-to-do-it-can-be-very-self-destructive.

Germain, David. "'Trespass' Is Breaking into Your Home Four Months Early." Associated Press. *Wilmington News Journal*, October 17, 2011.

Hanrahan, Harry. "Nicolas Cage Losing His Shit." YouTube, November 21, 2010. https://www.youtube.com/watch?v=4zySHepF04c&feature=emb_logo.

Joe Versus the Volcano. Directed by John Patrick Shanley. Burbank, CA: Warner Home Video, 2002. DVD.

Kohn, Eric. "Nicolas Cage's Next Act." IndieWire, May 23, 2018. https://www.indiewire.com/2018/05/nicolas-cage-movie-star-vod-mandy-cannes-1201967840/.

Lippiett, Nathaniel. "EXCLUSIVE: Nicolas Cage Reveals 'Nouveau Shamanic' Acting Technique." On Demand Entertainment, February 12, 2012. https://www.youtube.com/watch?v=Z1JyukEGjb0&feature=emb_logo.

Perez, Rodrigo. "David Gordon Green Talks 'Joe' & Reveals How He Convinced Nicolas Cage to Star in His Dark, Tiny Indie Drama." IndieWire, April 10, 2014. https://www.indiewire.com/2014/04/david-gordon-green-talks-joe-reveals-how-he-convinced-nicolas-cage-to-star-in-his-dark-tiny-indie-drama-87235/.

Schutte, Lauren. "Nicolas Cage Denies Vampire Accusations: 'I Don't Drink Blood.'" *Hollywood Reporter*, February 10, 2012. https://www.hollywoodreporter.com/live-feed/nicolas-cage-vampire-letterman-ghost-rider-289323.

Shira, Dahvi, and Oliver Jones. "Nicolas Cage Back to Work After Arrest." *People*, April 18, 2011. https://people.com/celebrity/nicolas-cage-back -to-work-after-arrest/.

Sperling, Nicole. "Nicolas Cage Back in 'Trespass.'" *Entertainment Weekly*, August 4, 2010. https://ew.com/article/2010/08/04/nicolas-cage-back -in-trespass/.

Stephanopoulos, George. "Nicolas Cage Interview 2014: Actor Gets Rave Reviews for 'Joe.'" *Good Morning America*, April 11, 2014. https://www .youtube.com/watch?v=caxMBk1__-Y.

Taylor, Drew. "Here's Why 'National Treasure 3' Never Happened." Collider, September 23, 2020. https://collider.com/why-national-treasure -3-never-happened/.

"Trespass." *Deadline*, August 3, 2010. https://deadline.com/2010/08/nicolas -cages-abrupt-departure-leaves-millennium-drama-trespass-in-lurch -59076/.

Acknowledgments

This book would never have happened if not for the help of many, so please indulge me in some thanks.

I'm grateful to have met my agent, Peter Steinberg, who believed in this project (and that I could write a book in the first place). Thanks also to the tireless Yona Levin.

It also couldn't have happened without Henry Holt and Company's James Melia, an editor who got what I was going for from the start and supported that vision all the way, while making invaluable improvements. Thanks also to Jenna Dolan for the thorough, thoughtful copyedit (and for catching a couple of embarrassing errors) and to Lori Kusatzky for all her help. And thank you to the rest of the team at Holt: Sarah Crichton, Maggie Richards, Amy Einhorn, Sarah Fitts, Chris O'Connell, and Meryl Levavi.

A lot of inspiration came from the cadre of longtime collaborators I've leaned on for years at the *A.V. Club*, the *Dissolve* (R.I.P.), and, currently, our podcast, *The Next Picture Show*:

Genevieve Koski, Tasha Robinson, and Scott Tobias. Scott in particular had many ideas and draft passages bounced off him over the last year and a half, some of them pretty half-baked. Thanks for helping me bake them fully. (A shout-out, too, to our podcast editor, Dan Jakes.)

I talked to a lot of knowledgeable film people who nudged me in the right direction while I pitched, researched, and wrote this book, some briefly, others at length: thanks to Carrie Rickey, Manohla Dargis, Isaac Butler, David Bordwell, Dana Stevens (not the one who wrote *City of Angels*; the other one), Jason Zinoman, and Chris Nashawaty.

When it comes to coaching me in navigating the book world, thanks to Steven Hyden, who pushed me along the way. Thanks also to Alan Sepinwall, for his help (and for listening to my horror stories). At the other end of the production cycle, thanks to my early readers, who offered opinions on various drafts at various stages: Rob Siegel, Josh Rothkopf, and Jean Kouremetis (just like in college).

Thanks to all the editors I've worked with on other projects during the course of writing this (and who've been understanding about my occasionally being busy): Frazier Tharpe at *GQ*; Sean Fennessey and Andrew Gruttadaro at the *Ringer*; Tim Surette at *TV Guide*; Jason Tabrys and Brett Michael Dykes at Uproxx; Phil Nobile Jr. at *Fangoria*; David Fear at *Rolling Stone*; Rachel Handler, Genevieve Koski (again), Ray Rahman, Chris Heller, and Neil Janowitz at *Vulture*; Matt Patches and Tasha Robinson (again) at the *Verge* and *Polygon*; and Nick Leftley at *Mel*.

I appreciate all those who took the time to talk to me—

namely, Martha Coolidge (a delight), Sam Pillsbury, Carol Hatfield, and John Dahl.

I also appreciate everyone in the circle of film and pop culture nerds whom I talk to regularly who've probably heard enough about Nicolas Cage without reading this book: Matt Singer, Mike Ryan, Jordan Hoffman, Alison Willmore, Kristy Puchko, Angelica Jade Bastién, Alan Scherstuhl, Vikram Murthi, Charles Bramesco, Jason Bailey, Kate Erbland, Emily VanDerWerff, Sam Adams, Bilge Ebiri (*Bad Lieutenant: Port of Call New Orleans*, good movie), Mark Pfeiffer, Brian Tallerico, Jen Chaney, Brian Grubb, William Goodman, David Sims, Alan Zilberman, Monica Castillo, Tim Grierson, Nick Allen, Robert Daniels, Katey Rich, Alissa Wilkinson, Josh Spiegel, and *Filmspotting*'s Adam Kempenaar and Josh Larsen.

When it comes to film writers, I want to single out two friends for special consideration in inspiring this book. In my capacity as an editor, I commissioned Noel Murray to write a piece about Nicolas Cage's early films. As part of that piece, he wrote about Cage using weirdness as a secret weapon. That got me thinking. Around the same time, Amy Nicholson published an *LA Weekly* article about how perceptions of movie stars can overwhelm their work, entitled "How YouTube and Internet Journalism Destroyed Tom Cruise, Our Last Real Movie Star." That got me thinking as well.

Thanks to my mom and dad, for letting me watch so many movies without asking too many questions. And thanks to Gregg Morton and Brian Hamilton for going to see *Raising Arizona* with me thirty-four years ago, though I'm not sure they wanted to.

This book is dedicated to her, but I have to thank my wife, Stevie, once again, because *none* of this would have happened without her. I also need to thank my daughter, Hannah, for watching some age-appropriate Cage movies with me. She recommends *National Treasure* and *The Croods*.

And though I doubt he'll ever read this, thanks to Nicolas Cage for being Nicolas Cage, because there is no actor like him, and the world is richer for it. *Omnia ab uno.*

Illustration Credits

1. Atlantic Releasing Corp.
2. TriStar Pictures
3. © TriStar Pictures
4. 20th Century Fox
5. MGM
6. Hemdale Film Corporation
7. Samuel Goldwyn Company/Photofest © Samuel Goldwyn Company
8. MGM/UA
9. Photofest
10. Photofest
11. Ron Galella, Ltd. / Ron Galella Collection / Getty Images
12. L. Cohen / WireImage / Getty Images
13. Paramount / Photofest © Paramount Pictures
14. Columbia Pictures
15. The Walt Disney Company
16. Lionsgate
17. First Look Pictures / Photofest © First Look Pictures
18. RLJE Films

About the Author

Keith Phipps joined the *A.V. Club* in 1997 and became its editor in 2004. Phipps later launched the influential movie site the *Dissolve* with Pitchfork in 2013 and served as editorial director for film and TV at Uproxx. He is currently a regular contributor to *GQ*, *Vulture*, *TV Guide*, and *The Reveal*, a film review site he created with longtime collaborator Scott Tobias. His work has also appeared in the *New York Times*, *Polygon*, the *Ringer*, the *Verge*, the *Daily Beast*, and *Rolling Stone* and on NPR.